Contents

On Healy's 'Investigation'—What the Facts Show *by Joseph Hansen*	5
Healy's Frame-up Against Joseph Hansen *by George Novack*	32
WSL Scores Healyite Frame-up of Joseph Hansen	36
Healy's Road to the Gutter—Statement by the Editors of 'Red Weekly'	41
A Statement on Healy's Frame-up of Hansen and Novack *by Betty Hamilton and Pierre Lambert*	44
'Socialist Action' Denounces WRP Smear Campaign	51
Notes on Healy's Role in Early Days of the British Trotskyist Movement *by Mary and John Archer*	53
When Isaac Deutscher Showed Healy to the Door *by Ernest Tate*	60
Healy's Smear Against Trotsky's Last Collaborators *by Sam Gordon*	63
Healy Caught in the Logic of the Big Lie *by Joseph Hansen*	70
The Verdict: 'A Shameless Frame-Up'—A Statement on the Slanders Circulated by the Healy Group Against Hansen, Novack, and the Socialist Workers Party (Signers of Statement)	113
Sara (Weber) Jacobs Recalls a Conversation With Trotsky	116
Charles Curtiss Condemns Frame-up	117
Ready to Participate in Jury of Honor (Statement by Tendance Marxiste Révolutionnaire Internationale)	118
Jean van Heijenoort's Opinion	118
Statement by Bala Tampoe	119
Statement of 'Bulletin Group'	120
Opinion of C. L. R. James	121

WRP Holds Frame-up Style Rallies 122
by Jim Atkinson and Skip Ball

Vyshinsky Rides Again 127
by Charles van Gelderen

LSA Adds Signature to Statement 129

Australian Healyites Revive Stalinist Methods of 1930's 131

Against Healy's Frame-up of Hansen and Novack! (Additional Signers of Statement) 133

Vereeken Regrets Healyite Taint in English Edition of His Book 135

Vereeken Begins Learning About Healyism 137
by Joseph Hansen

'These Attacks Must Stop' 140

Vereeken's Differences With Trotsky 142
by George Breitman

WSL Condemns New Brazen Moves in Healyite Frame-up 148

Healy's 'Political Bankruptcy' Shown in Frame-up of Hansen and Novack 153

Let Commission Investigate Charges of Healyite Violence! 157
by Dave Holmes

Introduction

In February and March 1975, *Intercontinental Press* published a document in which I detailed the circumstances that led me to leave the Workers League, an organization which I led for ten years. The Workers League was in political solidarity with the "International Committee," a body led by Gerry Healy of Britain, who broke from the Fourth International in 1963.

The document described the bizarre witch-hunt Healy launched against Nancy Fields, a national committee member of the Workers League, charging her with being a "CIA agent." When Fields stood up to Healy's bullying and I supported her, we were denounced in hysterical terms. I was removed from the post of National Secretary, and Nancy Fields was suspended from membership *before* a commission met to hear the charges against her.

A commission appointed by the International Committee later found the charges against Fields to be groundless, but barred her from holding any responsible position in the Workers League.

Nancy Fields and I had left the Workers League by this time, convinced that no organization that maintained such practices could construct a revolutionary workers party in the United States or anywhere else.

Joseph Hansen, the editor of *Intercontinental Press,* commented on what I had written in the March 31, 1975, issue. Hansen is a leader of the Socialist Workers party and has been a Trotskyist for four decades. He found my description of the events wholly plausible, in part because it was only the latest of a long line of purges and splits stemming from Healy's sectarian politics, antidemocratic organizational practices, and distorted personality. This was no new development, Hansen explained, but had roots in Healy's opposition to the reunification of the Fourth International.

Having already begun to reconsider a number of political questions, Nancy Fields and I were impressed by Hansen's evaluation. This opened up a process of discussion and collaboration which led us to join the Socialist Workers party at the beginning of 1976.

Our break with Healy was followed by further splits and expulsions from the "International Committee," in Britain, as well as in Greece and Australia.

Healy responded to Joseph Hansen's critique in a manner that has become characteristic of him. In October 1975, the Workers Revolutionary party launched into a campaign of character assassination, "indicting" Hansen as an "accomplice of the GPU," the Soviet secret police.

The Healyites accused Hansen of aiding the GPU in making possible the assassination of Leon Trotsky, and in "covering up" this and other GPU operations. This foul brew was spiced with charges of "FBI associations." Slanders of a similar nature were directed against the Socialist Workers party as a whole. To "prove" these slanders, the Healyites have resorted to faked quotations, lies, and crude amalgams.

Hansen disposed of the accusations in considerable detail in the November 24, 1975, and August 9, 1976, issues of *Intercontinental Press.*

When George Novack—another veteran SWP leader who played a key role in helping Trotsky to expose Stalin's frame-ups of revolutionists in the 1930s—denounced the charges as fraudulent, he too was branded an "accomplice of the GPU" by Healy's pen-pushers.

In the months that followed, leading representatives of virtually every current in the world Trotskyist movement, together with past and present associates of Trotsky, Hansen, and Novack, have denounced the frame-up, often contributing their own accounts of the facts.

Healy has reacted by having his "International Committee" declare Hansen and Novack "guilty as charged" pending a "trial" by an "international commission." Those who have repudiated Healy's slander campaign—including such figures as Vsevolod Volkov, Trotsky's grandson, and Marguerite Bonnet, an executor of Trotsky's estate—are declared by the Healyites to be "accomplices of the accomplices" of the GPU.

Thus virtually the entire world Trotskyist movement, along with most of the surviving associates of Trotsky, are now condemned by the Healyites as in league with the Stalinist secret police. The only exceptions are George Vereeken, an opponent of Trotsky who for his own reasons has joined in Healy's campaign, and Healy's dwindling band of followers, who are required by his dictatorial internal regime to support their leader's every word.

The resemblance between Healy's methods and those of Stalin in the Moscow Trials is striking. Unable to answer critics and opponents politically, the Healyites concoct "evidence" to smear them as longtime "agents" or "accomplices of the enemy."

This collection reprints everything published in *Intercontinental Press* on this subject. Together, this material not only explodes Healy's trumped-up case against two selfless revolutionists, but strikes an important blow for democracy within the workers movement.

Tim Wohlforth

In reply to a petty practitioner of the big lie

ON HEALY'S 'INVESTIGATION'—WHAT THE FACTS SHOW

By Joseph Hansen

The careful verification of every fact and every figure was typical of Ilyich. He based his conclusions on facts.

This eagerness to base every conclusion on facts is plainly revealed in his early propaganda pamphlets. . . . He did not foist anything on the workers, but proved his contentions with facts.

—N. K. Krupskaya,
Memories of Lenin, *vol. 1, p. 185.*

Last April 26, the AFL-CIO staged a "Rally for Jobs Now" in Washington, D.C. Called by the bureaucracy in response to pressure from the ranks resulting from the depression and mounting unemployment, the demonstration was widely recognized as an event of considerable significance. Not for decades had labor organized a political demonstration like this against government policies.

All the radical tendencies were there, marching with the contingents of the unions they belonged to and distributing their literature to the tens of thousands of participants.

Of uncommon interest was the leaflet passed out by members of a small sect, the Workers League. One side featured an argument pointing up the need for a labor party in the United States.

The other side carried an advertisement for a public meeting featuring Cliff Slaughter. Subject: "The World Crisis and the Fourth International—The International Committee of the Fourth International Answers the Attacks of Joseph Hansen *Socialist Workers Party.*"

Cliff Slaughter is one of the leaders of the Workers Revolutionary party, the British group headed by Gerry Healy, which maintains fraternal relations with the Workers League.

At his meeting in Washington, D.C., the British celebrity sought to voice the mood of the participants in the AFL-CIO "Rally for Jobs Now" by answering the attacks of Joseph Hansen.

Despite the fervor of Cliff Slaughter, however, his American followers seem to have concluded that he did not succeed in completely exorcising Joseph Hansen. Perhaps Washington, D.C., was not the right place.

About six months later they appeared at another important event, this time in Boston, where the second conference of the National Student Coalition Against Racism was held October 10–12.

The 1,300 activists at the NSCAR conference spent three days discussing a range of problems that have arisen in face of the efforts of a belligerent wing of the racists to kill busing, using Boston as a test area. The conference decided to launch a national campaign to defend school desegregation and fight racism.

The Workers League abstained from participating in the conference. The leaders had other fish to fry. A contingent outside the hall distributed a reprint of a four-page article taken from three issues of the *Workers Press*, "newspaper of the Central Committee of the Workers Revolutionary Party, British section of the International Committee of the Fourth International."

The title of the article: "WE ACCUSE JOSEPH HANSEN AND THE SOCIALIST WORKERS PARTY."

The fourth page of the throwaway carried an advertisement for a "Workers League Meeting." Subject: "We accuse Joseph Hansen."

No speaker was listed. Perhaps that was because the Workers League has no American leader whose name would draw a crowd; and the cost of flying an authority like Cliff Slaughter from London for the occasion was prohibitive.

Between the meeting held April 26 in Washington, D. C., and the one held October 11 in Boston, the subject on which the Workers League was seeking to create public interest obviously underwent a certain escalation. In Washington, D. C., "Cliff Slaughter, International Committee of the Fourth International," only answered "the Attacks of Joseph Hansen *Socialist Workers Party"* In Boston, the nameless speaker (or speakers?) was billed under a title indicating that the tables had been turned: "We accuse Joseph Hansen."

What put the Healyites on this kick? Why should a small isolated group of would-be revolutionists consider it more important to denounce the attacks of Joseph Hansen than to bring the message of socialism to workers marching in Washington, D. C., against the depression? Why should they consider it more important in Boston to "accuse" Joseph Hansen than to participate in a discussion with militants from all over the United States on how best to counter the murderous attacks of lynch-minded racists?

Clearly they consider it a matter of vital importance. The Revolutionary Workers party in Britain and the Workers League in the United States were shaken to the bottom, it would seem, by the attacks of Joseph Hansen. Their very existence as a political formation having been placed in doubt, all other considerations understandably went by the board.

The 'attacks' that staggered the Healyites

It should be understood that the word "attack" has a special meaning in the language spoken by the Healyites. In carrying on public polemics that could be of interest to quite a number of revolutionary-minded workers if the issues were argued on the basis of facts and principles, the Healyites include outrageous and even slanderous personal charges and characterizations.

If no response to such garbage is forthcoming, a campaign is mounted. Perhaps this will yield something that can be worked up into more articles. Often the campaign includes arrogant demands for a reply, as if the top body of the Healyites were a latter-day Inquisition holding special rights and powers.

If a response is made at any point, this is labeled an "attack," necessitating a vigorous "defense," which turns out to be a new attack, often more scurrilous than the first.

The Healyites obviously consider this polemical method to be one of their most attractive features; and I would be the last to attempt to persuade them otherwise. I ask only that it be kept in mind in what follows.

Somewhat more than a year ago, the name of Tim Wohlforth vanished from the pages of the *Bulletin,* the newspaper he founded and developed into a twice-weekly as the voice of the Workers League. His name also vanished from the pages of the *Workers Press.* This caused some speculation, inasmuch as he was the national secretary of the Workers League and one of the international leaders of the tendency headed by Gerry Healy, the general secretary of the Workers Revolutionary party.

The mystery was cleared up in a lengthy statement by Wohlforth, explaining what had happened to him and his companion Nancy Fields, which he made public in mimeographed form. Because of its obvious interest to the left as a whole, *Intercontinental Press* published it in four installments under the title "The Workers League and the International Committee."[1]

The appearance of Wohlforth's statement in *Intercontinental Press* caused considerable fluttering in the Healyite dovecote. The tactic of trying to dispose of Tim Wohlforth and Nancy Fields through silence had failed.

The February 21, 1975, issue of the *Bulletin* carried a statement by the "Workers League Political Committee," entitled "AN ANSWER TO THE SLANDERS OF ROBERTSON & WOHLFORTH." The statement was reprinted without comment in the March 1 issue of *Workers Press.*

"The circumstances of Wohlforth's resignation as presented by Robertson (and Wohlforth) are a pack of lies," the statement affirmed.

Furthermore: "In the revisionist circles, our

---

1. The first installment appeared in *Intercontinental Press*, February 24, 1975, p. 279. *Workers Vanguard*, the newspaper of the Spartacist League, published excerpts from the document in an article entitled, "Confessions of a 'Renegade': Wohlforth Terminated." The article was unsigned, but the style suggests James Robertson, the head of the Spartacist League, as the author.

> **Workers League Public Meeting**
>
> # THE WORLD CRISIS AND THE FOURTH INTERNATIONAL
>
> The International Committee of the Fourth International Answers the Attacks of Joseph Hansen
> Socialist Workers Party
>
> The liberation of Cambodia and the collapse of the Saigon regime are the greatest defeats for imperialism since the victory of the Chinese revolution.
>
> Throughout the capitalist world, the economic crisis is raging out of control. Global inflation and mass unemployment are on the agenda.
>
> These are the conditions for the construction of parties of the Fourth International in every country to lead the struggle for power.
>
> Saturday, April 26 4pm
> Elliot Junior HS 18th & Constitution Ave NE
> contribution: $1
>
> **Cliff Slaughter**, International Committee of the Fourth International

Leaflet distributed by Healyites at April 26, 1975, AFL-CIO march in Washington, D.C., against unemployment.

deep concern on these matters is put down to 'paranoia' about the CIA. Here is the petty bourgeois liberal face of all revisionist groups. This is just one of the profound differences between us and them."[2]

The admission that "all revisionist groups" have been referring to "paranoia" as a possible explanation for the peculiar concern of the Healyites

on these matters should be noted. It will come up later.

Wohlforth's account was directed to the members of the Workers League and the Workers Revolutionary party. He took up various theoretical and political issues of particular concern to these two organizations and sought to show that under Healy's leadership they were going badly astray. In this context, his description of Healy's organizational intervention in the Workers League was completely convincing.

Wohlforth described in the most concrete way, giving names, dates, places, and dozens of details as an eyewitness and one of the victims, how Healy whipped up a witch-hunt atmosphere at the group's summer camp in 1974 on charges that Nancy Fields was a possible agent of the CIA and that Wohlforth was guilty of not having obtained a "security clearance" for her.

At a session that began after midnight on August 31, Wohlforth was ousted as national secretary and Fred Mazelis named to succeed him. Nancy Fields was suspended.

Later an inquiry commission found that there was no substance whatever to Healy's charges. He had acted out of pure suspicion.

To this day, the Healyites have not attempted to refute any of the specific details in Wohlforth's account. That is because they cannot. They have made only *general* assertions, such as "a pack of lies." To help avoid answering, they have done everything possible to divert attention from the witch-hunt methods that were brought to public attention by Wohlforth.

By itself, Healy's performance at the summer

---

2. For the text of the statement, see "The Healyite Reply to Tim Wohlforth's Exposures," *Intercontinental Press*, March 24, 1975, p. 411.

camp of the Workers League remained completely enigmatic. No CIA agents had been trapped. Not a single one. Yet heads had rolled. They had rolled on the basis of nothing but *mere suspicion* in the mind of a single individual.

How could a leader claiming to be a *Trotskyist* do something like that? How could *Trotskyist* cadres—if that is what they were—permit it? What kind of thinking was it that had raised the question of "security clearances" to central importance in a group that believes it is following the practices of *Lenin* in party building?

In an article "The Secret of Healy's 'Dialectics'—The Logic of Factional Hooliganism," published in the March 31, 1975, issue of *Intercontinental Press*, I sought to show that the treatment of Tim Wohlforth and Nancy Fields was not an isolated incident but part of a general pattern to be seen in the group led by Healy. I pointed to the following examples besides this one:

- The severe beating administered to Ernest Tate by stewards of the Healyite group on November 17, 1966. Tate's crime, apparently, was to hawk a pamphlet entitled *Healy "Reconstructs" the Fourth International* in front of a Healyite meeting in London. When Tate protested by sending letters about the incident to working-class organizations, Healy responded by filing a lawsuit against him and two journals that published his letter.
- The experience of James Robertson at the April 1966 conference of the "International Committee" in London. Because Robertson did not offer a sufficiently abject apology for missing a session, he was ousted from the conference. Robertson had no discernible political differences with Healy; in fact, he went to considerable lengths to display his conformity.
- The expulsion of Alan Thornett, who sought to open an internal discussion in the Workers Revolutionary party. Thornett, along with about 200 other worker activists, was thrown out on the eve of the first annual conference of the organization, which was held in London December 15–17, 1974. The treatment of members of the Thornett group was strikingly like that meted out to Wohlforth and Fields.
- The details of Wohlforth's testimony. These corroborated the conclusions drawn by previous victims about the internal regime in the British Healyite group while offering invaluable new evidence along the same lines.

These cases taken together, I contended, proved beyond reasonable doubt the existence of a despotic regime in the Workers Revolutionary party. Such a regime, however, is in harmony with the ultraleft, sectarian politics of the WRP and in consonance above all with the leader's philosophical outlook, which amounts to a private religion.

> Wohlforth describes Healy's performance as "madness," [I said]. Would it not be preferable, and perhaps more precise, to use a modern term like "paranoia"?
>
> If the term fits, then the true explanation for Healy's obsession about CIA agents, police agents, and plots against his life, as well as his rages, "extreme reactions," and strange version of dialectics is to be sought not in his politics, philosophical methodology, or models like Pablo or Cannon, but in the workings of a mind best understood by psychiatrists.
>
> We also have a better appreciation of Healy's aversion to facts, and to the reflections of this foible in the *Workers Press*, making it one of the most unreliable journals ever produced in the radical movement.

In light of these considerations, I drew some additional conclusions from the facts that had come to public notice about the WRP and the "International Committee." For lack of space I will not repeat them here but refer whoever may be interested to the article.

The need to secure a 'sanity clearance'

There were several ways the Healyites could respond to these "attacks."

1. They could recognize the validity of the criticisms and seek in an open way to come to grips with the despotic internal regime, fighting to change it and to establish the norms of democratic centralism. In particular, the leadership could seek to modify Healy's obsessive concern over "security," putting into effect the principles observed by Leon Trotsky and James P. Cannon on this question.

2. Without making any public statements, they could simply proceed to make these changes for the better.

3. They could continue to operate in the old way without bothering to answer the "attacks."

4. They could seek to obtain a "sanity clearance" for their leader.

In accordance with the character of their organization, they chose the latter course.

This required proving that the real world is in conformity with the thought of their extraordinarily suspicious leader. Some difficult hurdles had to be surmounted such as proving that "Joseph Hansen and the Socialist Workers Party to which he belongs" were guilty of "criminal negligence in relation to the security implications of the death of Trotsky and the tasks of revolutionary security in relation to the defense of the Fourth International."[3]

It probably never occurred to these tacticians that taking this course might provide weighty evidence for the correctness of the diagnosis of "paranoia."

In view of the importance of getting a sanity clearance for the top leader, no expenses were to be spared:

> The International Committee is recommending to the Sixth World Congress that a special fund be started to provide resources for a thoroughgoing investigation into security in the Fourth International and the role of individuals such as Hansen.[4]

With ample funds at their disposal, the Healyite sleuths did a first-rate job from a certain point of view. We will examine their findings presently and trace how they worked up the raw material.

The guiding lines of their "investigation" are clearly indicated in the following paragraphs from an article, "Hansen's Campaign of Slander," published in the April 25, 1975, issue of *Workers Press*. Despite its length, the extract is well worth studying:

> The source of Hansen's outraged [*sic*] and slanderous attack on the International Committee of the Fourth International is the desertion by Wohlforth, ex-national secretary of the Workers League, following fully substantiated charges of negligence on internal security. His article explicitly defends the method—or lack of method-employed by Wohlforth in protecting the Workers League from infiltration, disruption and provocation by state police agencies. At the same time, he raises a frenzied witch-hunt against the International Committee and in particular Comrade Gerry Healy, general secretary of the Workers Revolutionary Party. Where Wohlforth undermined the *internal* security of the Workers League, Hansen sets out consciously to whip up a lynch atmosphere of violence to threaten the *external* security of the Workers League and the International Committee.
>
> There is not a shred of politics in the attack on Comrade Healy. Hansen is incapable of that. He resorts to personal abuse of the most slanderous kind with no other purpose than to frame him. A long time ago, Hansen earned a reputation for this kind of scurrilous abuse. In 1966 *The Newsletter* (forerunner of *Workers Press*) pamphlet, "Problems of the Fourth International" quoted a member of Hansen's Socialist Workers Party as saying:
>
> "When it comes to normal polemicizing against opponents there are all sorts of comrades who can undertake this task, but when Cannon wants to sharpen things up, with a real dirty below the belt job, all eyes on the committee turn automatically in the direction of Joe Hansen."
>
> ("Problems of the Fourth International" August 1966. Printed in *Trotskyism versus Revisionism*, Volume 4, New Park Publications, 1974.)
>
> Hansen joins Wohlforth in a dubious crusade which says that if the revolutionary leadership raises political vigilance on questions of security, it is, by definition, "mad". Hansen writes:
>
> Wohlforth describes Healy's performance as "madness". Would it not be preferable, and perhaps more precise, to use a modern term like "paranoia"? If the term fits, then the true explanation for Healy's obsessions about the CIA, police agents, and plots against his life, as well as his rages, "extreme reactions", and strange version of dialectics is to be sought not in his politics, philosophical methodology, or models like Pablo or Cannon, but in

---

3. See "Introduction" to the Healyite compilation *Security and the Fourth International*, p. vi.

4. *Workers Press*, April 26, 1975.

the workings of a mind best understood by psychiatrists.

(*Intercontinental Press*, March 31, 1975.)

These are gross slanders on Comrade Healy which have not the slightest foundation in fact. They must be repudiated. He has no "obsession" about CIA agents, nor has he ever voiced any fears about plots against his life. These are figments of Hansen's imagination produced to titivate the fraternity of sleek Philistines and well-heeled anti-communist liberals in his entourage. The use of the term "madness" and "paranoia" to avoid a scientific materialist analysis of the class basis of a political leadership does not signify an episodic aberration on the part of Hansen. On the contrary it is an expression of extreme, incurable and slanderous subjectivism, the complete disorientation of a petty-bourgeois revisionist and impressionist who tries to substitute intuition and belief and myths for the existence of a real material world independent of his mind.

The method employed by Hansen is not new and is itself an expression of the social and political crisis. Let us remember that one of the best-known epithets hurled against the defendants in the Moscow Trials was "mad dogs" and that Lenin too was subjected to an unprecedented barrage of lies by renegades and revisionists in October 1917 who described the seizure of power as the work of "people in the grip of madness". (See *Lenin* by D. Shub, p. 300, Pelican, 1966.) When Trotsky was fighting against enormous historical odds to build the youthful Fourth International under the continuous threat of assassination by Stalin's GPU, he had to contend with the slanders of the Stalinist and "liberal" Press which accused him of "persecution mania". In fighting against any complacency on security questions in the building of revolutionary parties, the International Committee of the Fourth International is carrying forward the tradition and principles of Marxism, Leninism and Trotskyism. If this is suddenly derided as "madness" then it is not the International Committee which has strayed, it is an expression of the complete political degeneration of Pabloite revisionism.

HEALY: Wins place in history for his contribution to art of building monolithic party through "security clearances."

The authors make some excellent points in that final paragraph. However, they evade the real question. Is a person in the "grip of madness" thereby shown to be a Lenin? Is a person suffering from "persecution mania" thereby shown to be a Trotsky? Is a person who wears a folded paper hat and poses with his right hand in his left armpit thereby shown to be a Napoleon?

Character assassins at work

Let us follow the spoor left by Healy and his sleuths. The long quotation above is as good as any to begin with.

Reread that short bit about Hansen resorting to "personal abuse of the most slanderous kind with no other purpose than to frame" Healy.

> A long time ago, Hansen earned a reputation for this kind of scurrilous abuse. In 1966 *The Newsletter* . . . pamphlet . . . quoted a member of Hansen's Socialist Workers Party as saying:
>
> "When it comes to normal polemicizing against opponents there are all sorts of comrades who can undertake this task, but when Cannon wants to sharpen things up, with a real dirty below the belt job, all eyes on the committee turn automatically in the direction of Joe Hansen."

Obviously the Healyites consider this quotation to be one of their most important bits of evidence concerning Hansen's character and reputation, which may well be so. The authors of the article in which it is cited constitute nothing less than the Political Committee of the Workers Revolutionary party.

The importance of the quotation is shown again by the fact that in the October 31, 1975, issue of the *Bulletin*, Jeff Sebastian used it as the opening paragraph of an article entitled "Spartacist—Errand Boys for Joseph Hansen."[5]

Sebastian voices the outrage of the Workers League at Spartacist pickets carrying signs in front of one of their meetings, one of which read: "WL SAYS: INVESTIGATE HANSEN! WHERE DID HEALY GET HIS SECURITY CLEARANCE?"

One change is to be noted in the source to which Sebastian ascribes the quotation. Instead of "a member of Hansen's Socialist Workers Party," he ascribes it to "a leading member of the Socialist Workers Party."

The quotation was used for the first time in an article by "G. Healy National Secretary of the Socialist Labour League" published in the September 10, 1966, issue of the *Newsletter*. Healy said the source was "a member of this leadership"; i.e., the "SWP leadership."

Let us examine the quotation a bit more closely. Whoever said it, clearly directed it more against James P. Cannon than against Hansen. It is Cannon who "wants to sharpen things up." Hansen merely accepts the assignment.

Note the conciseness of the quotation. It names Cannon, Hansen, and "the committee." It has "all eyes . . . turn automatically"—all this in a single sentence that also smears Hansen as a specialist in carrying out "a real dirty below the belt job." The author displayed uncommon literary ability to get so much in and yet to speak so casually.

Note some further peculiarities:

1. The author of the quotation is not named. In all three citations—by Healy, by the Political Committee of the WRP, and by Sebastian—it is ascribed to "a member" of the SWP, or to "a leading member" of the SWP, or to "a member of this leadership." Just who is *a member*? Or should we say, *A. Member*?

2. The date of the quotation is not given. It was "a long time ago," according to the Political Committee of the WRP. It was "once said," according to Healy. Sebastian agrees with Healy; it was "once said."

Why do these authorities avoid indicating even the year in which *A. Member* made his memorable remark?

3. The publication in which the quotation appeared is not divulged. Why are these investigators so secretive? Have they made a pact not to reveal the source of the quotation? Who are they trying to protect? What are they trying to cover up?

4. The political context of the damning quotation is not indicated by any of these polemicists. Yet as anyone can see by referring to the paragraph preceding the quotation, one of the charges leveled against Hansen is that there is "not a shred of politics in the attack on Comrade Healy. Hansen is incapable of that."

Where is the shred of politics in the decaying bit of cabbage contributed by *A. Member*?

To answer these questions, more material is required. The following quotation may prove to be enlightening:

> The reader may not know who Joseph Hansen is, so we will tell him.
>
> The Hansen we mean is a writer for the *Militant* and a spokesman for the Socialist Workers Party. When there is some ordinary criticism or other to make of us, there is mild and fun-loving strife at the meeting of the second stratum of SWP leaders (the first stratum meets only with himself, because he is The Founder) about who shall write it. But if there is some especially dirty, unscrupulous, lying, villainous job to be done on us, the eyes of all of them turn in silent spontaneity— some with admiration, some with relief—to the one in their midst whose bucket is never empty and hands are never dry. That's Joseph Hansen.

I hope everyone on reading this noticed the phrase, "When there is some ordinary criticism or other to make of us. . . ." The "us" refers to the Shachtmanites.

The article in which these lines appeared (as the opening two paragraphs, Sebastian may recall)

---

5. From the photograph in the *Bulletin* it is evident that besides "errand boys for Joseph Hansen"—which is about as low as you can sink—there was at least one errand woman.

was entitled "The Man With the Bucket." It was published in the December 7, 1953, issue of *Labor Action*, the newspaper of the Independent Socialist League. This group, headed by Max Shachtman, consisted of the remnants of the petty-bourgeois opposition that Trotsky battled in a faction fight in 1939–40.

The article was signed by Jonah Williams. I never met Jonah Williams and cannot say for sure who he was. At the time the article appeared, I suspected that "Jonah Williams" might have been a pen name used by Max Shachtman for this venture into the use of a bucket. But I must admit that I was rather indifferent to pinpointing the responsibility. A polemic on that level is generally a waste of time.

The political context was as follows. The Cochranites, an unprincipled faction that combined a wing of unionists, worn-out so far as revolutionary struggle was concerned, and a wing that saw possibilities in friendly activities in the periphery of the Communist party, had just split from the Socialist Workers party.

An article about the split was published in the November 16, 1953, issue of *Labor Action*.

This was followed by a rather long letter to the editor from Bert Cochran, correcting some factual errors that had appeared in the article and adding an explanation from his own viewpoint of the reasons for the split.

Cochran's letter, published in the November 23, 1953, issue of *Labor Action*, represented a rather surprising move. Why should Bert Cochran choose the pages of *Labor Action* to make the first public statement of his group following the split? What was the reason for his friendly tone?

In an article entitled "A Stalinophile Warms Up to a—Stalinophobe," which was published in the November 30, 1953, issue of the *Militant*, I took up the possible political reasons for Cochran's ploy.

The article by Jonah Williams was the response from the Shachtmanites to what I said.

In the light of this background, the question that leaps out is the doctoring of the original quotation. Who did it? Where? When? Why this manipulation of quotations in the tradition of the Stalinist school of falsification?

Other aspects should not be overlooked. How does Healy explain this pawing through the garbage can of the Shachtmanites? They dissolved their organization seventeen years ago to join the Social Democracy, where they vanished. Aren't the crusts they left behind rather moldy today?

Does Healy really see eye to eye with the late Shachtman on principled questions? If not, why is he willing to join with him in a knife job on the character of a militant who was upholding Trotsky's positions against both Shachtman and Cochran? Is such treachery proof of one's sanity?

Above all, why does Healy present Jonah Williams, a leading member of the Independent Socialist League, as *A. Member* of the Socialist Workers party?

Finally, I should like to observe how thoroughly the Healyites have proved my contention that the *Workers Press* is "one of the most unreliable journals ever produced in the radical movement."

Not a single one of its assertions can ever be taken at face value. All of them have to be checked against the original sources. Let everyone know that! It is not just a matter of congenital carelessness, although that is bad enough. It is a matter of *fabrications* prepared in the style of the authors of the charges in the Moscow Frame-up Trials.

More dishes from the Healyite kitchen

In the article in which he first used the doctored quotation by A. Member,[6] Healy included a few other items that attest to his methods. In referring to the differences between the Socialist Workers party and the Socialist Labour League over attempting to heal a long-standing split in the Fourth International involving the faction led by Michel Pablo, Healy said the following:

> Then Joseph Hansen entered the scene. His job was simple.
> "Eventually", said Cannon, "we cannot avoid discussion so your task Joe is to poison the political atmosphere inside the SWP against the SLL so that when we have to discuss our

---

6. The article, which first appeared in the September 10, 1966, issue of the *Newsletter*, was reprinted by the Healyites in the compilation *Trotskyism Versus Revisionism*, vol. 4, pp. 290–91. The compilation was issued by New Park Publications Ltd., London, in 1974. That means that after eight years consideration, the Healyites had decided their frame-up had withstood the test of time.

members will be dead against them."

By implication he was saying: "Never mind about principles and truth. We're pragmatists like President John F. Kennedy, so we do what is 'best' to preserve ourselves now."

And Joseph Hansen got to work.

His task as an ex-Mormon from Salt Lake City, was to discredit the SLL, not by political argument, but by poisonous slander and gossip.

I will begin with the last paragraph. It is true that I was born in Salt Lake City. However, an investigation, which I undertook in the pattern followed by Healy, shows that this must be viewed not as an absolute but a relative fact. The planets and the sun were in such position that being born in Salt Lake City at the precise moment was equivalent to being born in London. Healy's very unfavorable horoscope, on the other hand, shows that his place of entry into the world was equivalent to Frogtown, Utah.

Which explains a lot. Especially the voice that spreads "poisonous slander and gossip" in deep bass from the Healyite headquarters.

I must also plead guilty to having been born in a family that adhered to the Mormon faith. As for myself, I was never attracted to any religion, whether Mormonism, Catholicism, Buddhism, Zionism, or Healyism. The old-time atheism was good enough for me.

The words ascribed to Cannon, in which I am allegedly assigned the "task" of poisoning the political atmosphere, is a pure fabrication. The real author of these false phrases only reveals his hatred of Cannon and his readiness to resort to frame-ups if no facts can be found to support this pathological attitude.

Healy's exegesis of his own fabrication thus falls into the same category. "Like President John F. Kennedy"! A very instructive example—concocting phrases, putting them in the mouths of political opponents, and then interpreting them as confirmation of one's own positions! That's Gerry Healy. And that's the *Workers Press*.

Let me take another dish, fresh from Healy's cooker.

In the April 23, 1975, issue of the *Workers Press*, the Political Committee of the Workers Revolutionary party attempts to smear Bala Tampoe, the head of the Ceylon Mercantile Union and a leading Trotskyist in Sri Lanka, as "associated with the Central Intelligence Agency."

The charge was investigated six years ago by a commission at the 1969 congress of the Fourth International. It was found to be untrue.[7] The slander was based on a 1967 trip to the United States taken by Ceylonese labor and political figures in which Tampoe participated. The trip was sponsored by the Asia Foundation, one of many front organizations that received funds from the CIA. Among other things, the visiting Ceylonese delegation was addressed by Robert McNamara, who was at that time the civilian head of the Defense Department.

Observe now, how the Healyite "investigators" extend Operation Smear to Hansen:

> Reporting a visit he made to Sri Lanka in 1972, Hansen wrote, "Mr Robert McNamara, president of the World Bank, appeared to be very well briefed on the Ceylon situation." He was indeed—by, among others, one Bala Tampoe, Hansen's man on the island.

Lest anyone be misled by the grammar of the Political Committee of the WRP, that was McNamara, not Hansen, who made a trip to Sri Lanka.

So "Hansen wrote . . ." Did he really? Once again, let us check the original source. This can be found in *Intercontinental Press*, February 14, 1972, p. 144. The article, which is unsigned although I was editorially responsible, is entitled "A New Coalition Government in Ceylon?"

The part that has a bearing in our checking what "Hansen wrote" reads as follows:

> Robert McNamara, president of the World Bank, visited Colombo January 22–23 to discuss imperialist "aid" projects with the coalition government. His impressions of the prime minister were reported on the front page of the February 3 *Ceylon News*. The item, charming in its frankness, deserves to be quoted in full:

---

7. See "Healyites Smear Bala Tampoe," a statement by the United Secretariat of the Fourth International. *Intercontinental Press*, November 20, 1972, p. 1286.

> "Mr. Robert McNamara, President of the World Bank, has been 'deeply impressed' by Prime Minister Sirimavo Bandaranaike's 'outstanding qualities of leadership,' according to diplomatic circles in Colombo.
>
> "Commenting on the fact that Mr. McNamara appeared to be 'very well briefed' on the Ceylon situation, a senior western diplomat told the Daily News that Mr. McNamara had expressed his 'deepest admiration' for the quality of leadership shown by Mrs. Bandaranaike during the April insurgency and the skill with which she maintained what Mr. McNamara called 'a middle course in international relations'. . . ."

The "April insurgency" refers to the bloody suppression of the young revolutionists of the Janatha Vimukthi Peramuna, whose leader, Rohana Wijeweera, was defended in court by Bala Tampoe.

Check that source in *Intercontinental Press* again. Did "Hansen" write that McNamara "appeared to be very well briefed on the Ceylon situation"? No, not at all. It was reported by the *Ceylon News*.

And the *Ceylon News* made very clear that the source was a "senior western diplomat" in Colombo.

To convert what a "senior western diplomat" said in Colombo into a product from Hansen's typewriter may seem like a tall order. That, however, is to consider the operation only from the viewpoint of proletarian morality.

For the technicians in Healy's kitchen, it's as easy as turning out an omelet. Of course, you have to break a few eggs. So what?

Twenty-six articles to prove it's not 'paranoia'

From the foregoing examples showing how the "investigators" have proceeded in reconstructing reality to conform with Healy Thought—thereby demonstrating their leader's sanity—it can be seen that it is no easy task to examine every point they raise, particularly if you consider the abundance of the material.

Two series of articles have to be checked. The first, which began in the April 19, 1975, issue of *Workers Press*, consists of seven articles signed by the "Political Committee of the Workers Revolutionary Party."

The second series, which began in the August 14, 1975, issue of the same paper, consists of nineteen articles signed by the "International Committee of the Fourth International."

Why two sets of authors were put to this task is not explained. Perhaps there were not two sets but one, which uses the name "Political Committee of the Revolutionary Workers Party" and "International Committee of the Fourth International" interchangeably. There could be thirteen authors or one. The number, the differentiations, and the pecking order really do not make much difference, since the two committees are equally faceless and equally nameless.

In both the seven-article series and the nineteen-article series the authors (or author) pursue several themes. These can be listed as follows:

1. The Socialist Workers party is completely indifferent to infiltration by agents of the Kremlin, the CIA, the FBI, or other spies and agents provocateurs and considers concern about infiltration to be evidence of "paranoia."

2. The person chiefly responsible for this reprehensible attitude of the SWP is Joseph Hansen, who is a "dubious" person now discovered by investigators of the Workers Revolutionary party to be guilty of "criminal negligence"—if not more—in the assassination of Leon Trotsky.

3. In contrast to the SWP, the "security" system used by the Workers Revolutionary party is in accordance with the principles laid down by Lenin and Trotsky in this question and meets the dangers confronting the Trotskyist movement in the spy-ridden world of today.

Healy's "security" system amounts to a permanent witch-hunt in his own organization. Curiously enough, in the twenty-six articles summing up the results of their "investigation," Healy's disciples do not report a single example of the success of his method. Perhaps they had none to present that would stand examination.

Consequently, they base their case not on any positive results in the Workers Revolutionary party or the Workers League but on a presentation of cases elsewhere going back almost forty years.

Moreover, in following this strange procedure, their main criterion is the quantity of material published in the press of the Socialist Workers party over that long period. Even in twenty-six articles, and even if the "investigators" applied their tape measures honestly, the results could only be one-sided and distorted. We shall see in a couple of test instances the results that can be obtained with tape measures made of stretch hose.

However, this elastic approach is required by the main purpose of the two series, which is to heap slander on the leaders of the SWP, particularly Hansen, and to picture them as being soft on spies, if not in "association" with agents of the CIA, the FBI, or the GPU, thereby winning a "sanity clearance" for Healy.

So let us take up some of the charges leveled against the SWP, using a convenient condensation presented by the "International Committee of the Fourth International" in the September 9, 1975, issue of *Workers Press:*

> Nothing was revealed by Hansen about the infiltration of GPU agent *Sylvia Franklin* into the New York headquarters of the SWP as James Cannon's secretary; nothing was disclosed about *Floyd Cleveland Miller*, party name Michael Cort, who wrote for SWP publications as a military correspondent, and who betrayed to the GPU the names of Trotskyist seamen travelling to the Soviet ports of Murmansk and Archangel.
>
> How many seamen died on the high seas or disappeared in the Russian ports because Miller had tipped off the GPU in advance of their arrival?
>
> The late *Max Schachtman* [sic] raised questions about *Sylvia Franklin* before ex-Stalinist Louis Budenz made public her GPU role in Cannon's office. But although he pressed the leadership to conduct a security commission, his request was pushed aside. Cannon went on with a GPU bug on his phone and a Stalinist agent as his secretarial aide.
>
> Was this because Hansen was applying his anti-Trotskyist theory that it is better to have a spy in the organization than to take notice of "personal suspicions"?

It is true that Max Shachtman relayed to the leadership of the SWP what he had heard about the rumors being circulated by Budenz. It is not true that Shachtman was given the brush-off. On questions of defending civil liberties, of mutual defense against physical attack by goons, of uncovering infiltrators, or anything of common interest on that level, the Socialist Workers party has always cooperated with other sectors of the left despite the sharpest political differences.

Although we had heard from other sources that members of his group were themselves circulating the rumor, we thanked Shachtman for the information.

To assert that Cannon did nothing is a lie. The grossness of the lie can be judged by reading Cannon's article "An Answer to Budenz's Latest Frame-up," which was published in the August 28, 1950, issue of the *Militant*. Because of its general interest in connection with the problem of defense against infiltration, the article is being reprinted as a document in this issue of *Intercontinental Press*.[8]

Sylvia Caldwell (that was her party name) worked very hard in her rather difficult assignment of managing the national office of the Socialist Workers party, which included helping Cannon in a secretarial capacity. In fact all the comrades who shared these often irksome chores with her regarded her as exemplary. They burned as much as she did over the foul slander spread by Budenz.

Sixteen years later, in a letter dated November 12, 1966, James P. Cannon, discussing the function of the Control Commission in the Socialist Workers party, recalled how the slander had been handled.

"In another case," he said, "a rumor circulated by the Shachtmanites and others outside the party against the integrity of a National Office secretarial worker was thoroughly investigated by the Control Commission which, after taking stenographic testimony from all available sources, declared the rumors unfounded and cleared the accused party member to continue her work."

Why did Healy's "International Committee" decide to say nothing about Cannon's article in the *Militant* exposing Budenz's frame-up? Why did they decide instead to lie, declaring that the leadership of the SWP gave Shachtman the brush-off and refused to investigate the charges? Why did they

---
8. See p. 1654.

repeat the fabrications circulated by Budenz, who first served the GPU and then the FBI, as if they were gospel truth?

The reasons are perfectly clear—this course was required by the necessities of their own frame-up, which in turn was required by the imperative need to "prove" that Healy Thought is truly sane and in consonance with reality.

The case of Miller was the opposite of that of Sylvia Caldwell. After dropping out of the Socialist Workers party under guise of having developed political differences, he confessed that he had served as a Stalinist agent.

Miller was a free-lance writer who made his living doing mostly radio and later TV scripts. One of the maritime unions in which we had good relations with the leadership at the time relied on us for technical assistance in getting out the union newspaper. We assigned Miller to this task, through which he received the title of editor. Because of this assignment he was invited to attend meetings of our maritime fraction in New York.

As a Stalinist agent, he no doubt provided information to be used against us by the Communist party maritime fraction, particularly in the National Maritime Union, which was dominated by the Stalinists in that period.

Miller claimed that he was told by his Stalinist superiors to work himself as high as possible in the "hierarchy" of the party. He did not succeed in worming himself very high, never being included even in the leadership of the SWP's maritime fraction.

As a government witness in the 1960 spy trial of Dr. Robert Soblen, Miller claimed that "the Stalinists" were concerned about Trotskyist seamen sailing into Russian harbors with American supplies, particularly Murmansk.

"My job as a Stalinist," he continued (as reported by Healy's investigators), "was to keep track of the sailing of all Trotskyite seamen so a Stalinist agent would be at the port and have a surveillance on whatever Trotskyites entered the Soviet Union."

The Healyites parlay this assertion of a Stalinist agent into the question: "How many seamen died on the high seas or disappeared in the Russian ports because Miller had tipped off the GPU in advance of their arrival?"

The answer is *none*. If the Healyites had not concentrated so heavily on wielding their tar brush, they might have reached this conclusion themselves:

1. During the war, the destination of American ships was kept secret by the government. In signing on a ship at the union hiring hall, a seaman was not informed where it was scheduled to go. This information was given out only after the convoys were on their way.

It is true that some of us in the maritime fraction were sometimes able to guess from the type of ship or nature of the cargo where it might go. However, such guesses were always uncertain.

2. We suffered losses on ships carrying supplies to the Soviet Union just as we did in other theaters of the war. Seamen belonging to the Communist party suffered an equally high rate of casualties.

If the Healyites will stop to think, they may recall that German imperialist armies had invaded the Soviet Union, and that German submarines and bombers did their utmost to cut off supplies coming from the United States. Our casualties on the Murmansk run were caused by German torpedoes and dive bombers.

3. Trotskyist seamen whose ships reached Soviet ports were received as warmly as other seamen. Some of them tried to do a little propaganda work for Trotskyism. While they generally met with indignant rebuffs, nothing untoward happened to them.

4. Several Trotskyist seamen, whose ships were sunk by the Germans, managed, along with other members of the crew, to launch lifeboats and eventually make their way to Murmansk. Because of exposure in open boats in those waters, several of them had to spend months in the hospital. They were given first-rate treatment, and the staffs were very friendly.

Was this because Moscow had been tipped off by Miller?

The case of Robert Sheldon Harte

The job done on Robert Sheldon Harte by Healy's "International Committee" is particularly vile.

Harte was the young member of the Socialist Workers party on guard duty when a gang of Stalinists under the leadership of the painter David Alfaro Siqueiros raided the Trotsky home in Coyoacán on May 24, 1940. Harte was the one who opened the steel door to the street, letting them in.

After machine-gunning Trotsky's bedroom, the gang left, thinking they had succeeded in murdering Trotsky and his companion Natalia Sedova.

The gang kidnapped Harte, shot him in the head, and buried his body in a grave which they filled with lime.

As part of the cover-up for this crime, the Stalinist hacks accused Trotsky of having committed a "self-assault." They also did their utmost to throw suspicion on Harte.

I wrote about this in an article published in the August 1940 issue of *Fourth International*. Here are a few paragraphs indicating the line followed by the Stalinist propagandists:

> At the same time, in direct contradiction to its accusation of "self-assault," the GPU began a campaign against Robert Harte, charging that he was the "leader" of the assault, that he had "betrayed" his chief, that is, sold out to the GPU. . . .
>
> Beginning with May 27 . . . every conceivable type of vilification was launched against Harte in the Stalinist papers. It was said that he had a photograph of Stalin in his room at home warmly autographed by Stalin himself (a GPU slander which not even a telegram to the contrary from his father could dispel); in actuality he was not an American but a Russian who had just got off a boat from Russia a week or two before coming to Mexico; the references with which he landed a job with Trotsky were so fabulously good that Trotsky had not even checked them; his baggage was still plastered with Moscow labels; he was a typical gangster type; during the assault he ran about the patio in his pyjamas; he had been paid a fabulous sum for the betrayal; it was impossible to steal Trotsky's automobiles without Harte's connivance as he had control of the ignition keys (in reality they were always kept in the cars for emergency use); he did not come as an agent of the assassins but was bought by them in Mexico; he came as an agent but was won over by Trotsky and so only carried out a partial treachery; he acted as a driver of one of the automobiles which carried away the assassins; he was very nervous when he left with the assailants; he was very calm when he left with the assailants and spoke familiarly with one of them known as "Felipe"; he was completely in Trotsky's confidence and led the "self-assault"; he was snug and safe in his father's home in New York.
>
> These slanders were the moral lime with which the GPU hoped to obliterate all the trails leading to the body decomposing in the mountain cabin.
>
> For several days, as a matter of fact, the Stalinists succeeded in disorienting the police hunt. Two of Trotsky's secretaries were held for two days in jail for "questioning." Two friends of the Trotsky household, one a refugee from Germany, were held for four days in Guadalupe prison. The chauffeur of Diego Rivera was arrested. The house of Frida Kahlo, former wife of the painter, was searched. Seemingly the GPU was forging ahead with its campaign of moral assassination.

With that background in mind, read the following material published in the August 18, 1975, issue of *Workers Press*:

> The US State Department and the FBI were clearly concerned about Harte's disappearance. Official records show that a "rush" telegram was sent from Washington to the US Consulate on May 25, 1940, stating:
>
> "Please in your discretion make informal inquiry of (Mexican) Foreign Office regarding Harte's rescue. According to application on which father Jesse Samuel Harte was issued a departmental passport March 6, 1926, Sheldon K. Harte who was also included was born at Brooklyn, New York, on April 6, 1917. Strictly confidential. Report to the department any information discreetly obtainable regarding Sheldon Harte's activities."
>
> The cable was sent at 5 p.m. on May 25, a day after the raid. It was sent in "confidential code" from the State Department to the US consul and FBI men on the staff who were working under diplomatic cover. (The FBI was the predecessor of the Central Intelligence Agency in Latin America.)

The most curious aspect of the cable is the use of the expression "regarding Harte's *rescue*." But Harte hadn't been "rescued," he had been kidnapped by the Stalinist raiding party.

It is logical to assume that the US Embassy in Mexico would be briefed to discover the whereabouts of Harte, an American national, and to find out who had kidnapped him. Then why say *"rescue"*? [Presumably because his father would also want him rescued from the kidnappers.—J.H.]

This wasn't the only puzzling aspect of Harte's kidnapping.

He was the son of *Jesse S. Harte*, president of Intermediate Factors Corporation. Before Mr Harte, Snr, left for Mexico to join the search for his missing son, the State Department sent a message to the US consul advising them to meet him and take care of him since he was a friend of Mr Hoover's—J. Edgar Hoover, director of the Federal Bureau of Investigation (FBI).

Reports appeared in the New York newspapers that when police visited the missing guard's flat in New York, they found a photograph of Stalin on his wall. He had been a former member of the Communist Party, but then so had many of those freshly joining the Trotskyist movement.

When the chief of the guards at Coyoacan, Harold Robins, searched Harte's room, he found a Spanish-English dictionary. Inside the front cover he was surprised to find the

Headline on four-page throwaway distributed by Healyites at entrance to three-day Boston conference of National Student Coalition Against Racism. This was the sole contribution offered by Healyites at gathering that launched campaign in United States for continued busing of schoolchildren and more effective defense against murderous attacks of racists.

signature of Siqueiros.

Other evidence has emerged to show that while he was in Mexico, Harte became friendly with Ramon Mercader, alias Jacques Mornard, alias Frank Jacson. They went out drinking together.

On August 20, 1940, surrogate James A. Delehanty of New York granted letters of administration on the estate of Harte, aged 25. He left a total of $25,000 in personal property to close relatives.

The most this material shows is that Harte was born in a wealthy, conservative family, that he had become radicalized, and that he hid his revolutionary views from his family. The type is not unknown today.

It can also be deduced that Jacson made a special effort to win his friendship, that Jacson showed him about the town, and introduced him to a few others who might prove impressive to a youth fresh from New York and entranced by Mexico.

None of this alters in the least the conclusions we drew in 1940 concerning why Harte violated the rules and opened the door to the gang. Aside from the fact that they wore police uniforms, which would tend to dispel suspicion, he recognized the person at the door as a friend. It was because he could identify that person that he was murdered.

To bolster their effort to present Harte as another "dubious" figure in Trotsky's household, Healy's "International Committee" found a quotation in which Trotsky, as they put it, "deals with the suspicion that was aroused in Harte."

The suspicion referred to was the suspicion in Harte aroused by the GPU to help divert attention from Jacson by turning the police investigation in the direction of the murdered guard. Trotsky concedes in his article dated June 8, 1940, that "despite all precautions, it is, of course, impossible to consider as absolutely excluded the possibility that an isolated agent of the GPU could worm his way into the guard."

Trotsky then proceeds to show how implausible it was to suspect Harte of having been an accomplice in the assault.

Trotsky reaffirms his confidence in Harte: "I have not heard a single convincing argument to indicate that Sheldon Harte was a GPU agent. Therefore I announced from the outset to my friends that I would be the last one to give credence to Sheldon's participation in the assault."[9]

Thirty-five years later, Healy's "International Committee" remains unconvinced that it was right of Trotsky to display such confidence in Harte. Trotsky's attitude is seriously out of line with their approach. Thus they say in the August 21, 1975, issue of *Workers Press*:

---

9. The quotation is from Trotsky's own account of the May 24, 1940, assault. See "Stalin Seeks My Death," *Writings of Leon Trotsky (1939–40)* (New York: Pathfinder Press, 1969, 1973), pp. 311–334 [2012 printing].

No verdict can be passed on Sheldon Harte at this stage. The US State Department records do testify to the fact that he had a photograph of Stalin on the wall of his New York flat, but it could have been placed there: or it could have been a hangover from his days in the American Communist Party, though it would be a peculiar thing to keep around the house.

The report, according to the State Department records, emanated from Harte Snr's son-in-law, a lawyer named Morton Wild.

The odor of the old GPU slanders against Harte, we see, still persists in the headquarters of the Workers Revolutionary party. There is no thought there that Harte might have been victimized by Jacson the way Sylvia Ageloff was victimized. There is no admission there of the possibility that Harte could have been deluded into taking Jacson as a trusted friend just as Ageloff, who fell in love with Jacson, was deluded into believing that her love was reciprocated.

Through Ageloff, a trusted member of the Trotskyist movement, who did not have the faintest idea of his real identity, Jacson was introduced into the household in Coyoacán.

Through Harte, he was introduced into the patio with a squad of killers.

After kidnapping and murdering Harte to avoid detection, Jacson was able on the basis of his relationship with Ageloff to enter Trotsky's study on August 20, 1940, and carry out the assignment given him by Stalin.

The specialists functioning under the banner of the "International Committee" do not report Trotsky's final verdict on the martyrdom of Robert Sheldon Harte. What Trotsky said does not conform to their suspicions and the imperatives of their "security" system.

One month after the May 24 assault, Harte's body was discovered. On the following morning, after having confirmed that it was really Bob, Trotsky voiced his grief.

> The body of Bob Sheldon Harte proves in a tragic manner the falsity of all the calumnies and denunciations leveled against him. . . .
> . . . the version that Sheldon was an agent of

the GPU is completely crushed. His body is a convincing argument. Bob perished because he placed himself in the road of the assassins. He died for the ideas in which he believed. His memory is spotless.[10]

Drilling for oil in Coyoacán

The Healyite "investigators" devote considerable space to Mark Zborowski, the GPU agent who penetrated the Trotskyist movement in 1934 and gained the confidence of Leon Sedov, Trotsky's son.

Under the name "Etienne," he helped publish the *Bulletin of the Left Opposition* and participated in the day-to-day work of the small center of the Fourth International in Paris. Zborowski was implicated in the mysterious death of Leon Sedov in a Paris hospital on February 16, 1938.[11]

Insofar as smearing the SWP is concerned, this operation must be written off as a dry well. In Coyoacán, however, Healy's drillers act as if they had struck a gusher.

One of their main targets is the article I wrote at the time describing the assassination of Trotsky, "With Trotsky to the End." Here are some of the items they find extremely suspicious:

1. The title is immodest.

I plead not guilty. The title was placed on the article by the editors of *Fourth International* in New York.

2. Hansen displays "precision-like accuracy on the state of the cloud formations to the south-west of Coyoacan, but deliberate omissions and evasions on the visit to the US Embassy and the immediate events following Trotsky's assassination."

I will come to the "deliberate omissions and evasions," pausing here only to indicate why I included the detail about the weather.

"... Harold Robins received the visitor in the patio," I wrote in 1940. "Jacson wore a raincoat across his arm. It was the rainy season, and although the sun was shining, heavy clouds massed over the mountains to the southwest threatened a downpour."

If Robins had asked Jacson to leave his raincoat, the assassin would not have been able to accomplish his mission—at least on that day, for Robins might well have noticed that inside the raincoat Jacson had hidden a gun, a dagger, and an alpine pickax.

But Robins did not suspect Jacson any more than anyone else did in the household; and in view of the weather there was no reason to wonder about the raincoat.

3. The Healyite sleuths question my statement that Trotsky had dozens upon dozens of friends in Mexico whom the guards would not handle any differently than they did Jacson.

To imply that my account was inaccurate, they quote Gen. Leandro A. Sanchez Salazar of the Mexican secret police and author of *Murder in Mexico*; Isaac Don Levine, author of *The Mind of an Assassin*; and Isaac Deutscher, the author of Trotsky's biography.

General Sanchez offered his impressions of the appearance of Trotsky's home and what this, in his opinion, revealed about Trotsky. The description is reasonably accurate, and I would not quarrel with the small errors and overstatements it contains.

Nor would I quarrel with the paragraphs cited from Levine's book. In preparing his manuscript, Levine consulted me concerning the details of the assassination of Trotsky, and I think the information contained in the paragraphs approved by Healy's "investigators" reflect what I told Levine.

Similarly in the case of the quotations from the biography of Trotsky. Deutscher asked me to go over the chapter dealing with the assassination to check its accuracy. Unfortunately this was delayed until the book had reached the stage of page proofs, which limited the changes he could make. Nonetheless, in the light of my criticism, Deutscher made such corrections as appeared imperative to him, and I think this is reflected in the paragraphs approved by Healy's specialists in plots and conspiracies.

---

10. Trotsky's statement appeared in the July 6, 1940, *Socialist Appeal* (the name used for a time by the *Militant*). It can also be found in the *Writings of Leon Trotsky (1939–40)*. See "GPU Tried to Cover Murder With Slander." This was the title used by the editors of the *Socialist Appeal*. We are republishing the article in this issue of *Intercontinental Press* under the title "Trotsky's Tribute to Robert Sheldon Harte." See p. 1655.

11. In his biography of Leon Trotsky, Isaac Deutscher includes an account of the agent provocateur. See vol. 3, *The Prophet Outcast*. Also see *Our Own People*, by Elisabeth K. Poretsky. (Ann Arbor: University of Michigan Press, 1969).

4. The Healyites quote from my introduction to Trotsky's autobiographical work *My Life* in which I mentioned how I and Rae Spiegel, who served as Trotsky's Russian secretary, removed the small automatic on Trotsky's desk out of our concern over the emotional crisis he and Natalia were going through.[12]

According to our Healyite "security" experts this ". . . left Trotsky without a weapon to defend himself in the event of one of the 'dozens upon dozens' of visitors being a GPU assassin!"

What swine!

L.D. and Natalia were mourning the murder of their son Leon Sedov. They stayed in their room *without seeing anyone*—not even the guards and secretaries, outside of Rae, who made sure that food was brought to them and attended them in whatever way she could.

Moreover, it was not Trotsky's habit to carry a gun. He left his automatic on his desk in his study, which he did not enter in those weeks. Even when the most painful phase of mourning began to subside, he started to write in his bedroom, not using his study or a secretary.

The real security problem in this instance was not counteracting the danger accompanying visitors but helping L.D. and Natalia in a personal way through this very difficult period in their lives.

5. Attempting to prove that security in Coyoacán was exceedingly lax, the Healyites quote a letter from Harold Robins:

> When I arrived in Mexico in October 1939, as a member of the guard I found that none of the members of the guard had even fired their weapons in more than a year's time. For my part, I had never fired a gun in my life.

Marksmanship was not the sole criterion by which guards were selected. Expert drivers were just as badly needed. Robins had had experience

Advertisement in four-page Healyite throwaway distributed at October 10–12 antiracist conference in Boston.

as a New York taxi driver. Also Robins had proved his capacity as a union battler, even having served a term in prison for union activities.

As for stepping up the armed defense, that began after my arrival in 1937. Our first decision was to standardize the equipment as much as possible. For that we brought in .38-caliber Colts, which were easier to obtain in the United States in those days than they are now.

The guard included members with years of experience in handling guns, which naturally included keeping up their skill with a minimum expenditure of live ammunition.

6. Elsewhere in his letter, Robins, recalling details of the assassination, says:

> According to Joe's account he and I both arrived at the doorway of Trotsky's office at the same time. Hansen wrote that while he went to help L.D., Robins went into the office to take care of the assassin.
>
> Since the assassin held a 45-calibre "Star" pistol in his hand at that time, I posed the question when recounting the events of August 20, 1940, that Hansen did not reach the door with me because he would then have gone into the office to subdue and disarm the assassin. That action fell to me since I was first on the scene.

Robins wrote his letter, apparently, because of some "mixup of quotes," which he is trying to straighten out.

The Healyites are delighted. "Robins' letter alone," they say, "calls for a fresh inquiry into the

---

12. For the details, see the introduction to *My Life* (New York: Pathfinder Press, 1970), pp. 33–4 [2015 printing].

circumstances surrounding Trotsky's death."

That's what they say!

Here is what I wrote in the article "With Trotsky to the End":

> As I entered the door connecting the library with the dining room the Old Man stumbled out of his study a few feet away, blood streaming down his face.
>
> *"See what they have done to me!"* he said.
>
> At the same moment Harold Robins came through the north door of the dining room with Natalia following. Throwing her arms frantically about him, Natalia took Trotsky on to the balcony. Harold and I had made for Jacson, who stood in the study gasping, face knotted, arms limp, automatic pistol dangling in his hand. Harold was closer to him. "You take care of him," I said, "I'll see what's happened to the Old Man." Even as I turned, Robins brought the assassin down to the floor.

Does that call for a "fresh inquiry"? Let the inquiry consist of reading the two quotations again.

Trotsky's study opened onto the dining room. Robins and I reached the *dining room* about the same time. The entrance to the study was closer to the door through which Robins had rushed in from the patio than it was to the library door through which I entered from the opposite end of the dining room. Therefore Robins was closer to Jacson than I was.

I could have fired at Jacson from where I stood, and I would not have missed. It was imperative to take him alive, however. That was why I told Robins, "You take care of him." Which Robins did, while I turned my attention to L.D.

Everyone clear on the position of the various rooms, the three doors, and the sequence?

So much for that oil-drilling operation.

And where was Healy?

In their "investigation," the Healyites concentrate on the single question of measures that might have led to the unmasking of Jacson or at least of discovering concealed weapons on anyone coming near Trotsky.

This, of course, follows from their concept of "security," which is to create the highest possible level of mutual suspicion among comrades working together.

Because of this they remain glued to the actual course that our defensive measures—feeble though they were because of limited resources—compelled the GPU murder machine to take.

Because of this, the Healyites leave out of account other security problems that were of great concern to us in Coyoacán.

1. Sappers could tunnel from an area in the neighborhood and dynamite the house. This method had been used by the GPU against revolutionists in Europe. If I recall correctly, Trotsky mentioned that this had occurred in Poland.

2. The place could be bombed by a small plane. We weighed the feasibility of setting up steel nets. But this was not within our means and it might not have proved workable.

3. We could be machine-gunned on the highway or on a street in Coyoacán. This seemed to me to be an especially vulnerable point. We tried to meet it with careful procedures and split-second timing on all trips that included L.D.

4. Package bombs could be tried.

5. Poisons could be introduced through food brought into the house. We tried repeatedly to lower this possibility, but it always remained a danger.

6. The place could be attacked by demonstrators mobilized by the Mexican Stalinists. This was a very real threat. Several times, the Stalinists seemed to be organizing for this; but our countermeasures proved effective.

Our chief problem, however, was our fixed position. We had no way of changing our base the way guerrillas do, thereby constantly disrupting the plans of attackers. Of course, we had a few places that could serve as temporary hideouts for Trotsky and that we actually used when the situation appeared particularly dangerous. Under GPU surveillance, however, these could prove to be deadly traps.

It is well understood today how difficult it is for even a powerful government to safeguard its top political figures from individual assassins. It can be imagined how much more difficult it is for an individual to block one of the most powerful governments in the world that has determined to kill him, particularly if that individual is pinned down, as we were, to a spot known to everyone.

As one of the world's great military figures, Trotsky was perfectly aware of this. Yet all of us shared his determination to make the struggle as difficult and as costly to Stalin as we could.

It is possible, of course, that Healy had some proposals in those days that might have improved our defense. Unfortunately they were never called to our attention in Coyoacán.

If they were published anywhere, Healy would seem duty bound to state what publication they appeared in, or even to reprint them with some comments on the lessons to be drawn thirty-five years later.

The fact is that Healy belonged to a clique that stood in opposition to Trotsky as long as Trotsky was alive.

This did not prevent Trotsky from being concerned about them. In 1938 he asked James P. Cannon to stop in London, talk with them, and try to persuade them to send a delegation to the founding congress of the Fourth International.

They said no to Cannon and Trotsky. I have never heard what the reasons were, and I suppose that in the final analysis the reasons are not of much interest. Perhaps the clique thought of the width of the Channel and the likelihood of a choppy crossing, and put "security" first.

A few years after Trotsky's death, Healy made a self-criticism and tried to follow the example set by Cannon in party building. There was considerable hope in the Fourth International that this would help Trotskyism to become rooted in Britain. However, Healy veered in a sectarian direction around 1956, became more and more preoccupied with "security," and is still traveling down that road.

As for Slaughter, was he in the Communist party when Trotsky was murdered, doing for Stalin what he now does for Healy? Or did this come later?

FBI 'associations'—a geyser of mud

In the September 6, 1975, issue of *Workers Press*, under the title "The Role of Joseph Hansen and Pabloite Revisionism," the "International Committee" presents its chief finding, a report by Robert G. McGregor, an aide to the American consul in Mexico City, of a conversation with me, which was sent to the State Department. The State Department later included it in materials open to public inspection.

McGregor's report, as quoted by *Workers Press* (which may account for the British punctuation), is as follows:

> Mr Joseph Hansen, secretary to the late Mr Trotsky came in on Saturday morning in order to discuss matters connected with the assassination of Mr Trotsky. I told him of my desire to be in possession of as much information as possible regarding the relationship of the assassin and Miss Sylvia Ageloff with the United States.
>
> Hansen repeated his assertions that this crime was engineered from the United States. He pointed to the fact that Mornard (the assassin) had made a journey to the United States between the dates of the first attempt upon Trotsky's life and the second successful one. He declared that undoubtedly the desk clerk at the Hotel Pierpont in Brooklyn could give some information and seemed to attach considerable importance to the packages that Sylvia states Mornard kept in the safe at the hotel. Hansen likewise believes that the Ageloff family could furnish some valuable information as to who Mornard saw while on his last trip to New York.
>
> It is Hansen's opinion that Mornard himself will be unable to give much more authentic information concerning names of persons acting as his principles in this matter. For, while Hansen is convinced that the murder is a GPU job, that very fact makes it hard to unravel. Hansen stated that when in New York in 1938 he was himself approached by an agent of the GPU and asked to desert the Fourth International and join the Third. He referred the matter to Trotsky who asked him to go as far with the matter as possible. For three months Hansen had relations with a man who merely identified himself as "John," and did not otherwise reveal his real identity.
>
> I had hoped that Hansen might cast some suspicion on persons in the United States but most of his suspicions seemed to attach themselves to persons now in Mexico. In this connection he mentioned a Mr Frank Jellenek

who came to Mexico in November 1937 from France and was at that time writing a book on the French Commune. He represented himself as the correspondent for the *Manchester Guardian* and had close connections with Mr Frank Kluckholm, former correspondent for the *New York Times* in Mexico. Hansen said that Jellinek's actions led him to believe that he is a GPU agent in Mexico.

Hansen declared that he shared the opinion expressed to me personally by the late Mr Trotsky that Mr Harry Block, an American citizen residing in the Federal District, is the direct agent here for Mr Oumansky, Soviet Ambassador in Washington. Oumansky, Hansen said, is a police officer whom Trotsky knew personally when in authority in Russia and that Trotsky always felt apprehensive of Oumansky's presence in Washington.

I asked Hansen what his impression was of President Cardenas' recent statements condemning the communists. He said that he was afraid this was the "swan song" of the investigation of the assassination of Trotsky. He seemed to have little faith in the sincerity of the endeavours of the police to unravel the crime.

Missing from McGregor's report is any explanation of the objectives of my visit to the American consulate. Yet I must have had some reason other than the pleasure of "associating" with an FBI agent, as the Healyites suggest.

The report itself, however, indicates that it concerned the identity of the assassin. McGregor, in reporting to his superior, implies that he took the initiative in this: "I told him of my desire to be in possession of as much information as possible regarding the relationship of the assassin and Miss Sylvia Ageloff with the United States."

Again: "I had hoped that Hansen might cast some suspicion on persons in the United States. . . ."

It is also completely clear from the report (for which, of course, I do not take any responsibility whatever) that everything I said was directed against the GPU and was intended to further the investigation of the identity of the assassin.

Now let us turn to the way in which the nameless and faceless members of Healy's "International Committee" seek to utilize this material to cast the foulest suspicion on me and the Socialist Workers party.

"One document in particular," they say, "raises questions about Hansen himself. It is a statement that he made to an FBI agent who was operating under diplomatic cover at the American Embassy in Mexico City. Hansen made a statement to him on August 31, 1940, 11 days after Trotsky had been killed by the GPU agent Ramon Mercader."

They say again (in the September 9, 1975, issue of *Workers Press*):

"Until the International Committee discovered the existence of a statement he gave to the FBI agent at the US Embassy on August 31, the movement knew nothing of it. Why?"

In the whole series of twenty-six articles, the Healyites in no place indicate the basis of their charge that McGregor was "an FBI agent who was operating under diplomatic cover at the American Embassy." I will indicate a possible source of the charge further on. For the moment it is sufficient to note how the Healyites use this label to suggest that at Coyoacán I was in "association" with an agent of the FBI.

To bolster the impression they seek to create, they make further insinuations in their article, "The Role of Joseph Hansen and Pabloite Revisionism":

> The tone of the opening sentence of the US Consul McGregor's report hints at a familiar relationship with Hansen. Perhaps this is why they made a Saturday morning rendezvous. It raises the question whether Hansen had met McGregor before. How many times? What had they discussed?

Why doesn't Healy make the same insinuation in relation to a more important figure than Hansen? McGregor states: "Hansen declared that he shared the opinion expressed to me personally by the late Mr Trotsky. . . ."

Doesn't that raise the question whether Trotsky had actually met McGregor? How many times? What had they discussed? How is Trotsky's "association" with an alleged FBI agent to be explained?

Everything else in McGregor's report pales in

comparison with that question, for whatever Hansen did quite obviously was in accordance with a relationship established by Trotsky himself.

That this is the case can easily be shown from other reports from the consulate reprinted by the "International Committee" in *Workers Press*.

1. In a report to the State Department,[13] Geo. P. Shaw, the American consul in Mexico City, said:

> This matter was first brought to my attention by Mr Charles Cornell, who came to the Consulate General to report the disappearance of Mr Harte.... I immediately delegated Consul Robert G. McGregor, Jr. to accompany Mr Cornell to Trotsky's residence to verify the statements made and to ascertain any other interesting facts available.

Healy's net has caught another "dubious" figure, Trotsky's secretary Charles Cornell, in "association" with an alleged FBI agent.

2. In a confidential memorandum, McGregor reported how Cornell drove him to the residence of "Mr Leon Trotsky, in Coyoacan," where Cornell showed him the grounds and described the May 24 assault. Cornell's affability hints at a familiar relationship!

WORKERS PRESS
SLAUGHTER: Brings American workers Healyite message on importance of maintaining "security" against Hansen.

3. Continuing his report, the alleged FBI agent said: "I entered the house proper and was confronted by Mr Trotsky. He was most polite and talked with me in his office for about ten minutes....

> "I explained that my interest in the matter was to seek means whereby Harte could be rescued and in this connection to co-operate fully with the Mexican police."

Healy has now enmeshed the most "dubious" figure of all—Leon Trotsky. Why doesn't he try to land him, the way he did Hansen?

4. McGregor reported still another conversation with a member of Trotsky's guards, this time Walter O'Rourke, on May 27, 1940. The conversation was about the May 24 assault, Stalin's possible motives, the identity of the attackers, and whether Harte could have been an accomplice.

> He [O'Rourke] said that he was sure that Harte was not a party to the crime because he said that all the guards employed by Trotsky were sent here after very careful observance of their activities by members of the Party in the United States, and that Harte would have had to be a superb actor to have consistently concealed the intention for which he was sent, and that he did not believe the boy to be capable of masquerading as a Trotskyist, with all of the careful observation to which Trotsky's aides are subjected.

O'Rourke, too! Score another "association" with the FBI for Healy's probers.

5. In still another memorandum to the State Department, McGregor reported a confidential conversation he had with Trotsky on June 25, 1940. McGregor wanted to know Trotsky's reaction to interpretations of a statement he had made to the press.

Healy's bloodhounds have really exposed the "dubious" Trotsky. He was in "association" with the FBI agent at least *twice*, according to the agent's report and not just once as in the case of Hansen.

In this confidential rendezvous with Consul McGregor, Trotsky said that his statement had been misinterpreted. He also gave McGregor the names of certain Stalinist figures who might provide information concerning the May 24 attack. McGregor included in his report the following item:

> In a strictly confidential and private manner Mr Trotsky told me that he suspected

---
13. As published in the August 21, 1975, issue of *Workers Press*.

the orders for this attempt on his life came through the Soviet Ambassador in Washington, Mr. Oumanski, who according to Trotsky is a GPU agent.

When I followed this same line in my conversation with McGregor following the assassination of Trotsky, Healy's "International Committee" took this as proof of my "dubious" character:

"Hansen makes another puzzling statement to the man from the embassy. He says that he believed that the Stalinist murder plot originated in the United States. But all the evidence demonstrates that the center was in Paris. This was easily deductible by even the most amateur observer."

And why doesn't the same reasoning apply to Trotsky? It is because at this point Healy is not interested in smearing Trotsky. His immediate target is Hansen.

An item worth noting in connection with this point is the testimony years later of Budenz, in whom the Healyites place great confidence as we have seen. Budenz publicly implicated members of the Stalinist machine in the United States in the murder of Leon Trotsky.

Demands were raised in the United States to bring Budenz and his accomplices to trial. A grand jury actually questioned Budenz, but nothing came in response to public insistence that he be indicted.

Let me now bring into focus the material brought forward by the members of Healy's "International Committee."

Among the chores assigned to Trotsky's secretaries in Coyoacán was diplomatic relations with the Mexican government and with the embassies of other governments when necessity arose. Most of this work, naturally, involved the Mexican government, which had granted political asylum to L.D. and Natalia. The American secretaries were assigned to cover the American consulate. That was why, aside from Trotsky, the names dug up of those who "associated" with the consulate were all Americans—Cornell, O'Rourke, Hansen.

On my first visit to the American consulate, Trotsky explained the procedure to follow. For me it was a valuable lesson in the protocols of diplomacy. Trotsky's parting words as I set off, were: "Go play poker with them."[14]

The purpose of the visit was to make an informal inquiry as to what would be the probable reaction of the State Department if Trotsky were to apply for a visa to visit the United States. The purpose of the visit would be to make a tour of the battlefields of the Civil War to help in writing a book comparing that conflict with the civil war in Russia.

The aide in the consulate assigned to talk with me about this was McGregor.

When I reported back, Trotsky speculated that McGregor might be an attaché assigned to topics of interest to the FBI, and he explained how all the embassies of all countries include attachés who follow special fields of interest. However, he was never firm about this possible identification, and of course it would have made no difference to Trotsky. First of all, we were not responsible for the personnel in the embassy. Secondly, we had no choice in the matter.

The response that came back from the State Department on Trotsky's inquiry, and that was relayed to me by McGregor on a subsequent visit, was that if Trotsky applied no visa would be granted.

Now let's turn to the inquiries I made at the American consulate following the assassination of Trotsky. The inquiry was made, of course, in consultation with Natalia Trotsky, with Albert Goldman, and with other members of the household, of whom I might mention especially Evelyn Reed.

One purpose of the inquiry was to do everything possible to suggest that the State Department utilize its resources to help ascertain the real identity of the assassin. McGregor was generous with his time and I mustered all the arguments I could think of.

Another—and important—purpose of the inquiry was to probe the probable reaction of the State Department to an application by Natalia Trotsky and her grandson for visas to come to

---

14. On some occasions when he was relaxing, such as on a visit to Taxco, Trotsky played a simple game of cards with other members of the household. I tried to inveigle him into learning poker. He played for a time with interest. However, after being bluffed a few times, he argued that it was unfair. The rules permitted someone with almost nothing to win against a much superior hand! Whether because of this or because he really did not care for cards he did not take up the game.

the United States where we could safeguard and take care of them much better than we could in Mexico.

The response to the inquiry soon came and McGregor called Coyoacán, asking me to come to his office.

There he gave me the information concerning the origin of the false passport that Jacson said he had burned on the way to Coyoacán. He also gave me a copy of the photograph on this passport, and mentioned that the consulate was turning the same information over to the Mexican police, who would release it publicly.

This was the source of the photograph of Jacson and the information about his false passport used by the press of the Trotskyist movement.[15]

As for Natalia and the grandson of Trotsky, McGregor said that Natalia would be turned down but the grandson would be permitted to enter the United States.

After agonizing over this response, Natalia felt that she could not bear the separation, and that it would not be good for the orphaned Seva.

As I have already pointed out, the direction taken by the frame-up artists of the "International Committee" is to smear Trotsky with the tar brush of "association" with an FBI agent, although they have not yet gone that far.

If they are contemplating further steps along this road, I can offer them testimony which they may consider to be first-rate for their purposes. This is the "confession" written by Jacson to help cover up the GPU in case he should happen to be killed by Trotsky's guards. Here is the pertinent paragraph:[16]

> One day, speaking of the fortress, which his house had become, he [Trotsky] said: It is not only to defend myself against the Stalinists, but also against the Minorityites which meant that he desired the expulsion of various members of the party. Precisely in connection with this house, which he said very well had been converted into a fortress, I asked myself very often, from where had come the money for such work, since in reality the party is very poor and in many countries does not have the possibility of bringing out a daily paper, an indispensable means for the struggle. From where came this money? Perhaps the consul of a great foreign nation who often visited him could answer this question for us.

Should that not be quite explicit enough for Healy's purposes, it could be reinforced by the direct charge made by Oscar Greydt Abelenda in the March 1940 issue of Lombardo Toledano's crypto-Stalinist magazine *Futuro* that Trotsky "as is logical" placed himself in the "service of the Federal Bureau of Investigation (FBI) of the United States."[17]

In echoing such charges, the nameless and faceless "International Committee" follows a path, we can see, that converges with that of the assassins of Leon Trotsky.

Their way versus Lenin's way

Is there a discernible political issue in this reeking package?

A single point stands out. This is Healy's difference with the Socialist Workers party on how to uphold the security of a revolutionary organization against infiltration.

In his article "An Answer to Budenz's Latest Frame-up,"[18] James P. Cannon has outlined the principles observed by the SWP.

In opposition to these principles, Healy maintains a *permanent witch-hunt* in the Workers Revolutionary party and the Workers League. This witch-hunt is highly disruptive.

Which method is in the Leninist tradition of party building?

I indicated Trotsky's views on the question in my article "With Trotsky to the End." The outline is accurate, and I will repeat it:

> Each day in this period of world war, of factional struggles, was of immeasurable value to the new generation of revolutionary cad-

---

15. A good reproduction can be found on p. 25 of *Leon Trotsky: The Man and His Work.*

16. For the full text of Jacson's "confession," see *The Assassination of Leon Trotsky,* by Albert Goldman, pp. 5–8.

17. Quoted on p. 8 of my article "The Attempted Assassination of Leon Trotsky" in *Leon Trotsky: The Man and His Work.*

18. See footnote No. 8.

res. Trotsky knew it better than anyone. He wanted to hand us intact the entire heritage of Bolshevism which was in his charge, even down to the smallest item. He knew what that heritage had cost, what it was worth to us in the epoch now opening before us. The time was so short!

Since September 1937 Trotsky's secretaries tried to institute a system in the household whereby everyone who entered would be searched for concealed weapons. They also attempted to make it an iron rule that Trotsky was never to talk with anyone alone in his study. Trotsky could not endure either of these rules. Either we trust the people and admit them without search, or we do not admit them at all. He could not bear having his friends submit to search. No doubt he felt that in any case it would be useless and could even give us a false sense of security. If a GPU agent succeeded in entering, he would find some way of setting at naught what search we could make. Trotsky had dozens upon dozens of friends in Mexico, whom the guards—so far as their vigilance was concerned—placed in the same general category as Jacson before the assault. As to our second proposal that someone should always remain with him in his study, this too was never effective. So many of his guests had personal problems—would not talk freely in the presence of a guard! Sometimes I was able to remain in the room merely by sitting down contrary to Trotsky's instructions to leave, but both he and I felt uncomfortable about it, and he would never permit this discourtesy from anyone else. Trotsky was the builder of the political party and a worker in the field of ideas. He preferred to trust his friends rather than to suspect them.

All of Trotsky's guards tried to make themselves suspicious of everyone. Trotsky, however, was interested not only in being guarded, but in teaching his guards by example some of the fundamentals of organizing a political movement. Mutual suspicion in his eyes was a disintegrating force much worse than the inclusion of a spy in the organization, since such suspicions are useless anyway in uncovering a highly skilled provocateur. Trotsky hated personal suspicion towards the members and sympathizers of the Fourth International. He considered it worse than the evil it was supposed to cure.

Whenever this subject came up, he was fond of telling the story of Malinovsky, who became a member of the Political Bureau of the Bolshevik Party, its representative in the Duma and a trusted confidant of Lenin. Malinovsky was at the same time an agent of the Czar's secret police, the dread Okhrana. He sent hundreds of Bolsheviks into exile and death. Nevertheless, in order to maintain his position of confidence, it was necessary for him to spread the ideas of Bolshevism. These ideas eventually caused his downfall. The proletarian revolution is more powerful than the most cunning police spy.

From their viewpoint, the Healyites correctly single out these paragraphs for some of their most venomous attacks. The picture of Trotsky that emerges does not fit what the ranks of the Workers Revolutionary party have been led to believe; that is, that Healy was shaped in the image of Trotsky, and if you've seen Healy in operation then you've seen Trotsky.

For instance, they say in "The Role of Joseph Hansen and Pabloite Revisionism":

> There is no doubt that the social revolution is definitely more powerful than the secret police. But Hansen is saying something quite different.
>
> He is using Trotsky's anecdote about Malinovsky to suggest that such agents provocateurs inevitably find their way into revolutionary parties: They are obliged to play a progressive as well as a revolutionary role; and no matter, in due course they will be flushed out when the revolution occurs.
>
> With this kind of conception, why bother about security at all? Hansen suggests that having a spy in the organization is better than an atmosphere of "mutual suspicion." He opposes one to the other. We are for neither.

Instead of trying to learn from Trotsky, the Healyites try to shift Trotsky's view onto Hansen and in that way dispose of it as coming from a "dubious" source.

Nonetheless, Healy's argument is really against Trotsky and ultimately Lenin, for Trotsky was only passing on to us the attitude taken by Lenin.

In his biography of Stalin, Trotsky reports Lenin's defense of Malinovsky:

STALIN: His "security" methods are aped by leaders of the WRP in Britain.

> Lenin's opponents subjected him to a prolonged and cruel barrage for "sheltering" Malinovsky. The participation of a police agent in the Duma fraction, and especially in the Central Committee, was, of course, a great calamity to the Party. As a matter of fact, Stalin had gone to his last exile because of Malinovsky's betrayal. But in those days suspicions, complicated at times by factional hostility, poisoned the atmosphere of the underground. No one presented any direct evidence against Malinovsky. After all, it was impossible to condemn a member of the Party to political—and perhaps even physical—death on the basis of vague suspicion. And since Malinovsky occupied a responsible position and the reputation of the Party depended to a certain extent on his reputation, Lenin deemed it his duty to defend Malinovsky with the energy which always distinguished him.[19]

19. Leon Trotsky, *Stalin* (New York: Harper & Brothers, 1941), p. 151.

Krupskaya recalls that in the summer of 1914 doubts about Malinovsky crossed Lenin's mind:

> Rumours about Malinovsky being an *agent provocateur* had been circulating for a long time. These rumours came from Menshevik circles. Elena Fedorovna Rozmirovich had strong suspicions in connection with her arrest—she had worked with the Duma fraction. The gendarmes who questioned her possessed information about details which they could have obtained only from spies inside the organisation. Bukharin also had certain information about Malinovsky's conduct. Vladimir Ilyich thought it utterly impossible for Malinovsky to have been an *agent provocateur*. Only once did a doubt flash across his mind. I remember one day in Poronin, we were returning from the Zinovievs and talked about these rumours. Suddenly Ilyich stopped on the little bridge that we were crossing and said: 'It may be true!' and his face expressed anxiety. 'What are you talking about, it's nonsense,' I answered deprecatingly. Ilyich calmed down and began to abuse the Mensheviks, saying that they were unscrupulous as to the means they employed in the struggle against the Bolsheviks. He had no other doubts on this question.[20]

After the February 1917 revolution, evidence in the tsarist archives proved that Malinovsky had indeed served the police as an agent provocateur. Lenin appeared before the investigating commission. The following summary of his testimony indicates his views:[21]

> I did not believe—testified Citizen Ulyanov before the Extraordinary Investigating Commission of the Provisional Government—in provocateurship here, and for the following reason: If Malinovsky were a provocateur, the

20. N.K. Krupskaya, *Memories of Lenin*, vol. 2 (New York: International Publishers, undated), pp. 131–32.

21. Cited in *Three Who Made a Revolution*, by Bertram D. Wolfe (New York: Dial Press, 1948), pp. 553–54. Wolfe devotes a chapter to the career of Malinovsky, including facts drawn from rather extensive research.

Okhrana would not gain from that as much as our Party did from *Pravda* and the whole legal apparatus. [In which Malinovsky played a key role.—J.H.] It is clear that by bringing a provocateur into the Duma and eliminating for that purpose all the competitors of bolshevism, etc., the Okhrana was guided by a gross conception of bolshevism, I should say rather a crude, homemade (*lubochnii*) caricature. They imagined that the Bolsheviks would arrange an armed insurrection. In order to keep all the threads of this coming insurrection in their hands, they thought it worth while to have recourse to all sorts of things to bring Malinovsky into the Duma and the Central Committee. But when the Okhrana succeeded in both these matters, what happened? It happened that Malinovsky was transformed into one of the links of the long and solid chain connecting our illegal base with the two chief legal organs by which our Party influenced the masses: *Pravda* and the Duma Fraction. The *agent provocateur* had to serve both these organs in order to justify his vocation.

Both these organs were under our immediate guidance. Zinoviev and I wrote daily to *Pravda* and its policy was entirely determined by the resolutions of the Party. Our influence over forty to sixty thousand workers was thus secured . . . [*Vestnik Vremmenago Pravitelstva*—News Bulletin of the Provisional Government, June 16, 1917. p. 3.]

In November 1918 Malinovsky returned to Russia. He was put on trial, convicted, and shot for his crimes.

The few facts I have cited are sufficient to prove, I believe, that Trotsky's views on the problem of infiltration and how to counteract it were not different in general from those of Lenin. It will also be agreed, I think, that Cannon's views were in the tradition of Lenin and Trotsky.

Healy's concept is the polar opposite. It falls within the tradition of Stalin, including Stalin's frame-up methods.

Let us note another very important fact. The Bolsheviks and other revolutionary currents in Russia had to operate in the underground against one of the most oppressive governments of the time. The lives of hundreds of comrades were at stake. If they were not executed, they were imprisoned or exiled for years.

The Workers Revolutionary party operates in a country where democratic traditions are still very strong. One of the sights in London is cops who do not even carry guns. The WRP can conduct public meetings, march in the streets, post pickets, sell its paper and other literature, without the least interference from the authorities.

Nonetheless, Healy's obsession with "security" causes the WRP to act as if it were deep underground, fighting against terror squads and a police that might seize and torture to death any WRP members they can lay hands on. In other words, the WRP seems to see little difference between Harold Wilson and Chile's Pinochet.

Thus "security" is an *absolute* under Healy's regime. There is nothing at all relative about it. No adjustments for varying degrees of oppression are admitted.

It is, of course, possible that Britain, too, may go the way of Chile. Healy might argue that this is the real prospect and that the organization must be prepared well in advance for it.

If this prognosis proves to be correct, it can safely be predicted that the WRP will be permeated with such a false sense of security that it will be helpless before the infiltrators, some of whom may turn out to be as skilled as the fabled Malinovsky and as high up in the Healyite hierarchy.

As my final bit of evidence to show the superiority of the tradition upheld by the Socialist Workers party, I should like to point out that at no time in the forty years or more for which we have definite proof did the FBI succeed in disrupting the SWP or in creating a poisonous atmosphere among its ranks. This includes the years of McCarthyism in which a general witch-hunt atmosphere affected the entire country.

It was only by strictly adhering to the principles and the methods taught us by Trotsky that we were able to inculcate an attitude of mutual confidence among party members that enabled us to survive McCarthyism and the pressure emanating from the FBI.

Now finally, in the wake of the defeat suffered by American imperialism in Indochina and the wave of exposures of government corruption and government lawbreaking, the Socialist Workers party has been able to turn the tables on the FBI.

Through its $27 million lawsuit against Nixon, et al., the SWP took the lead in exposing the FBI's infamous Counterintelligence Programs. Its success in compelling the FBI to release some 4,000 pages of documents detailing the illegal actions of its agents in connection with the SWP has inspired others to press similar actions.

The achievements of the SWP against the FBI can already be accounted one of the most inspiring victories yet won in this field in the United States.

And Healy's method? It has succeeded only in disrupting his own organization, in making it more vulnerable to infiltration by the Special Branch or other agencies—if they have any interest in his sect—and in bringing shame and condemnation on his head from partisans of the truth.

NOVEMBER 14, 1975

'Shameful and Sinister Motives'
HEALY'S FRAME-UP AGAINST JOSEPH HANSEN
By George Novack

Gerry Healy, general secretary of the Workers Revolutionary party, has been seized by a passion for historical research. The press of his entire movement from London to Sydney has dedicated itself, week in, week out, to scrutinizing the circumstances surrounding Trotsky's assassination in August 1940 and its aftermath. Why has this event that occurred thirty-five years ago so suddenly and totally obsessed the leader of the sectarian International Committee?

Certainly not because of any desire to establish or amplify the true facts about the affair, which a scrupulous scholar like Isaac Deutscher might do. Healy's campaign has more shameful and sinister motives and his researches pursue other objectives. He is impelled to slander and discredit his political opponents in the Socialist Workers party and the Fourth International, even if that tends to dishonor Trotsky himself and his son Sedov. Then he seeks to serve notice on present or potential critical minds in his own ranks that if they voice dissenting opinions, they are liable to the same kind of abuse as has been heaped upon Tim Wohlforth, Nancy Fields, Alan Thornett, and others who have gotten crosswise with the unchallengeable guru.

The third reason is the most despicable, petty, and spiteful. That is his personal vendetta against Joseph Hansen, editor of *Intercontinental Press*. Healy is bent on destroying by the vilest means the reputation of this veteran revolutionist who has most persistently and effectively exposed his theoretical incapacity, political errors, and organizational methods. In actuality, his efforts only provide proof of Hansen's diagnosis that Healy has a streak of paranoia in his makeup. This psychological factor accounts for the frenzied drive and unrestrained viciousness of the false accusations and insinuations Healy and his acolytes have launched against Hansen in the pamphlet entitled *Security and the Fourth International: An Inquiry into the Assassination of Leon Trotsky*.

In it Healy charges that the SWP leadership of that time was "criminally negligent" in failing to prevent Trotsky's assassination (he discovered this only after breaking off years of collaboration with them); that Joseph Hansen, as one of Trotsky's secretaries, was the chief culprit; and he insinuates that Hansen may be either an FBI or a GPU agent or both. Such lies and slanders are the ammunition with which reactionary forces have often bombarded honest revolutionists. Healy has resorted to their techniques because he feels more at ease on this level than in the give and take of political debate. That demands talents beyond his capacities.

I am writing this reply to his poison-pen attacks, not only as a longtime leader of the SWP and intimate co-worker of Hansen's for over a third of a century, but as one of the most authoritative living witnesses to the developments upon which Healy bases his false indictment. Let me briefly indicate, for those unacquainted with my early career, what my credentials are in relation to the events leading up to and following upon Stalin's assassination of his arch-antagonist.

For six years, from 1934, shortly after I joined the Communist League of America, until the day of Trotsky's death in August 1940, I was more or less occupied by assignment with matters pertaining to Trotsky's security.

In 1934, when the Russian exile was in France, being hounded by fascists and Stalinists alike—in response to a desperate appeal for help, I initiated a committee of American intellectuals that sought to obtain entry for Trotsky into the United States. We retained Morris Ernst, then general counsel of the

American Civil Liberties Union, to see Roosevelt at the White House to intercede with the president. The effort failed and Trotsky remained "a man on the planet without a visa" until the newly elected Norwegian Labor government gave him asylum in 1935.

When the first Moscow Trial was staged in 1936 and the Norwegian cabinet under pressure from the Kremlin interned Trotsky and Natalia so they were gagged and unable to defend themselves against Prosecutor Vyshinsky's infamous accusations, that early committee was revived under the name of the American Committee for the Defense of Leon Trotsky. I served as its national secretary. This body had the objectives of obtaining asylum for Trotsky and promoting the formation of an International Commission of Inquiry into the Moscow frame-ups.

We realized both of these aims. In December, through the mediation of the writer Anita Brenner and the artist Diego Rivera, President Cárdenas agreed to welcome the Trotskys as guests of his government. I can vividly recall how Max Shachtman and I relayed that cheering news by phone from New York to Oslo through Walter Held. In January we met Trotsky and Natalia upon their arrival in Tampico and escorted them on the presidential train to Frida Kahlo's home in Coyoacán.

After helping to bring it together, I accompanied the Dewey Commission of Inquiry to Mexico in April 1937 where it held the memorable hearings, recorded in *The Case of Leon Trotsky*, that attracted world attention and dealt the strongest blow to the credibility of the Moscow Trials.

After that, together with comrades of the SWP and others assigned to that duty, I worked to safeguard Trotsky in every way possible against the death warrant issued against him by Stalin's henchmen. I was especially entrusted with raising the funds needed for the extensive defense measures that were instituted both before and following the May 24, 1940, Siqueiros assault on the household. Indeed, one of the last letters Trotsky wrote, shortly before he was struck down, was addressed to a sympathizer friend who had contributed generously for that purpose.[1]

I was also apprised of the investigations undertaken to check on persons connected with the household after the May assault and the additional measures taken to strengthen the defenses.

During that same time, because of my contacts in different circles, I was placed in charge of securing documents and visas for Trotskyists in Western Europe whose lives and liberties were menaced by the Nazis and their agents. I collaborated with several voluntary agencies and negotiated with government officials in this cause and succeeded in bringing to safety a number of endangered Jewish and non-Jewish comrades. For example, I made all arrangements for Walter Held (Heinz Epe) and his family to come to the United States, invoking the aid of high government officials, but he was apprehended by the Soviet secret police in transit through the USSR and executed. Unknown to us at that time was the presence of one GPU agent among those we brought to safety. That was Mark Zborowski (Etienne) around whom Healy has raised his hue and cry decades later.

It was better to save ten good comrades even if included in the company was one treacherous agent whose identity was in any event then unknown and unproven. If a similar situation should recur in Western Europe or elsewhere, we of the SWP would follow the same policy. We would not wait to check out the bona fides of every individual in our movement to the nth degree before coming to their rescue.

During this entire period I worked in fraternal association with Trotsky and enjoyed his confidence, as did Hansen and Cannon. This is more than Healy can claim.

What Healy does claim is that we abused that confidence and were guilty of not taking better precautions and thereby preventing Trotsky's assassination. This turns the situation upside down. It is true that we did not prevent Trotsky's death. Despite the tightest defense and constant vigilance, it is not easy, and it is in fact hardly possible, to hold off indefinitely a determined band of assassins, armed with inexhaustible resources, from carrying out their deadly objective. They can be staved off for a while, as happened by accident in May. But in the long run their chances of success are optimal, as Trotsky himself was well aware.

With all the forces at their command the Russian

---

1. See *Writings of Leon Trotsky, 1939–40*, pp. 440–41.

tsars and the two Kennedys became victims of assassins. How could an isolated exile with scant resources and a few friends in a foreign land have been expected to succeed where the entourage of these mighty heads of state failed?

That is one side of the matter. Of great importance was the positive fact that thanks to our efforts and intervention, Trotsky was enabled to enjoy a moratorium of three and a half years from January 1937 to August 1940. The execution of the death sentence was put off during those final years in which he continued to lead the Fourth International and wrote some of his most valuable contributions. In 1935 Trotsky stated in his *Diary in Exile* that he needed five more years of uninterrupted work to pass on to the oncoming generation his knowledge of the revolutionary method. He managed to receive those five years, although they were far from uninterrupted.

By August 1940 virtually all the other defendants in the Moscow Trials except the Old Man had already been done to death by Stalin. The vengeful Healy is unwilling to give Cannon, Hansen, and their colleagues any credit for that achievement. It was much more significant than the incapacity of Trotsky or his protectors to see from what quarter and through what channel the next and final long-anticipated deathblow would be delivered.

Healy likewise does not see that Hansen and the others are only secondary figures in the drama. The principal actors were Trotsky and Sedov themselves who trusted Etienne and allowed Jacson entry into the household. By aiming at the American Trotskyists Healy strikes at the victims themselves.

Not only that. His reckless and indiscriminate allegations insinuate that Trotsky's nineteen-year-old guard Sheldon Harte; Sylvia Caldwell, Cannon's secretary; and Lola Dallin, who helped save so many antifascist refugees, were likewise GPU agents, although he provides no new probative evidence to that effect. Anything goes in his frantic endeavors to cast a net of suspicion around Joseph Hansen and his colleagues.

During my political career I collaborated not only with Trotsky but with Joseph Hansen and Gerry Healy. I have been a close associate and literary partner of Hansen's since we jointly wrote the introduction to Trotsky's last work, *In Defense of Marxism*, in 1942. From 1951 to early 1953 I worked on a daily basis with Healy in England. I know both men well.

From this personal experience and direct knowledge I believe I am as qualified as anyone living on either side of the Atlantic to judge the probity of both men and assay the charges Healy has leveled against his former associate. I may cite a further qualification. Since the Scottsboro case in 1931 I have been involved in defending civil liberties and labor's rights in a series of cases here and abroad too numerous to itemize. The best known are the Tom Mooney case, the Moscow Trials, the Minneapolis Case, the Kutcher Case, and currently the SWP suit against the FBI, CIA, etc. As a result I have learned to smell the frame-up of a militant from miles away and have time and again organized movements to defend the victims on a national and international scale. As an expert on frame-ups of all kinds, I feel well equipped to render a verdict on this one. It stinks to the heavens.

Apart from the total absence of a shred of evidence Healy can bring forth, to anyone who has known Hansen at the closest range for decades, it is a psychological impossibility that he could be an agent of the Soviet secret police or the FBI. On the other hand, I know that Healy is quite capable of spreading false reports about his opponents for the sake of factional advantage, especially against those who tread upon his ego.

In my judgment Healy is in this case a shameless liar, an unmitigated rascal, and a political hooligan. I state this, less to exculpate Hansen and Cannon, who do not need my defense, than to characterize Healy for what he has shown himself to be. In all my experience I have rarely seen so odious and flimsy a frame-up as this spicy dish he has concocted.

His stupid calumnies against Hansen and Cannon are as detestable and unfounded as Stalin's accusations against Trotsky and Sedov in the Moscow Trials. Why does he refrain from including Dobbs and Novack, who were equally involved in and responsible for planning Trotsky's security—or are we being reserved for a second round?

Or, to come closer to London, they are as unwarranted as the British government's accusations when it interned Trotsky in a German prisoner-of-war camp in Nova Scotia on his way to Petrograd in April 1917. They said he was a German agent.

When the news reached the Petrograd Soviet, the *Pravda* under Lenin's direction answered:

> Can one even for a moment believe the trustworthiness of the statement that Trotsky, the chairman of the Soviet of Workers' Delegates in St. Petersburg in 1905—a revolutionary who has sacrificed years to a disinterested service of revolution—that this man had anything to do with a scheme subsidized by the German government? This is a patent, unheard-of, and malicious slander of a revolutionary.[2]

At that time Trotsky had served less than half the years in the service of the revolutionary cause that Hansen has. Healy's charges against Hansen, et al., are as baseless—and as base—as the British government's against Trotsky. We in 1975 refute them as vigorously and unequivocally as Lenin did in 1917: "Can one believe even for a moment Healy's atrocious slanders against the irreproachable Joseph Hansen?"

Until Healy withdraws his accusations and insinuations, the dishonorable brand of an unconscionable slanderer will remain on his forehead for all to see.

NOVEMBER 20, 1975

---

2. Leon Trotsky, *My Life*, p. 388.

WSL SCORES HEALYITE FRAME-UP OF JOSEPH HANSEN

The following article appeared in the December 31, 1975, issue of *Socialist Press*, the fortnightly paper of the Workers Socialist League. Under the title "WRP FRAMES HANSEN," the statement presents the position of the WSL on the efforts of the Workers Revolutionary party to frame up the editor of *Intercontinental Press*.

In an accompanying note, the Workers Socialist League declares:

> As our recently published International Perspectives document *Fourth International—Problems and Tasks* shows clearly, the Workers Socialist League has major political differences with the U.S. Socialist Workers Party.
>
> But our differences do not prevent us speaking out in a principled manner to defend one of the leading members of the SWP, Joseph Hansen, from a lying and scurrilous attack from the press of the Workers Revolutionary Party.

The opening paragraph of the article refers to a police raid "on the Derbyshire education centre of the Workers Revolutionary Party." For information about this raid see the following articles in the October 20, 1975, issue of *Intercontinental Press*: "Police Raid WRP School," p. 1439; "WRP Solicitors Protest Conduct of Police," p. 1440; "The 'Observer' Article Used as Pretext for Police Raid," p. 1437; and "Defend the Democratic Rights of the WRP!" by Joseph Hansen, p. 1394.

For further information about the Workers Socialist League see "Healy Purges 200 Dissidents From WRP," in the January 13, 1975, issue of *Intercontinental Press*, p. 25, and "Alan Thornett's Contribution to the Discussion in the WRP," in the February 10, 1975, issue, p. 199.

A subscription to *Socialist Press* can be obtained by writing to 31 Dartmouth Park Hill, London NW5 1HR. The cost is £1 (US$2.02) for six issues.

In the text below we have corrected a few obvious typographical errors. The subheads appear in the original.

The police raid on the Derbyshire education centre of the Workers Revolutionary Party and the subsequent stonewalling by the Home Office and police authorities, underline the increase in police attention and harassment directed at organisations of the revolutionary left.

The same point was highlighted by a right wing Labour MP in November, who spoke in a Parliamentary debate on the public spending cuts, congratulating Wilson on his mutilation of the social services, but pleading that spending on police forces should be *maintained* to the full.

And indeed the two go hand in hand. As the Labour leaders are forced by the economic crisis to launch an all-out assault on the gains of the working class movement, the state apparatus limbers itself up for disruption, harassment and frame-ups of revolutionaries and left-wingers.

At the same time the economic and political crisis thoroughly tests out every "revolutionary" organisation—its cadre, its programme and policies, its defence of principle, and its ability to fight and build within the workers movement. Any "party" which is unprepared, in which routine has replaced the ferment of revolutionary politics, in which the line has become an everyday implement of polemic, must inevitably be thrown into a severe internal crisis.

Thus it is with the Workers Revolutionary Party, which a year ago set the seal to its political degeneration by expelling wholesale the opposition tendency (later to form the Workers Socialist League) which was fighting for a return to communist methods and to the Transitional Programme of the Fourth International.

It is against this background that we must assess the long series of articles published by its General Secretary, Gerry Healy, together with the WRP leadership, on *Security and the Fourth International* (Workers Press: 7 articles April 19th–26th, 1975, and 19 articles August 14th–September 9th, 1975).

Purpose

The prime purpose of these series is very simple, as is made clear in the concluding articles. It is to *frame* Joseph Hansen, along with other members—alive and dead—of the world Trotskyist movement.

Hansen, who is now a leading figure of the American Socialist Workers Party (sympathising organisation of the "United Secretariat of the Fourth International"), was in charge of the bodyguards at Coyoacan, Mexico, on August 20th, 1940, when Trotsky was murdered by Stalin's agent. The articles in *Workers Press* accuse him (in assertions thinly veiled as questions, or in insinuations) of being, since before 1940, an agent of the FBI, *or of* the Stalinist GPU, *or both!*

The preceding articles—which draw almost entirely on materials that are published and have been known for some time—are all designed to lead up to this conclusion: that for *forty years* the SWP has had a police spy in its political leadership, and that the struggle, since the split of 1963, between Healy and Hansen has been, in reality, a struggle against police provocations.

As the WRP leadership say, their accusations (*if true*) raise very grave problems for the SWP and the world Trotskyist movement. But it is worth noticing that these accusations also seek to *solve* some problems for Healy and the WRP leadership—they relieve them of the need to carry out a political struggle!

For what is the point of mobilising and convincing the membership in a struggle to defend the Transitional Programme, to sharpen and resolve the crisis in the world Trotskyist movement—if your principal adversaries are not genuine *political* opponents but police spies?

Evidently, none! And that is why, hand in hand with the WRP's political degeneration and paralysis, has come a rich harvest of such accusations.

Rigged

But what of the specific charges against Hansen? Hansen *himself* (*Intercontinental Press*, 24th November) easily demolishes the main points as simple lies and rigging of the evidence. We take just one example from the mountain of circumstantial titbits under which the WRP "investigators" seek to bury him: a report from Robert G. McGregor, a US diplomatic official in Mexico City, of his conversation with Hansen on Saturday, August 31st, 1940—i.e. 11 days after Trotsky's murder.

To this report (in the form of a memorandum forwarded to the State Department by the US Consul) Healy's "investigators" add evidence or qualification, as "fact" that McGregor was an *FBI agent* (at this time the FBI had not been replaced by the CIA on overseas work), and draw the following inferences:

1. That Hansen was familiar with an FBI official and met with him probably "clandestinely," and certainly out of office hours (i.e. on a Saturday).

2. That Hansen deliberately attempted to direct the search for the GPU network which planned Trotsky's assassination away from Europe (where it was mainly based) towards the USA.

Twisted

In order to steer towards these conclusions Healy's journalists—unfortunately for them—are obliged to twist the facts in the most barefaced way:

1. They deliberately disguise the fact that Hansen was only *one* of at least *four* members of the Trotskyist movement—the others being two Americans, Charles Cornell and Walter O'Rourke, *and Trotsky himself*—who had private discussions with McGregor both before and after Trotsky's death.

These conversations were all, no doubt, reported equally swiftly to the State Department, especially after the failure of the May attempt by the Stalinists on Trotsky's life and the kidnapping (and later murder) of his young American bodyguard, Robert Sheldon Harte.

2. The WRP imply—contradicting their own main insinuation that Hansen was an FBI agent—that Hansen was both misleading the FBI *and*, it is implied, the Trotskyist movement by guiding the search for those who planned Trotsky's murder towards the United States, instead of France.

This is then used to bolster the additional accusation that Hansen deliberately covered up the role of the most important Stalinist agent in the Fourth International, Mark Zborowski ("Etienne"), who was implicated in the murder of Trotskyists in Paris in the 1930's, and later came to America and spied on the Trotskyist movement there.

In fact (as Hansen's reply makes clear) there were excellent reasons for the Trotskyist movement to try and protect itself by using the resources of the capitalist states and (in particular in this case) to try and persuade the FBI to probe clandestine Stalinist activity *in the USA* (the country where the FBI was in charge) for clues as to the murder of Trotsky. In August 1940 this required concentrating the attention of the State Department on anti-Trotskyist conspiracies by the GPU *inside* the USA.

Loose end

The ideas that Hansen could both *be an agent of the FBI* and deliberately misleading them are one glaring loose end in the WRP frame-up—there are many others. This is the case even though Healy's "sleuths" include at least *one* man—Mr Alex Mitchell, editor of *Workers Press*—with detailed knowledge of police and espionage techniques. And what they make no attempt to explain is why—if Hansen was the FBI's agent—he should maintain contact with them (as is implied) by meeting *in public* with a US official well-known to several other Trotskyists and why a report on this contact should be sent *using his real name* in the normal correspondence, to later finish up among publicly available State Department papers—while Hansen is still a leading SWP member?

Such conduct would contradict *every* ground rule of clandestine work. It is, of course, *logically conceivable* that while Hansen's meeting with McGregor was wholly legitimate (and McGregor's report does nothing to suggest otherwise) he was simultaneously in undisclosed contact with the FBI through quite different channels—but the WRP produce not one shred of evidence to support such a verdict.

Their fraudulent manner of handling facts and evidence carries right through the series *Security and the Fourth International*. For example, they uncritically accept all aspects of the testimony (before American criminal courts and witch-hunting committees of Congress) of a range of ex-Stalinist stool pigeons and exposed Soviet spies, busy "singing" to save their skins.

One such is Louis F. Budenz, a notorious Judas throughout the US labour movement, a one-time GPU agent, and subsequently managing editor of the American CP's *Daily Worker*. In October 1946 Budenz announced his renunciation of communism and his return to the Roman Catholic Church. A month later he was a star witness before the McCarthyite House Un-American Activities Committee, slinging mud at every brand of "communist."

For years he made a living from slanders and inventions, mainly against the Stalinists. But this is not all—*Budenz* played (according to testimony before congressional committees) a big role in driving Trotsky to Mexico from Norway in 1936.

It was Budenz, then New York editor of the *Daily Worker*, who supplied the "confidential evidence" of violent plots by Trotsky which was used by Stalin's ambassador in Oslo to twist the arm of the Norwegian government into placing Trotsky under house arrest at the height of the Moscow purge trials, and then expelling him.

But for *Workers Press* Mr Budenz is all good stuff. They are quite content to use fragments from his writings and testimony to cobble together their "investigations" of Trotsky's murder, and to help frame Hansen. Budenz opens his autobiography (*This Is My Story*, 1957) with a prayer to "the Mother of God, Mary of the Magnificat" and rejoices that "but for her amazing assistance" his story could not have been told. Precisely the same can be said of the story told by the WRP's "investigations"!

What makes the matter even more serious is that the slanders to which Hansen replies are by no means an isolated instance. In the last two years or so similar insinuations, in writing or verbally, have been levelled by Healy and the WRP leadership against a number of individuals and tendencies in the labour movement, including:

1. The "Bulletin" group, sympathising organisation in Britain of the "Organising Committee for the Reconstruction of the Fourth International."

2. Members of the 1974 opposition within the WRP which, after its unconstitutional expulsion by Healy, fought on to form the WSL.

3. Tim Wohlforth, former leader of the Workers League, sympathising organisation of Healy's

"International Committee" in the USA.

4. Members of the "International Spartacist Tendency" in Australia.

This cascade of mudslinging—neither substantiated nor withdrawn—serves in no way to assist in removing the *real* police and Stalinist agents who undoubtedly operate in the ranks of the Trotskyist movement.

It serves only to *divert* from political struggle on the life-and-death issues now facing the international working class—of the struggle for revolutionary programme and for resolving the crisis of leadership within the working class and the Trotskyist movement itself.

Healy's calumnies, therefore, run parallel to one of the main pursuits of the police agencies themselves—the circulation of false and disruptive accusations that revolutionaries involved in internal political battles are themselves police provocateurs.

Provocation

For example, among the FBI files released as a result of congressional investigations and legal moves taken by the leadership of Hansen's Socialist Workers Party are documents showing that in January 1962 the New York Office of the FBI attempted an elaborate provocation which involved feeding the SWP leadership forged evidence that Jack Arnold (a member of the minority tendency supported by *Healy* within the SWP) was an FBI informant.

The aim was to disrupt the political struggle by having Arnold expelled.

In fact, it appears, the FBI's scheme got nowhere because the SWP refused to act on anonymous "evidence" which they considered fake.

But Healy and the WRP leadership, as we have seen, readily resort themselves to the faking of evidence. This is all the more criminal since the WRP leadership now includes Alex Mitchell, who has studied in some detail the methods of British police and intelligence agencies and who must be aware that such frame-ups are a standard technique.

Mitchell, present editor of *Workers Press*, was previously employed as a journalist on the *Sunday Times*. And in the late 1960's he acted as research assistant in the writing of a book by members of the *Sunday Times* staff on the Philby-Burgess-Maclean affair* and its widespread repercussions in the British intelligence services (*Philby, the Spy Who Betrayed a Generation*, by Page, Leitch and Knightley, 1968).

As the *Preface* makes clear, research for this book involved not only study of publicly available material, but extensive "off-the-record" contact with those prepared to give an "inside" account to journalists regarded as reliable.

Presumably Mr Mitchell no longer involves himself in Saturday morning conversations with such characters. We mention this past employment not in order to accuse him of anything (given the WRP's leadership's scrupulous attitude to "security" we assume they investigated his past in the most thorough manner before recruiting him, never mind making him editor of *Workers Press*). The point is rather that, if other tendencies were to adopt the method of the WRP school of falsification (of whom Mr Mitchell has shown himself an able student), then the editor of *Workers Press* himself would be an obvious and easy target for slander and insinuation.

As we have said, the slanders and frame-ups of Healy and the WRP leadership are not an accident. They are part of a swift *political* degeneration.

Turning their backs on the fight for principles and programme in the mass movement, with a membership confused and paralysed by—for example—the WRP's participation in the "corporatist" Ryder committees at British Leyland—the WRP leadership head into an insoluble *political and organisational* crisis. They have now publicly declared that they are £50,000 in debt, and that unless a "crisis fund" of this amount can be raised by February, *Workers Press* will be in jeopardy.

Slander fund

But how, and from who, was this huge debt incurred? Part of it was (as is stated in *Workers Press*) used in the "special fund" allocated by the International Committee to send journalists to France and the USA to prepare the special series on "Security

---

* Philby was the Soviet agent who, after the war, was put in charge of British intelligence operations against the Soviet Union, and, later, liaison with the CIA. His exposure caused, to put it mildly, a major shake-up in the methods and personnel of the British intelligence apparatus.

and the Fourth International"—i.e. to manufacture slanders against Joseph Hansen and others!

There is another, equally serious, implication of the WRP's £50,000 "crisis fund"—if their own published figures are to be believed. At the time of the WRP conference in December 1974 at which the expulsion of the opposition was rubber-stamped the leadership publicly claimed 8,000 members. With an *active* membership of this size it should be no serious problem to raise £50,000 in two months (it would only mean £3.12½ per month each!). But the claimed membership was and is clearly a lie. This is shown also by the fact that even with the support of other political organisations and trade union contingents they mobilised only about 1,400 on the demonstration in November against the police raid on their premises—and even Workers Press claimed only 5,000!

Uncontrolled

But the issue is not simply how big the WRP membership is or isn't. It is that the WRP has, since at least 1974, *inflated* its real "active" membership with a huge "halo" of paper members—many "signed up" on street corners and on doorsteps in the WRP's liquidationist election campaigns. These "recruits" never really had any political agreement with the WRP, are inactive most of the time and not under the discipline of the leadership, and who (as the "crisis fund" bears witness) will not even contribute to Party funds. *But such a "membership"—uncontrolled and politically responsible to no-one—is precisely the environment in which police spies and provocateurs flourish.*

WRP members who are being asked by Workers Press to hand over half their wage packets for six weeks have a right to know what the money is being used for. And the true answer is—*not* for the building of a revolutionary leadership—but to have journalists for the manufacture of frame-ups, and to give a lease of life to the politically bankrupt clique which has led the WRP into its present acute crisis.

Healy's Road to the Gutter
THE FRAME-UP OF JOSEPH HANSEN AND GEORGE NOVACK

The following is a statement by the editors of *Red Weekly*, newspaper of the International Marxist Group, British section of the Fourth International. It appeared in the January 29 issue of *Red Weekly*.

On 5 January 1975, *Workers Press*, the "daily organ of the Central Committee of the Workers Revolutionary Party," accused Joseph Hansen and George Novack—well-known American Trotskyists, long-standing members of the Socialist Workers Party and numbered amongst Trotsky's closest collaborators during his last exile in Mexico—of being "accomplices of the GPU" (the Stalinist secret police).

Under most circumstances we would not even bother to deal with such ravings. When Joseph Stalin swung the resources of the Soviet State behind manufacturing a gigantic lie, Trotskyists were obligated to reply charge by charge; when Gerry Healy uses his detailed knowledge of the Moscow trials to imitate the methods of the prosecutors, we can safely leave this question not to political and factual refutation but to the medical study of mental degeneration in the epoch of capitalist decay.

This is particularly the case when the sole "evidence" which Healy produces is that of the capitalist state, self-confessed GPU agents and similar riff-raff, ex-Trotskyists who have unfortunately degenerated to the point where they place in the same breath GPU agents and Palestinian commandos and IRA fighters, and elements such as Vereecken—newly elevated by Healy to the rank of "veteran Trotskyist"—who were described by Trotsky himself as "placing themselves outside of reality politically" and characterised by the founding congress of the Fourth International as having "utilised their formal membership in the movement of the Fourth International to flout its principles, sabotage its discipline, and give aid and comfort to its enemies."

On Healy's method, of course, he is an "accomplice" of all these elements. Fortunately for him he isn't an "accomplice," or "agent"—he merely illustrates the rule that if you descend into the gutter all you will come up with is filth.

Healy's record is also public for the world to see. He sits in the ruins of a smashed and wrecked organisation. The International Committee of the Fourth International has gone through the vile methods used against the Spartacists, the split with the Lambertists, the disgusting expulsion of Alan Thornett, the hounding of Tim Wohlforth, and now it is reaping the whirlwind. The explosion of its organisation in Australia and the collapse of its forces in the United States are merely the harbingers of the destruction of its cult society in Britain. As Gerry Healy looks back on his life he can truly record, "everything I built turned to dust."

But the political decline has now led to a moral and personal degeneration as well. We no longer have merely sectarian positions, social democratic errors, and violent methods—now we have organised and conscious lying on the largest scale which Healy's resources will permit.

The historical path to this is clear. First the "International Committee" used little lies to aid arguments a bit—after all, as the "Pabloites" of the Fourth International are objectively agents of capitalism, then if the SLL/WRP couldn't find the evidence it could "serve the interests of the working class" by inventing it. Then unfortunately Healy's lies were exposed and he was unable to reply. The answer was clear—just censor the membership a bit and step up the lying.

But once Healy opened the door just that inch

to the lying and abandonment of principles, he embarked with iron logic on the road to the political gutter.

As for the proposal in *Workers Press* for a world investigation on this matter, it is beneath contempt even to discuss seriously whether Joe Hansen is an accomplice of the GPU. Healy learnt that trick from the textbook of any tenth rate bourgeois lawyer, from the Stalinist methods in the Comintern, and from the arsenal of Joseph McCarthy. The technique is simple—make the most absurd charge, which no one would believe, but then if you can get a body set up to "investigate" it the lie is given some respectability and perhaps people will think there is something to it.

We have no intention of giving respectability to a charge whose sole record will be as a dirty and sordid footnote in the annals of pathology. The only "investigation" we suggest for any student of the byways of history is to describe in detail, if anyone has a strong enough stomach, how an organisation like the SLL/WRP, which started as an enemy of the capitalist system, prostituted the highest cause in the world to the methods of the gutter and in so doing led its leaders to utter political and moral degeneration. That is the sole interest of the *Workers Press* "charges" for the working class movement.

As for Joseph Hansen, he doesn't need anyone to vindicate him—history has already done it. Joe Hansen for four decades and more has served the only cause worth serving—the interests of the working class. For those same decades he has sought to defend the only ideas worth defending—the ideas of revolutionary Marxism. He did so as Trotsky's secretary and through the long years of repression, witch-hunt and isolation of the 1940s and 1950s.

Whether history will judge him right or wrong on any question, he sought to defend revolutionary socialism and the cause of the working class in the only way it can be defended—through scrupulous attention to truth, through serious study and effort, and through a consistent fight for what you believe to be true. His stature as a revolutionary and a political fighter is irreproachable.

As for Healy and his bunch of liars, they were only too pleased, in saner days, to have the support of Joe Hansen during the 1950s—even quoting proudly the "accomplice of the GPU" in praise of their organisation. And as for the other "guilty party" George Novack, not merely was he working *personally* for years in day-to-day collaboration with your leadership but you, Mr Healy, put your own signature to public articles which were in reality written by this "accomplice of the GPU."

The publication of Healy's attack in a journal claiming to be Marxist, however, does not represent the paranoia of a single individual, no matter how powerful he or she may be within the WRP. It represents something much graver. It marks the complete and utter political degeneration of a sect which has claimed adherence to Trotskyism. It is the ultimate logic of sectarian politics, and it should be a terrible reminder to other groups on the left of what can happen when you *start* political debates by distorting the positions of your opponents and slandering them personally in no uncertain terms.

There were always traces of this in the WRP's predecessor, the Socialist Labour League (SLL), but in the 1950s and early '60s the slanders were milder, the distortions less outrageous, and the internal regime of the organisation marginally more flexible. The roots of the present degeneration can be traced back to the events surrounding a major schism in the Fourth International in 1953, the subsequent emergence of two currents, the International Secretariat and the International Committee, and the failure of Healy to participate in the reunification of the two currents in 1963.

Healy's explanation of these events has always been in terms of a supposed revision of Marxism—and therefore transfer to the camp of the class enemy—carried out in the early 1950s by Michel Raptis (Pablo). This was supposedly concretised in a whole series of historic betrayals carried through by the International Secretariat of the Fourth International—and, after 1963, also carried out by the SWP. A shibboleth had been established, and the SLL was subsequently to spend much time, energy and resources in explaining to the British working class the evils of "Pabloite revisionism."

The fact that Pablo's views were not those of the majority of the International Secretariat, that even if they had been these *theoretical* differences did not justify a split, was of no account. The battlelines had been drawn, the main enemy identified, and the battle had to take place. Small matter that the International Secretariat denied most of the slanders; small matter that the opponents of Healy were straw persons; and small matter that Trotskyists had been attacking these methods of debate in the workers movement for decades.

The political sectarianism became intensified when the victory of the Cuban revolution and a common attitude towards it helped to reunify the mainstream of world Trotskyism. The SWP, barred by reactionary legislation from affiliating to the Fourth International, declared its support for the reunification. But Healy stayed away. The SWP had clearly capitulated to "Pabloite revisionism." At all costs the disease must not be allowed to spread. Their own ranks must be inoculated against it. And so they were.

Having embarked on a sectarian trajectory, Healy began to pay the price. In his current's total obsession with themselves they now denied that the Cuban revolution had taken place. Castro was qualitatively no different from Batista. Here we have a model example of sectarian subjectivism. Since the victory of the Cuban revolution goes against our immediate sectarian interests, let's not even admit that it's taken place. It's in Latin America in any case, and none of our members will know enough about it to seriously challenge the assumption.

For self-proclaimed revolutionaries in an advanced capitalist country to deny the reality of a socialist revolution—albeit in a small, far away island—because to do so would weaken their factional arguments against their opponents, was certainly an innovation in the Trotskyist movement. Stalin had applied a similar criterion to Yugoslavia after Tito had refused to accept Stalinist dominance over the Yugoslav party and state apparatus. Stalin had then also resorted to calling Tito every name under the sun and had been loyally echoed by Thorez in Paris and Togliatti in Rome. Purges in the Eastern European parties had wiped out all supposed "Titoist deviationists."

Healy has taken his time, but now employs similar methods against his opponents within his own "party" as well as his factional opponents in other groups. This sort of degeneration is political. If you have a sectarian political line, you have to build an organisation where it is never seriously challenged. Sectarian politics of necessity require a monolithic organisation. Sectarian training of members in verbal violence opens the way to physical violence against your opponents.

If you tell your members that the dreaded Pabloite revisionists are the agents of the petty-bourgeoisie in the workers movement pretending to be Trotskyists, or are police agents or agents of the Soviet bureaucracy, the door is then open for physical attacks on all political opponents both inside and outside your own sect. This has also occurred in the sect now led by Gerry Healy, Mike Banda et al.

When a workers state degenerates we call for a political revolution. When a working class organisation degenerates we call on its members to wage a fight against this degeneration.

We therefore appeal to the members of the WRP: comrades, study the history of the movement of which you claim to be a part. Study the writings of Trotsky, the documents of the Left Opposition, the documents (all of them) related to the polemics in the Fourth International, and ask yourselves whether the methods being used by your leaders are more akin to Stalinism or Trotskyism. Ask yourselves whether or not there was something wrong with the way in which Alan Thornett and his comrades were expelled from your ranks.

Follow the advice given by Marx to his daughter—"doubt everything." In particular, doubt everything your leadership tells you without studying the case of your opponents. Ask yourselves why it took Healy nearly four decades to discover that Hansen and Novack were "GPU accomplices." We doubt whether you will be able to save your organisation, but it is certainly the only way you will be able to save yourselves as revolutionary militants!

The real targets are Cannon, Trotsky, and the Fourth International

A STATEMENT ON HEALY'S FRAME-UP OF HANSEN AND NOVACK

By Betty Hamilton and Pierre Lambert

The following article, translated by *Intercontinental Press*, appeared in the February 27–March 4 issue (No. 740) of *Informations Ouvrières*, the weekly publication of the Organisation Communiste Internationaliste (OCI), whose headquarters are in Paris.

Betty Hamilton, who has been in the revolutionary Marxist movement for fifty years, was one of the founders of the Socialist Labour League (later the Workers Revolutionary party). She is thus able to speak of the methods followed by Gerry Healy from years of firsthand experience.

Pierre Lambert is editor of *Informations Ouvrières* and one of the leaders of the Comité d'Organisation Pour la Reconstruction de la Quatrième Internationale, the international formation to which the OCI adheres. Together with Healy, he was one of the leaders of the sector of the International Committee that rejected joining in the reunification of the Fourth International in 1963. However, because of deepening political and organizational differences, the OCI broke from the Healyite wing in 1971.

We have read the indescribable articles written at the orders of G. Healy attempting to prove that Joseph Hansen and George Novack are agents of the CIA and the NKVD.[1] We confess that we found it very difficult to force ourselves to read these "articles." But we considered it our duty as representatives of our organizations in the International Committee of the Fourth International—which was formed in 1953 by the Socialist Workers party (SWP), the Socialist Labour League (SLL), the PCI (Parti Communiste Internationaliste, now the Organisation Communiste Internationaliste), and the Swiss and Chinese organizations—to express our solidarity and sympathy with the SWP. We decided to draft this statement not only as founding members of the International Committee but also as representatives of the SLL and the OCI (PCI), which, in disagreement with the SWP, decided in 1963 to maintain the International Committee.

We accuse Gerry Healy of unscrupulously rigging up a whole scenario in the hope that it would prove difficult to unravel such a tangle of lies, baseless insinuations, and gratuitous suppositions from facts no one denies. He did this to try to create an impression of "impartiality" so as to justify the slanderous amalgam he is putting together against the SWP and two of its leaders.

False accusations, slander, and lies have always been a specialty in which the representatives of ruling and oppressor classes have excelled. But the direct representatives of the ruling class have clearly been surpassed in this by those in the workers movement who subordinated themselves to the interests of the bourgeoisie. The Mensheviks, for example, had to maintain that Lenin was an "agent of the Kaiser," just as later the Stalinists were to claim that Trotsky was an "agent of the Gestapo." So, in a historical period when the struggle for the emancipation of humanity is inseparable from the fight to free the working class from leaderships chained to imperialism, through the struggle to rebuild the Fourth International, it is extremely important to keep this counterrevolutionary tradition of lies and slanders from filtering into the ranks of the vanguard.

The only justification for the monstrous accusations raised against Joseph Hansen and George

---

1. In *Workers Press,* the organ of the Workers Revolutionary party (WRP) of Great Britain, three series of articles devoted to the question of "security in the Fourth International" have been published—seven, beginning with the April 19, 1975, issue; nineteen, beginning with the August 14, 1975, issue; and finally eight, beginning on January 5, 1976.

Novack—and, in fact, as we will show later, against the SWP leadership and against Leon Trotsky himself—would be if they were based on grave evidence against them, on proofs, on documents from which it could logically be deduced that whether or not they were guilty of the crimes charged against them that at least an inquiry was necessary.

A very peculiar logic

However, the elaborate fabrication of G. Healy collapses like a house of cards the minute you begin to apply this basic criterion. When it comes to Hansen and Novack (the nominal targets of this attack), the scheme is reduced to a very peculiar brand of logic which Vyshinsky tried to make respectable but which certainly has nothing to do with the traditions of our movement.

Joseph Hansen had a meeting with the U.S. consul in Mexico. Well, an American consul has to be an FBI agent. So, Hansen, since he had a meeting with an FBI agent, is himself one, or could be.

What conclusions, then, should we draw from the fact that after the murder of L. Sedov, Leon Trotsky not only filed a complaint with the French authorities but also ordered activists to testify to the police who were conducting the investigation? If we followed the same line of reasoning that G. Healy does, we would have to conclude that since L. Trotsky made a complaint to the French imperialist authorities, since he called on comrades to testify to the police of French imperialism, L. Trotsky was an agent of imperialism and of the French police! The procedure G. Healy has resorted to is typically Stalinist.

The slanderer G. Healy does not stop there. He turns to arguments appealing to authority (because I say it is so, it is so).

For example, in 1938, a GPU agent entered into contact with Hansen. Hansen explained that Trotsky told him to "maintain the contact." How does Healy respond to this?

"We state categorically that Hansen is lying when he says that Trotsky told him to consort with the GPU agent 'John' Rabinowitz. It is inconceivable that the Bolshevik leader would instruct the head of his security arrangements at Coyoacan to meet a GPU agent over a period of three months." No evidence whatever is offered to support this assertion. It is enough that Healy thinks that what Hansen says is "inconceivable." You have to believe G. Healy because he has spoken. Has G. Healy ever thought about this: The international apparatus of the Kremlin and its national agencies are controlled by the GPU. At every step, at every moment, Trotskyists have come in contact with CP leaders who are often agents of the GPU. Hidden under Healy's virtuous indignation is petty-bourgeois philistinism.

Some may say that we are judging the "basis" for this case in advance when we speak in a general way of the monstrousness of the accusations raised against Joseph Hansen. In fact, we do not think that Comrade J. Hansen in any way stands "in the dock," or that he is a man "on trial" who must prove his innocence. When Trotsky had to face the abominable lie-machine of Stalinism, he offered, as the first *proof* of the absurdity of the accusations lodged against him, the record of his public political activity.

Joseph Hansen's continuous activity, for more than forty years now, as a member and leader of the American Trotskyist organization, his role in the history and debates in the Fourth International—where, although there have been deep differences between us, he has always stood within the framework of Trotskyism—are in themselves the best answer to the allegations of those who are impugning his honor as a revolutionist.

Is this to say that because of this work Comrade Hansen enjoys a kind of immunity? By no means. But if the "trial" in which Healy wants to play the role of prosecutor were not rigged from start to finish, it is this aspect that he would have attacked first, while he does not mention it even once. And, what is more, in the long pages of *Workers Press*, which if they were all put together would make a book, Healy has not been able to offer a trace of evidence or a single document coming either from Hansen or from the former GPU agents who went over to the FBI (whom Healy, without any verification, seems to regard as the bearers of the truth) that can support his monstrous charge that Hansen is "an accomplice of the GPU."

So, if we spend a little more time dealing with these charges—before coming to the political conclusions—it is not in order to defend Comrade Hansen, it is to show that the method used by

Gerry Healy stands in fundamental contradiction to the principles and traditions of the Fourth International and the workers movement.

An incoherent detective thriller

The serial that has filled four pages in each issue of *Workers Press* in the last month before it ceased publication takes the form of an incoherent detective thriller in which any precise facts that can be gleaned have been long known, and where unfounded speculations, gratuitous assertions, and contradictions abound.

Let's take one example. *Workers Press* makes a big to-do about a visit Joseph Hansen made to the American consul McGregor, a visit he made as Trotsky's secretary eleven days after Trotsky was murdered. The fact that it took place on Saturday and not on a workday is used to justify an insinuation that there was something odd about it, that Joseph Hansen might be linked to the FBI (as if, by the way, Trotsky's murder was not an event of sufficient international importance for the American consul to give up part of his Saturday morning!).

Let us follow the curious line of "reasoning" of *Workers Press*. From this "proof," which is no proof at all, it concludes that Hansen could very well have maintained relations with the FBI, and then it goes on as if such a link had been established. But this curious line of "reasoning" is itself contradicted by the charges its authors make against Joseph Hansen. What did Hansen tell the consul—according to the latter's report? That the GPU was responsible for the murder and that the crime must have been engineered from the United States. He pointed out that "Mornard had made a journey to the United States between the dates of the first attempt upon Trotsky's life and the second successful one," and so he insisted that the American police check out the hotel where Mornard stayed in New York.

What conclusion was drawn by *Workers Press?* That Joseph Hansen was trying to deceive the Fourth International, because the murder was engineered in Paris by Zborowski and not in New York. But if this had been the case, according to the previous accusations, Hansen would have been deceiving his alleged "employers."

But, the imaginative editors of *Workers Press* might reply, what if Hansen was an agent of the GPU? Then one would wonder why he insisted on the guilt of the GPU. But (slanderers always have a ready comeback), his role as a Trotskyist leader obliged him to do this.

Then (if we agree to accept a trial framework briefly for the sake of clarity), in any case, this was an official conversation with the U.S. consul and precisely because it was official, it proves nothing, it is outside the framework of the debate! In fact, we will have to come back later to the reasons for using this conversation.

Let us add that Gerry Healy "forgot" that J. Hansen gave his reason for this visit—to try to establish the exact identity of the murderer, which was then unknown—and that from this standpoint the approach to the consul produced results.

Cynical disregard of the truth

Let's be serious. The center where Trotsky's murder was decided on and prepared was the Kremlin. As his confessions in 1956 have since shown, Zborowski acted in Paris, operating as an agent provocateur in the Fourth International, playing a central role in setting the stage for the crime. In this, however, other links in the chain were needed in the United States and in Mexico. At the stage where the investigation stood eleven days after the death of Trotsky, no one endowed with a minimum of good sense and honesty could find anything "reprehensible" or "strange" in the fact that Joseph Hansen pressed for the American police to make an investigation in the United States. He was only doing his duty as a revolutionist. In this respect, he was following the example of Trotsky, who advised Ignace Reiss to place himself under police protection.

But the spirit in which *Workers Press* has conducted its investigation is indicated by the thread running through all the attacks on Comrade Hansen; that is, that he is supposed to have tried to divert attention from—to "cover up"—Stalinist agents planted in the SWP and operating in the United States.

The consul's report establishes the contrary. With his very special brand of logic Gerry Healy finds in this fact a new "indictment." Such contradictions can no doubt be resolved by Healy's version of dialectics, which is on a par with his logic! But this contradiction establishes very clearly that what is involved here is not an attempt to uncover the truth or to clarify the problems of "security in the Fourth International." On the contrary what we see here is an application of the method that "anything goes," and the old maxim that "if you throw enough mud, some of it will stick."

Other examples testify to a cynical disregard for the minimum requirements of telling a credible story. The main thing is to pile up enough disparate elements to, if not convince, at least sow doubt.

In the case of Robert Sheldon Harte, the young bodyguard who was found murdered after the assassination attempt on May 24, 1940, while not categorically asserting that he had a responsibility in this, *Workers Press* implies that he might have been an accomplice of the assailants, who later got rid of him. The SWP leadership maintains the position it took after the crime—which was held, moreover, by Trotsky. Robert Sheldon Harte remained faithful to Trotskyism and was a victim of the GPU. Once again, one might wonder what Healy is trying to prove, and what relationship this question has to the charges made against Joseph Hansen.

If it were shown (and we note that *Workers Press* offers no new evidence) that Trotsky and the SWP leadership were mistaken about Sheldon Harte and that he was a GPU agent, how would this prove that Hansen and other SWP leaders "covered up for GPU agents," how would this justify advancing even as a "hypothesis" this infamous charge, which, inasmuch as Trotsky did not think Robert Sheldon Harte was a provocateur, is directed jointly against Hansen and L. Trotsky?

Criminal irresponsibility

However, what interests us here, again, are the methods of Gerry Healy. He quotes the following passage from Julian Gorkin's book on Trotsky's assassination:

"If it were admitted that Sheldon was a spy, that would place the question of responsibility in the chief Trotskyists in New York, who had sent him to Mexico. We do no more than mention this aspect of the question. Let each one draw his own conclusions." And he describes Julian Gorkin as "an authority on the crimes of Stalin." He neglects to say that from the standpoint simply of histori-

cally verifiable facts, much new evidence has come to light since Gorkin wrote this book. He also neglects to say that Julian Gorkin was one of the leaders of the POUM (which he left while in exile) most hostile to the Fourth International and that his book was written in collaboration with General Salazar, the chief of the Mexican police, who sought to pin as much of the blame as possible on Trotsky's entourage.

It was this aim of the book that *Workers Press*, to use a term it is fond of, "covered up." This did not prevent him from presenting in another article, for his purposes, statements—which were rather confused—of a former bodyguard of Trotsky's, Harold Robins, who accuses Hansen of covering up the slanders of the Mexican police!

One final example: *Workers Press* plays up the fact that it was the SWP leadership that helped Zborowski return to the United States.

Do we have to point out how absurd it is to blame the SWP comrades for the fact that Zborowski was among certain cadres of the Trotskyist movement who were brought to the USA through the work of members and leaders of the SWP at the time of the Hitlerite victories in Europe? As *Workers Press* notes, moreover (as an "argument" against Joseph Hansen), Zborowski's area of activity was Europe. It was by integrating himself among the cadres of the Trotskyist movement in Europe that he became a member of the international leadership, recognized by Leon Trotsky as a close collaborator of Leon Sedov. As the leader of the Fourth International, Leon Trotsky entrusted Zborowski with organizing the founding conference of the Fourth International in September 1938.

The absurdity of this slander is striking. In 1940, Zborowski had not been unmasked as the GPU agent he was. If he blames the SWP leadership and Hansen for organizing his trip to the USA, G. Healy should naturally put the blame for this on L. Trotsky and draw the conclusion that the latter, like Hansen, was an agent of the GPU. Let us note again that it is hard for revolutionists to force themselves to dig through all the mud thrown by G. Healy, who in his irresponsibility pays no attention to the damaging blows he is dealing to the Fourth International, to which he still claims to adhere.

We repeat: What particular guilt can be attributed to the SWP cadres? And even if it were maintained that they should have been more "vigilant"—which, we stress, would be a gratuitous remark—how would this justify calling them "accomplices"? Unless the mere fact of associating with Zborowski, as L. Sedov and L. Trotsky himself did, without immediately identifying him as an agent provocateur constitutes guilt within the "Healyite theory of evidence." But, then, we repeat, Healy's search of "accomplices" would take him far beyond Joseph Hansen and George Novack, and even the leadership of the SWP.

Let us repeat again, in the voluminous inquiry of *Workers Press,* there is not the slightest document or fact that would justify raising—even as a possibility that would still have to be proved—the infamous accusations lodged against Comrades Joseph Hansen and George Novack.

What is infamous—and degrading for the authors—is having raised such charges. The method they used, their cynical contempt for the truth, disqualifies them politically. This is criminal irresponsibility contrary not only to the principles of the Fourth International but also to the most basic traditions of the workers movement.

We should, however, take up G. Healy's strange brief from another standpoint.

At the beginning of this statement we referred to the way that G. Healy and his "investigators" used the visit Joseph Hansen made to Consul McGregor. In this case, Joseph Hansen quite correctly said that G. Healy stirred up a "geyser of mud." But the mud has only washed over G. Healy himself.

In the first place, the way this episode was exploited illustrates G. Healy's political perfidiousness. He, as much as any comrade holding responsibilities of leadership in the revolutionary workers movement, knows that the contact Joseph Hansen had to maintain with the American consulate was only a particular expression of a much more general reality. Political activity must involve all aspects of the struggle, that is, also the need for diplomacy, for "contact" with the enemy camp. It is this that for Gerry Healy constitutes the proof of Joseph Hansen's "guilt." But can anyone fail to see that such "guilt" would have to be assigned first of all to Leon Trotsky? As the official reports indicate, other members of Trotsky's guard, Charles Cornell and Walter O'Rourke, were in touch with the consul, as well as Leon Trotsky (and, in the case of the founder of the Fourth International, the consul visited him in his home!). There were, thus, to divulge a "dreadful secret," regular contacts between the U.S. consulate and Trotsky and his entourage. It is not so difficult to understand what could be grasped by the representatives of American imperialism, who banned Trotsky from their territory with ferocious determination. In view of what Trotsky represented, relations with this isolated exile took on a certain government-to-government nature. And, from the stand-point of his security, Trotsky had a stake in such relations.

As Comrade Hansen correctly notes, G. Healy and his investigators are on a path that tends to converge with that of Trotsky's murderers.

The old method of the amalgam

There is yet another aspect, which may appear minor but which we think is significant, since it shows how rotten something is in the little kingdom of Clapham High Street (the national headquarters of the WRP in London).

This is the practice of the "classical"-type Stalinist amalgam. The articles in *Workers Press* talk about a Stalinist agent planted in the SWP, Floyd Miller, who was later unmasked. Since this agent functioned in the maritime fraction of the SWP, *Workers Press* says that his work enabled him to point out to the GPU who the Trotskyist sailors were that were on their way to the USSR. On this question Hansen says simply, in passing, that this Miller never occupied a leadership position, even at the level of the maritime fraction, and that in any case no Trotskyist sailor ever disappeared. And he adds:

> Several Trotskyist seamen, whose ships were sunk by the Germans, managed, along with other members of the crew, to launch lifeboats and eventually make their way to Murmansk. Because of exposure in open boats in those waters, several of them had to spend months in the hospital. They were given first-rate treatment, and the staffs were very friendly.

This is the comment these lines inspired from *Workers Press:*

"Soviet Weekly", the English language Stalinist newspaper produced by the CPSU, has a two-page article on wartime Murmansk in its edition for December 20–27, 1975.

It is a putrid piece of public relations for the Stalinist bureaucracy concerning a visit to Murmansk by one Ian Highet, a radio officer on board a British ship.

"Of Murmansk I have happy memories despite the bitter cold of January and the indescribable devastation. The cold was more than matched by the warmth of the Soviet people who extended to us a most tremendous welcome with typical Soviet hospitality, a hospitality that had to be seen to be believed."

The only thing to match this gushing description of wartime Murmansk comes from the pen of . . . Joseph Hansen. . . .

The similarity between these two excerpts shows an affinity which should not pass the attention of any class-conscious worker or youth.

This sort of thing requires no commentary, or rather only one. There is scarcely any need to call the attention of any conscious workers and youth to the similarity between this kind of proof and those of the Stalinist apparatus.

Who is the target?

One of the rare new elements reported by *Workers Press* is that the Sylvia Callen who was cited in 1969 as a codefendant in the trial of the Stalinist agent Robert Soblen was none other than Sylvia Franklin who was the secretary of James P. Cannon, the leader of the SWP. She had been accused by Louis Budenz, an ex-Stalinist leader in the United States who went over to work for the FBI. An SWP Control Commission was, after investigation, to reject these charges. Moreover, James P. Cannon denounced Budenz, assuring that Sylvia Franklin was "an honest comrade who gave years of valued service to the cause."

We do not know if the Sylvia Callen *Workers Press* talks about is really Sylvia Franklin, but we are convinced that if new facts require it, the SWP will review the conclusions of its Control Commission.

However, supposing that *Workers Press* were right and that Sylvia Franklin, James P. Cannon's secretary, were a GPU agent, how would this justify writing: "Joseph Hansen and George Novack have protected and covered up for SYLVIA FRANKLIN, the GPU agent in the Socialist Workers Party . . ."?

It was James P. Cannon who denounced Budenz's statements as lies. An SWP Control Commission confirmed this position. Why doesn't *Workers Press* follow its argument to the logical conclusion? Why didn't it say that James P. Cannon "covered up for a GPU agent"? There is more so-called "evidence" against him than against Hansen and Novack. Why doesn't it accuse the SWP leadership and J.P. Cannon for "covering up" for a GPU agent?

It is true that the fact that Cannon is remembered as the founder and builder of Trotskyism in the United States and as a major figure in the international workers movement makes this a difficult job. It is more expedient to make insinuations than to take the risk of making such a statement.

Nonetheless, this is where the logic leads. Naturally, this would also mean that Lenin covered up for Malinovsky, and was therefore the latter's accomplice, and that Trotsky and Sedov covered up for Zborowski and were his accomplices.

Behind Hansen and Novack, other targets can be seen. The first that comes to view is the SWP. The introduction to the last series of articles published in *Workers Press* said:

> WE ACCUSE Joseph Hansen and leaders of the Socialist Workers Party (USA) of deliberately covering up GPU murder and penetration of the Trotskyist movement. . . .

This vague article by unknown authors is one more outrage, but the target of the slander is clearly indicated. It is the SWP, which they try to represent as a hotbed of GPU agents, an organization with a number of leaders who were "deliberate" accomplices of the GPU. Clearly, they try to represent the SWP as an organization "kept" by the Stalinist apparatus.

But the SWP has played a considerable role in the history of the Fourth International. It was not only one of the strongest sections but the one whose leadership had the most direct ties with Leon Trotsky. The SWP was the battleground of a struggle decisive for the future of the Fourth International, the one over the question of the defense of the Soviet Union. If we had to accept Gerry Healy's standards for determining the truth, we would have to conclude that this struggle was conducted by a group, a majority of whom were "accomplices" of the GPU.

An attack against the Fourth International

Behind the SWP, the real target is the Fourth International itself, Leon Trotsky and his work. The Fourth International appears to be an organization "manipulated" by the GPU, in fact a creation of the GPU.

It would be unfair to compare Vereecken's book with the articles in *Workers Press*.[2] But it is interesting to note that *Workers Press* often quotes this work without reservation or comment. While it is undeniable that provocateurs such as Zborowski poisoned relationships inside the international movement, they could not conjure away the real political questions. It was on these questions that the break occurred between Vereecken and Trotsky. And what makes Vereecken's book a false and biased brief is that he wants to prove that it was the maneuvers of these agents that explain his break with Trotsky.

Referring to Vereecken, *Workers Press* writes:

"Today the International Committee of the Fourth International is getting the same slanderous treatment that others in the pre-war years in Europe endured."

---

2. *La Guépéou dans le mouvement trotskyste*, G. Vereecken, Éditions de la Pensée Universelle. Vereecken was a member of the Left Opposition in Belgium, with whom Trotsky was forced to break because of his sectarian positions.

Should we conclude that the decision to found the Fourth International was inspired by the GPU?

The abominable campaign conducted against the leaders of the SWP can only serve the enemies of the Fourth International and facilitate the work of those who in the interests of imperialism or Stalinism are trying to undermine and disrupt our movement.

An index of the profound political degeneration of the WRP leadership, this campaign is dealing a grave blow to Trotskyism in England. It is more than a coincidence that the publication of *Workers Press* ended almost immediately after the appearance of this series of slanderous articles.

Rejection of such methods, and the kind of politics that allows them to develop, is indispensable for moving forward to the reconstruction of the Fourth International.

As Trotskyists who have been in the fight since the prewar years when the program of the Fourth International was elaborated under the leadership of Leon Trotsky, we considered it necessary to make this public statement. We think that all the militants, whatever differences may exist between their organizations, who claim to adhere to Trotskyism, who have participated in the fight for the Fourth International, must take a position on this question. We think that all organizations that claim to be Trotskyist must also condemn the methods of G. Healy, methods that serve only the enemies of the Fourth International. This is the same struggle that was taken up in 1923 against Stalinism, which L. Trotsky denounced as a dreadful sickness afflicting the world workers movement.

Frame-up concocted in Stalinist tradition

'SOCIALIST ACTION' DENOUNCES WRP SMEAR CAMPAIGN

The following statement appeared in the February–March issue of *Socialist Action*, the newspaper of the League for Socialist Action, a group based in London.

The Workers' Revolutionary Party (WRP) is hardly known for its savoury polemics with other left tendencies. Its latest offering is, in most respects, even less savoury than previous ones. In a recent series of articles, entitled "Security and the Fourth International," the Healyites open an investigation into the death of Leon Trotsky.

Such an investigation is not inspired, as in the case of an honest biographer like Isaac Deutscher, by a real desire to discover the facts but by far more sinister motives. Its aim is to "indict" former Trotskyist secretary, Joseph Hansen, of "criminal negligence" in Trotsky's death, if not of being an "accomplice of the GPU."

It may seem strange that the Healyites should devote more space in their fast-ailing "daily" to witch-hunting a leading Trotskyist militant than to covering key issues such as the national struggle in Ireland. The answer is not so strange, however, as it may at first appear.

Set-backs

Since its split with the OCI, its sister organization in France a few years ago, the WRP has suffered some severe set-backs. It recently lost several leading members of the Workers' League, a sympathising section in the USA, and, closer home, launched a witch-hunt against over 200 trade union members in its own ranks who had the audacity to oppose the leadership's sectarian political line.

The cause of these set-backs—which have left the WRP more isolated than ever before—was analysed by Joseph Hansen in a hard-hitting article in *Intercontinental Press* (Vol 13 No 12). In particular, Hansen singled out the politically sectarian course followed by the WRP and its well-known organisational "thuggism" which denies its own members elementary rights—like thinking for themselves.

Unable to reply politically to such an argument, the Healyites have reverted to the level of politics where they feel most at home: personal slander. Healy no doubt hopes, by concocting frame-ups in the Stalinist tradition against his critics, to cloud the issue and divert the members of the WRP from probing the real reasons for these set-backs and the lack of rights they possess in his monolithic set-up.

New victim?

The slanders directed against Joseph Hansen, a leading member of the world Trotskyist movement for over 30 years, need not be refuted. They are based on rumours culled from self-confessed GPU and CIA agents. A clear, factual reply to them can be found in the pages of *Intercontinental Press* (Vol 13 No 42).

What is worth refuting is the method used by Healy in dealing with political tendencies he has differences with. It can serve as an object lesson for young radicals as to the ultimate logic of sectarian politics.

Hansen himself, in his reply, notes how, for the Healyites, "All other political tendencies . . . are regarded as agencies of the bourgeoisie to be dealt with accordingly." This attitude on the part of the WRP is, of course, merely a substitute for taking up and arguing against the political ideas advanced by rival tendencies. There is no point, after all, discussing with ones' political opponents if they are "agencies of the bourgeoisie." On the contrary, the task is to "expose" them, even if this means juggling with the facts.

Such a premise leads, quite inevitably, to the

wildest slanders and frame-ups (in the Stalinist tradition) to prove the "case." The accusations against Joseph Hansen are not new, in this respect, but merely the spiciest dish yet to be seen from the Healyite kitchen.

The April 23rd issue of *Workers' Press* tried to "smear" Bala Tampoe (leading Trotskyist and head of the Ceylon Mercantile Union) as "associated with the CIA." Tim Wohlforth, last year expelled from the Workers' League, was accused of "harbouring and covering for a CIA agent" and, most recently, Alan Thornett, who was expelled from the WRP for exercising the right to think for himself, was described by the General Secretary as a "police agent."

'Big lie'

The fact that Healy should be reduced to labelling every political opponent—inside and outside the WRP—as some form of police agent is not just a simple question of paranoia. It is an attempt to "shield" the dwindling membership of the WRP from the political arguments of rival tendencies by the use of what can only be called Stalinist methods.

It is an attempt to divert attention away from the fact that the leaders of the WRP have turned a once-promising group into a barren sect unable to relate to the real issues facing working people and unable to tolerate any real criticism of this course.

We can assure the WRP however that the time when it could pass such false coin as "Trotskyism" is long past. The WRP broke with Trotskyism, politically and in its organisational practice, long ago. The technique of the "big lie" will not hide this fact.

NOTES ON HEALY'S ROLE IN EARLY DAYS OF THE BRITISH TROTSKYIST MOVEMENT

By Mary and John Archer

1. As far as we know, Gerry Healy first contributed to the Trotskyist movement in Britain in the summer of 1937, before he was admitted as a member. He worked with us in the industrial region of Yorkshire, where we were building the "Militant Group"[1] and penetrating the Labour Left. We understood that he had been put in touch with us by the comrades of our group in London.

He worked with energy, helping us to run open-air meetings and to sell our paper, the *Militant*. This paper was published as the organ of the Militant Group in the Labour Party and not as an openly Fourth Internationalist journal. Healy was not at this time as far as we knew, a member of the Labour Party. He had evidently read little or nothing of the writings of Trotsky. We did not know then, and still do not know, how he came to break with the Communist Party or the Young Communist League. We have a record, however, of his own statement that he had been in the Young Communist League, in the minutes of the London aggregate meeting of members of the Militant Group dated November 14, 1937. He did not tell us how he had got in touch with our movement, but we were told later by Jock Haston that there was a loose grouping in 1935 and 1936 of former members of the Communist Party who called themselves the "Hyde Park Group" and who were attracted by the pamphlets produced by Pioneer Publishers and the New York *Militant*. We do know that in the autumn of 1936 some of these comrades, including Haston himself, joined the Trotskyist group which shortly afterwards became the Militant Group. Haston said that at first Healy had been very hostile to the Hyde Park Group and was pro-Stalinist. However, we have very little information about his origins or earlier activities.

Healy joined the Militant Group in August 1937, and stayed with it for about five months. The minutes of its national conference show that he was accepted into probationary membership at the conference on the motion of the late Denzil Harber, seconded by John Archer. The minutes of the London aggregate for November 1937 show him as formally a member of the Paddington branch in London. We recall, however, that he had some kind of publicity job which involved travelling round the country and staying only a short time in any one place. We cannot, therefore, say what his political work in Paddington amounted to. We do know, however, that the Paddington branch was joined in August 1937 by four comrades from South Africa whose arrival was to have a great influence on the subsequent history of our movement in Britain. The most politically developed of these four South African comrades was Ralph Lee; his companion, Millie Lee, had conspicuous administrative and secretarial talent.

2. The work of the Militant Group advanced in 1937, but in the course of that year it suffered two severe blows. The first was the success with which the Stalinists penetrated the Labour Left. The second, a consequence of the first, was the liquidation of the left-reformist organisation in the Labour Party, opposing the leadership, called the "Socialist League."

These blows meant that entry work would have been difficult for even a mature and experienced group, because the Left as a whole had been thrown back and disorganised. The group was not, indeed, mature enough to formulate with precision the political character of its problems and to overcome

---

1. The Labour Party entrist group recognised by the International Secretariat of what was to become the Fourth International.

the difficulties of its day-to-day work. Its problems, therefore, became expressed in conflicts between individuals and groups tending to be based on personal associations.

Extreme bitterness was fortuitously injected into the situation when a Stalinist slander followed Ralph Lee from South Africa. This comrade blamed the leadership of the group for failing to protect his revolutionary honour and for manoeuvring to exclude him and Millie Lee, as he thought, from positions of responsibility for which their abilities might be thought to qualify them.

Afterwards, the International Secretariat concluded that the Stalinists' accusations were pure calumnies, and censured the leadership of the Militant Group for mishandling the situation. However, while the affair was being discussed in Britain, and before any of the underlying political causes of friction in the organisation had been elucidated, let alone cleared up, a number of members headed by Ralph Lee and including Haston, Healy and Grant, walked out of the Militant Group and started a rival group, the "Workers' International League."

We have the minutes of the successive meetings of the London membership and of the leadership of the Militant Group in November and December 1937, together with a number of contributions from members to the internal discussion. These papers show that on December 19, 1937, Haston, Healy, Grant and seven others walked out of a London aggregate meeting, after a motion condemning a split had been passed by 25 votes to 6, with 9 abstentions.

The evidence suggests that the split was headed by Ralph Lee and that Healy played no prominent part in it. However, Healy had spoken at the preceding aggregate, that of November 14, in a vein which was in later years to become better known. The minutes read:

> H[ealy] (Paddington) said that he thought he had left slander and intrigue behind when he left the Y.C.L. The action taken by D.D. H[arber], E. S[tarkey] J[ackson] and Co. had shown that they had acted in a bureaucratic manner, their only excuse being that they had acted "for the good of the group". If rank and file comrades were arrested would these people still [be] acting for the good of the group [If they] give information to the police?

The minutes of London aggregate meetings were circulated to the branches of the Militant Group, and this report raised something of a furore. We have a letter, in Healy's own handwriting, addressed to the Executive Committee of the Militant Group, as follows:

> Dear Comrades,
> I had intended to correct the minutes of the last GMM[2] at the next GMM but in view of the conclusions drawn by people who were not present at the meeting as a result of reading the circulated materials I now think it necessary to send in a statement for circulation. The minutes give the impression that I accused leading members of the group of being likely to give information to the police. I report my speech below and shall move the same as a correction at the next GMM.
> (For Circulation)
> I stated that when it became clear that many members of the Group not members of the E.C.[3] knew about the rumours concerning R[alph] L[ee]: "We are asked to believe that these people were acting for the good of the group. In the event of comrades being arrested by the police, and information concerning these comrades reaching the police." Referring to the fact that these people were gossips "Would we be asked to accept the same excuse that they were acting in the interests of the group".
>
> *Yours fraternally,*
> *G. Healy.*

This not entirely coherent statement is undated, but evidently it was written some time between the London aggregate of November 14 and that of December 19.

There has also survived a letter which suggests that the split may have been premeditated before

---

2. General Members' Meeting

3. Executive Committee.

December 19. This is signed with the name of J.R. Strachan, a political name which we believe Healy used in the early 1940s. Dated December 23, 1937, it is addressed to a certain Willie Watson, an old Glasgow syndicalist who had bought Trotskyist literature from time to time. The letter invites him to subscribe to the new journal which the Workers' International League promised shortly to produce. The new journal did indeed appear very soon afterwards, so soon that we might ask Healy today to tell us whether the preparations for it were not already in hand before the walkout of December 19.

The Militant Group noted at its next conference, at Easter 1938, that the split had cost it four branches and one-third of its members. The political damage to our movement was, however, more serious.

3. In 1938, of course, the leading members of the Workers' International League were Ralph Lee and Jock Haston. Healy played a quite subordinate role. However, we encountered him in Yorkshire in that year, trying to disrupt our work, hanging round our contacts and young members with slanders about the leadership of the Militant Group, building nothing and leaving nothing behind. One of the people whom he recruited to the Workers' International League out of the Labour Party League of Youth is today a prominent right-wing Member of Parliament! Healy's name is not, indeed, mentioned in any of the documents which passed between the Workers' International League and the International Secretariat in the summer and autumn of 1938 when the fusion of the British groups was being negotiated and the Workers' International League was invited to join in, in preparation for the Founding Conference of the Fourth International and in anticipation of the early outbreak of the war.

The Workers' International League rejected Cannon's invitation to join the fusion, and its leaders had, of course, to try to justify their separate existence, as against the International Secretariat and, in due course, the Founding Conference. The documents of the Workers' International League show how it set in circulation certain falsifications of the history and theory of our movement which were later to grow into a positive mythology. They were used to defend false political positions against "entrism" and have prevented—not only in Britain but internationally—later generations even up to the present time from drawing fully on the results of our prewar discussions about and experience of entrism. Some of the sectarian nonsense which has subsequently plagued the British movement can, indeed, be traced back to the self-justificatory errors of the Workers' International League in 1938, to which Healy has given currency in later years.

The leaders of the Workers' International League inevitably cut themselves off from all the preceding experience of the British movement. In later years Healy has used their argument that nothing happened before they came on the scene, to pretend that nothing happened before the one and only Healy took charge, and that our experiences from 1931 to 1938 did not exist!

There is, however, no evidence that he had any direct hand in originating the falsifications. Comrade Joe Hansen has correctly pointed out in *Intercontinental Press*, November 24, 1975, that

> Healy belonged to a clique that stood in opposition to Trotsky as long as Trotsky was alive. This did not prevent Trotsky from being concerned about them. In 1938 he asked James P. Cannon to stop in London, talk with them, and try to persuade them to send a delegation to the founding congress of the Fourth International. They said no to Cannon and Trotsky.

The Workers' International League did actually send a representative to ask to be seated in the Founding Conference. They wanted, however, to be seated on the condition that they would not have to join in the fusion of the British groups. The Founding Conference rejected this condition, and the representative of the Workers' International League was not admitted.

Fortunately we do know the political reasons which they gave at the time for "saying no to Cannon and Trotsky". To resurrect and state their arguments is not, of course, to imply that they were right. Nonetheless their arguments are of considerable interest, not merely to us in Britain, where "entrism" is a life and death question, but wherever in the world "entrism" is a necessary stage in the construction of the party. In addition, a look at the whole prewar discussion on "entrism" in the British movement strikes a deathblow at the pretentious nonsense of Healy's "Problems of the Fourth International".

The statement of the International Secretariat said that there was no justification for the existence of the Workers' International League. The statement reads:

> The IS also considers it its duty to condemn energetically the action of Lee and his companions in this affair (his ultimatistic manner of posing the question before the GMM of 11 November [sic] and which brought them to split the MG[4] and create a new, minute, independent so-called "Trotskyist" Group, on a basis devoid of all political meaning.

We have three documents produced by the Workers' International League leadership during the summer and autumn of 1938 which show how they tried to establish some political justification for their separate existence as well as the political atmosphere which Healy breathed in those early days.

The first document is entitled "Contribution by Workers' International League to the Discussion on the Tasks of Bolshevik-Leninists in Britain". This attempts to explain why the members of the Workers' International League, having split from an "entrist" organisation without apparently realising why it was an "entrist" organisation, were continuing to work as members of the Labour Party after the split. The document contains, to be sure, a few faint echoes of the earlier and richer discussions which had gone on before any of the members of the Workers' International League had come on to the scene. However, the document cannot be said, even with the utmost charity, to go to the heart of the matter. It ends by basing the tactic of the Workers' International League on the expectation that the Independent Labour Party would return to the Labour Party.

The record of the discussions between Fenner Brockway and Jimmie Maxton, the leaders of the Independent Labour Party, and the leaders of the Labour Party are now all available for study. The expectation that the Labour Party would readmit the Independent Labour Party was not fulfilled, and the negotiations broke down because the Labour Party would not permit the Parliamentary Group of the Independent Labour Party to vote against majority decisions of the Labour Parliamentary Group. The Independent Labour Party effectively broke up in 1946 and some of its members, including Fenner Brockway, joined the Labour Party as individuals, being denounced for doing so by Maxton almost from his deathbed.

The "Contribution by Workers' International League to the Discussion on the Tasks of Bolshevik-Leninists in Britain" accordingly contains the political basis for the sectarianism which flourished in the Workers' International League during the war, when some of the Labour Party organisations closed down after 1939, and which dominated the policies of the Revolutionary Communist Party[5] from its foundation in 1944 to its collapse in 1949.

The second document is a statement issued by a meeting of the Workers' International League, dated June 27, 1938, attacking the International Secretariat.

After taking up a number of minor debating points, the document offers an explanation as to why those who walked out of the aggregate of December 19 did not appeal to the National Conference, the highest body of the Militant Group. First, says the statement, "the national membership of the 'Militant Group' is fictitious". The writers of this article have the best of reasons for knowing that this claim was untrue, since we had a group of some twelve comrades working actively in the Labour Party in Leeds and were in regular and frequent contact with other branches of the Militant Group in Hull, Liverpool, York, and Glasgow. Secondly, the minutes of the first annual conference of the "Militant Labour League", the cover organisation which the Trotskyists in the Labour Party promoted as the open expression of their work on a partial programme, record that in the autumn of 1938 it had 150 members, with six branches in London and seven in provincial cities.

The second document of the Workers' Interna-

---

4. Militant Group.

5. The Revolutionary Communist Party was formed in Britain in spring 1944 by the fusion of the Revolutionary Socialist League, the official British section of the Fourth International, with the Workers' International League.

tional League goes on to say that the expulsions[6] were accepted because "the actions of the leadership after our expulsion re-inforced the conclusion we formed that both the leadership and the remaining membership were irresponsible". It concluded by rejecting totally the resolution of the International Secretariat on the "R. Lee" affair which denounced the split.

The third document states:

> . . . the attempt to characterise our organisational separation from other groups as arising from "purely personal grievances" is simple mis-representation. [It goes on:] . . . to attribute the failure of the delegates [of the International Secretariat, i.e., Cannon, Shachtman, and Gould] to present a convincing case for organisational fusion to the resistance of leading members of our Group is sheer misrepresentation.

They also blame Harber [a delegate to the Founding Conference from the Militant Group] and Cannon for the fact that their statement was not presented to the Founding Conference. We do not know to what document they refer.

Healy went along with this, as far as we know, in 1938, but changed his mind about it later. He was to write in the summer of 1947:

> An additional factor which aggravates the sectarian sickness of the Revolutionary Communist Party is the past history and evolution of the present majority leadership [Haston, Grant]. Their unprincipled split from the Fourth International [in 1938], which they defend to this day, is a constant source of mis-education in the party . . .

Not a word about what he himself was doing and saying in 1938, but, more important, not a word about how the decision to stay out of the Fourth International was arrived at, and, therefore, no lessons drawn from the experience.

4. A page in the history of the European Trotskyist movement still remains obscure. It is said that a minority in the Workers' International League in 1939 and 1940 recognised that its attitude to the Fourth International was a bad one. This minority appears to have established some connection with elements of the French Parti Communiste Internationaliste (Frank-Molinier), on the basis that they all wanted somehow to reverse the judgement of the Founding Conference.

While Pierre Frank and Raymond Molinier took some positive steps at the time, members of the Workers' International League circulated disparaging remarks about the good faith of Cannon and his recommendations to the International Secretariat and the Founding Conference . . . even to the point of saying that Cannon was drunk when he was supposed to be negotiating between the British groups and trying to get the Workers' International League to come in.

These statements are still being circulated. It is historically important that they should be cleared up and any hitherto unpublished documents concerning the moves made at that time be made public. There are already more than enough little sectarian groups attacking the tradition of "Orthodox Trotskyism" and only too ready to pick up any bits of scandal to suggest that "there never really was a Fourth International" or "there never really was an international leadership".

5. The misguided efforts of the Workers' International League to justify its separate existence in 1938 were no more than the scratch which, in 1942 and 1943, developed into virulent sectarianism and finally into Healy's gross falsifications of history and theory.

In the period following the German imperialist invasion of Soviet Russia, the Workers' International League succeeded in establishing contact with certain layers of workers, especially in engineering, whose demands could find no expression through either the official trade union apparatus or through the Stalinist-controlled shop-stewards movement. This development surprised the official British section of the Fourth International, the Revolutionary Socialist League, which was the

---

6. The minutes of the General Members' Meeting of the "Militant Group" on December 19, 1937, show that a motion was carried, stating ". . . it will be the duty of all members loyally to accept the decision of the majority. No Bolshevik can consider splitting the Group on such an issue or at such a moment." Ten of those present, including Healy, then walked out of the meeting. Their expulsion was thereupon carried by 25 votes to 6.

result of the fusion in the summer of 1938 of all the British groups except the Workers' International League.

At the outbreak of the war the majority of the leadership and some of the rank and file of the Workers' International League departed from London to the neutrality of Southern Ireland, in the mistaken expectation that either London would be bombed to destruction from the air or that there would be immediate police action against those who opposed the war.

Healy went with the other leaders, and his relations with them in exile were far from harmonious. A document dated February 15, 1943, issued by the Political Bureau of the Workers' International League provides an almost ludicrous picture of his relations with the rest of the cadres. It is an explanation to the members as to why the Central Committee came to a unanimous decision at its February 7 meeting to expel him. (They took him back later.) The document provides a telling description of the capricious and unreliable temperament which made him impossible as a member of a team.

The emigration to Ireland has to be mentioned for another, more specific reason. There is in circulation in European Trotskyist circles a curious myth that the leadership of the Revolutionary Socialist League, the British section of the Fourth International, collapsed at the outbreak of the war in September 1939. Some kind of parallel is drawn between what is supposed to have happened in Britain and the alleged collapse of the Parti Ouvrier Internationaliste in France. If this myth is not corrected it will be used as further support for Healy's falsifications of the history of the British movement. It was the Workers' International League which collapsed at the outbreak of the war. We cannot allow Healy to score off those who are defending Hansen and Novack against him by posing—quite falsely—as one who stood up to the outbreak of the war, as did the leadership of the Revolutionary Socialist League. The work of the Revolutionary Socialist League is, in fact, mentioned in the report of the 1940 Emergency Conference of the Fourth International, which once again called upon the Workers' International League to join with it and spoke of the "substantial progress" achieved by our cover organisation, the Militant Labour League.

Towards the end of 1941, following the German imperialist invasion of Soviet Russia, the membership of the Workers' International League began to grow. It was soon in position to produce an attractive, printed paper, and to attract some notice. Its successes were, regrettably, transient, because practically everything which it gathered during these years disappeared after 1945. Nonetheless, at the time, its gains were more than the Revolutionary Socialist League, the official section, could claim. (We do not enter here into the political problems of the two groups during the war. They are of great theoretical interest and we hope that work will soon begin on the plentiful documents which have survived. It remains only to record that in all the years since 1947, when Healy began to have control of "his own" group, hardly a word has been written on these problems. They were raised *once* in *Labour Review*[7] at the end of the 1950s, and that was all.)

The majority of the new recruits to the Workers' International League during 1941–43 knew nothing about the prewar experience of the Trotskyist movement, whether nationally or internationally. They knew nothing about the peacetime Labour Party and were told nothing about the theoretical and historical foundations of "entrism" or the discussions before 1938 about it. The new recruits did, however, want to know why the Workers' International League, which claimed to be working for the Fourth International in Britain, was not recognised as the official section. Accordingly the leadership produced a document, sometime in 1942 or 1943—it is undated—which claims to "present a short factual summary of the early development of the Fourth International in this country . . ."

This document expands grossly on the claims which the Workers' International League had made in 1938 that the national membership of the Militant Group was fictitious and that the leadership and membership were irresponsible. It presents a much more fully developed mythology,

---

7. *Labour Review* was a theoretical journal published by the Healyite organisation in the 1950s. It began as a very modest mimeographed affair, but from January 1957 until 1963 it was attractively printed. Its earlier issues after the shake-up of Stalinism in 1956–57 gave promise of distinguished theoretical development.

which later research into the plentiful surviving documents of our movement is in process of destroying point by point.

One of its central arguments was: There never was a Trotskyist movement of any seriousness in Britain until the Workers' International League was formed. This claim involves obliterating and grossly slandering the original Groves-Wicks group, slurring over the lessons of the "entry" into the Independent Labour Party in 1934–36, and not saying a word about the work in the Labour League of Youth and the Labour Party which laid the basis for the development of the Militant Group in 1937.

Another central argument was to excuse the refusal of the Workers' International League to accept Cannon's suggestion to join in the fusion with the Militant Group which produced the Revolutionary Socialist League in 1938, on the ground that "there was no political discussion of tactics and perspectives for Britain".

We do not know who drafted this document, which has served Healy well in later years. We doubt that he had any hand in its authorship.

To close: A copy of a report found in Cannon's papers has been made available to us. This is headed: "Brief Outline of the British Movement (very much subject to correction)". Internal evidence suggests that it was written by a Canadian comrade who was prominent in the British section, and dates from 1936. It mentions Harber as a possible secretary for Trotsky, and, in addition, refers to the role of Margaret Johns and one of the present writers. It does not mention Healy, or, for that matter, anyone else later to become connected with the Workers' International League.

We have referred to a number of documents in this brief survey. We can locate them all and have copies of most of them.

FEBRUARY 27, 1976

WHEN ISAAC DEUTSCHER SHOWED HEALY TO THE DOOR
By Ernest Tate

It is not necessary for me to deal with Gerry Healy's slanderous accusations against Joe Hansen and George Novack—I think Joe Hansen's reply to the charges more than adequately exposed Healy's latest frame-ups[1]—but I think by relating some personal experiences I had in Britain, I can throw some light on how damaging Healy's methods can be—to Healy.

Readers of *Intercontinental Press* will be aware that I became one of Healy's victims when members of the Socialist Labour League physically assaulted me outside one of the organization's public meetings, on November 17, 1966, at Caxton Hall in London, England, where I was selling the *International Socialist Review* and the pamphlet, *Healy "Reconstructs" the Fourth International*.[2] In the beating, which took place in the presence of Healy, my glasses were smashed. After I got up from the pavement, I was forced to go to a hospital for treatment.

The beating was not just an isolated incident. It followed a series of threats against the political group I was active in—the sympathizing group of the Fourth International in Britain, which later became the International Marxist Group, the official British section of the Fourth International.

In the weeks preceding the incident outside Caxton Hall, members of our group had been threatened by Healy's followers and prevented from selling literature at an SLL meeting held during the Labour party annual conference in Brighton. And of course there was the open threat leveled against us in Healy's paper, the *Newsletter*, in connection with our selling the pamphlet, *Healy "Reconstructs" the Fourth International*:

> We shall not hesitate to deal appropriately with the handful of United Secretariat agents who hawk it around the cynical fake-left in England.

At that time our group was very much involved in mobilizing public sentiment against the complicity of the British government in the U.S. imperialist intervention in Vietnam. Our main activity was in the Vietnam Solidarity Campaign, but we were also helping the Bertrand Russell Peace Foundation in the organizational work of the War Crimes Tribunal which sought to bring together some of the world's leading intellectuals to hear and pass moral judgment on the American aggression against Vietnam.

It was through this work that I had the good fortune of meeting Isaac Deutscher, the Marxist historian and biographer of Trotsky.

Deutscher was very much committed to making the War Crimes Tribunal a success. He had spoken in the United States on the American aggression and had undertaken speaking tours throughout Europe on the question, putting aside some of his major historical writing to do so. He also took an active part in trying to solve the day-to-day practical problems that inevitably arose in making such a broad international undertaking as the War Crimes Tribunal a success.

As far as I am aware, this was the first time that Deutscher since leaving Poland had become publicly and personally involved, in an organizational

---

1. See "On Healy's 'Investigation'—What the Facts Show" by Joseph Hansen, *Intercontinental Press*, November 24, 1975, p. 1636.—*IP*

2. The pamphlet *Healy "Reconstructs" the Fourth International* as well as a series of documents concerning the beating of Ernest Tate have been included in a 253-page book, *Marxism Vs. Ultraleftism: The Record of Healy's Break With Trotskyism* (New York: Pathfinder Press, 1974).

sense, in political activity on the left.

My impression of Deutscher was that he saw his writings as his main contribution to the struggle for socialism. He remained aloof from the various groupings in Britain, but was, in general, sympathetic to the Trotskyists (but not the state capitalists!) although what he thought was the needless factionalism and polemics they conducted against each other was not to his taste.

I remember once discussing the Socialist Labour League and Healy with Deutscher. I had heard that in the past Deutscher had had a collaborative relationship with Healy and that articles by him had appeared in *Labour Review*, the theoretical organ of the SLL. I also knew that he had discussions with Healy from time to time.

Deutscher readily conceded the sectarian and political weaknesses of the SLL; but, he asked, which of the Trotskyist organizations in England at that time were as organizationally serious or as prepared to build a working-class leadership as was the SLL? And indeed, despite the serious political differences I had with Healy, I had to admit the element of truth in what Deutscher was saying.

At that time, the disease of sectarianism seemed to be rampant in most of the Trotskyist groups. Of them all, the SLL was the largest. Even though it abstained from participation in activities around the Vietnam war and was hostile to the War Crimes Tribunal, it nevertheless held some of the largest and most impressive meetings in London and had an atmosphere of seriousness surrounding it that was absent from the other groups.

The day following the incident outside Caxton Hall, I had occasion to see Deutscher in connection with some work concerning the War Crimes Tribunal. He could see that I was not in good shape, being bruised and having difficulty walking. He told me he had heard that I had been beaten, and asked me about it. I described briefly what had occurred.

Deutscher became angry and upset. If what I was saying was true, he said, he could not have such a person as Healy coming to his home. He felt that it was necessary for him to confront Healy with my accusation.

Deutscher asked me to come to his home to face Healy while he personally questioned him about the incident. I, of course, agreed to be present.

This is not to say that Deutscher was sympathetic to me in the affair—indeed, he told me that to sell such a pamphlet as *Healy "Reconstructs"* outside an SLL meeting was far too provocative.

I disagreed, but I felt that this implicitly was more of a condemnation of the SLL, because the material in the pamphlet stood on its own merits.

I think part of Deutscher's motivation in asking for the meeting was that he viewed himself as a friend of the left as a whole and was alarmed at the apparent degeneration in political relations between two Trotskyist groups. He thought he could use his own personal and intellectual authority—which stood high with the left in Britain—to intervene in the dispute and bring some sort of resolution to it.

Healy brought Michael Banda and Eileen Jennings with him to the meeting at Deutscher's home. Banda was editor of the *Newsletter*, if I recall correctly, and Jennings was the leader of Healy's Young Socialists. I brought Geoff Coggan, who at that time was on the staff of the Bertrand Russell Peace Foundation.

Deutscher confronted Healy with the charge I had made against him. Although I was boiling underneath, I did not say anything. Under Deutscher's questioning, Healy admitted that the people who had carried out the assault were members of the SLL. He admitted that I had been kicked while lying on the pavement. But he refused to take responsibility himself for what had happened.

He said that I had provoked the SLL members or supporters by saying things critical of the SLL.

Then he had the gall to say that I, Tate, *had attacked and beaten up his people*!

Deutscher wanted to know how it was possible for someone lying on the ground and being kicked to carry out this feat.

Indeed, Healy said, he had intervened personally and prevented me from receiving a worse beating.

Well then, Deutscher asked, didn't you see to it that Tate received attention for his injuries?

Healy had no answer.

Deutscher turned again to the question of responsibility. "As a leader of the SLL, don't you accept responsibility for the action of its members?"

Healy refused to accept this and Deutscher

quoted Lenin to him on the question of leadership responsibility.

Yes, in that sense I am responsible, Healy replied.

Deutscher, obviously very angry, ordered Healy to get out. He rose to show the SLL leaders to the door.

As they started to leave, Healy shouted at Deutscher; and Banda, who had been silent until then, joined in. They denounced Deutscher as "petty bourgeois" as they walked out.

What is instructive in this episode, in my opinion, is that Isaac Deutscher, who alone among the intellectuals of stature in Britain could be considered a friend of the SLL, was forced to break off personal relations because of an action of its leader that violated proletarian morality. The SLL thus lost a valuable asset because of the practices of the Healy leadership.

The "Tate incident" continued to give the SLL trouble. Some time later, Tony Garnet, the well-known television producer, who was sympathetic to the SLL, organized a meeting, ostensibly to discuss our group's policy on Vietnam, at which representatives of the SLL could present their views. We had known for some time that the SLL was trying to influence a number of politically inexperienced people in television work, who were moving to the left and who had participated with us in our Vietnam war protest activities.

The meeting took place at Garnet's home and the representatives of the SLL were no less than Gerry Healy and Cliff Slaughter. Also present at the meeting were participants in the *New Left Review*, most notably, Robin Blackburn. The meeting was essentially a debate between two from our group, Connie Harris, and myself on one side, and Healy and Slaughter on the other, concerning the antiwar movement in Britain and how our respective organizations could best defend the Vietnamese revolution.

The debate soon shifted to what was for Healy the real business of the gathering—a discussion of "the Tate affair." Healy went to great lengths to plead his personal innocence and I stated the facts as they happened outside Caxton Hall, explaining that witnesses were available who could verify what had occurred and the conclusion that Healy was entirely responsible for the assault upon me by his people. No matter how much he wriggled, Healy could not evade that central question.

Of course there was no way that particular gathering could really determine the truth about Healy's personal role, even if it wanted to, so the meeting broke up inconclusively in the small hours of the morning. From the discussion it was obvious that "the Tate affair" was disturbing to some of the people present, and this was creating problems for the SLL in winning them. In fact, the staging of the debate was in its own way a tacit recognition by Healy of the justice of my demand that a commission based upon working-class organizations be set up to investigate the beating, a demand that the SLL had categorically rejected.

I am sure, when the final balance sheet is drawn on the Workers Revolutionary party, Healy's distinctive technique (is it so unique?) of dealing with the ideas of political opponents, even in his own organization, through lies, slander, frame-ups, and general thuggery, will be seen to be a key element in the decline and isolation of that organization. I am confident that the attempt to besmirch Joe Hansen and George Novack will be an important contribution to that process.

The tragedy is that many good militants who are now members of the WRP may be lost to the cause of revolutionary socialism as a result.

Key Target Is the SWP
HEALY'S SMEAR AGAINST TROTSKY'S LAST COLLABORATORS
By Sam Gordon

The Gerry Healy circus, masquerading as the "International Committee of the Fourth International," has for some time been engaging in a completely unbridled smear campaign against the Socialist Workers party. This campaign has included a series of articles (over thirty-five to date!) in the daily newspaper misnamed *Workers Press*,[1] alleging that old-time leaders of the party like Joseph Hansen and George Novack, intimates of the coleader with Lenin of the Russian revolution during his last exile in Mexico from 1937 to 1940, were "accomplices of the GPU" and practically responsible for not forestalling the assassination of Leon Trotsky ordered by the Kremlin!

In support of the allegations against Joseph Hansen and George Novack (and by implication, posthumously against James P. Cannon), Healy's committee offers excerpts from testimony recorded in U.S. government documents, the opinions of long-time political enemies of Trotsky and Trotskyism, and the assistance of one old-timer, Harold Robins, a politically erratic worker comrade who is apparently backing the American Healyite organization in his old age.

What is the purpose of these tirades that have been one of the main features of the Healyite press in both Britain and the United States for an entire year?

Clearly the purpose is first of all to becloud the issues for Healy's own followers in the Workers Revolutionary party (formerly the Socialist Labour League). The issues, extending from philosophy and politics to organizational methods, have been publicly debated for a number of years. The outcome was to expose Healy's bankruptcy more and more thoroughly. Sizeable groups arose in opposition within his organization, only to be promptly expelled. Among these were the Bulletin group and the Thornett group (now the Workers Socialist League). They were smeared with the epithet "revisionist," and banished before any serious two-sided discussion could begin *inside* the organization.

In contrast, the SWP has, as long as I have known it, been open to criticism. It is not monolithic. In fact, it welcomes discussion and debate. Often debate continues with internal minority oppositions for years.

Healy's monolithism has reached the point where something qualitatively new is involved. We are now faced with the question of combatting foul witch-hunts and frame-ups like those featured in *Workers Press*. The whole logic of Healy's exercise there, whether he is aware of it or not, is to discredit the very idea of the Fourth International and with it the historic movement of Trotskyism.

It is impossible in a relatively brief article to undertake a thorough analysis and refutation of the International Committee's "exposures." But this effort hopes to make a contribution.

1. Should the SWP have investigated and publicized *any* charge in connection with the matter brought forward in the 1950s? Did it have the resources then, at the height of McCarthyism—a daily paper perhaps? Healy can tell, but he does not.

2. Where was Healy at the time? Did he make a public protest or even a private one to the SWP for its supposed dilatoriness? From personal experience I know that he was fully aware of Floyd Miller's testimony before the HUAC—the House (of Representatives) Un-American Activities Committee of the U.S. Congress—shortly after it was

---
1. *Workers Press* ceased publication February 14, 1976. Its reappearance under a new name has been promised.

given. He had read it in the columns of the *New York Times*. What action, if any, did *Healy* take at the time?

3. The Healyites charge that Sam Gordon, "alias" J.B. Stuart, was linked to Mark Zborowski, alleging that the GPU agent was a "close confidante [sic]," no less, of mine. As far as I can make out, this is a totally manufactured lie.

In international collaboration during the early 1940s, I knew only the French comrades Jean van Heijenoort and Rigal (fleetingly), the Germans Johre (Weber) and Louis (Ludwig), the Czech Jan Frankel, the Spaniard Grandizo Munis, the Brazilian Lebrun, a Chilean whose name escapes me at the moment (he attended the 1940 SWP convention as an observer).

If the Healyite charge had any correspondence whatever with the truth, Zborowski would presumably have spoken for the Russian Left Opposition. I never met any Russian Bolshevik-Leninist outside of Trotsky and Natalia. Nor did I meet any one-time Polish revolutionary socialist until I met Isaac Deutscher and a handful of others long after the war was over.

4. According to Healy, Hansen has "suppressed the fact that in 1941 it was the Socialist Workers Party who helped bring Stalin's No. 1 anti-Trotskyist agent, MARK ZBOROWSKI, into the United States from France."

As Novack patiently explained,[2] in what proved to be a vain effort to tap a vestige of a sense of class solidarity, it was he who participated in the broad committee that helped bring socialists of *all* denominations from Vichy France to the United States.

So far as I know, Novack never met or corresponded with Zborowski.

The actual affidavits for Zborowski—and affidavits are required for all immigrants—were signed by Mr. and Mrs. David Dallin.[3] David Dallin was a leading Russian Menshevik who had settled in America. His wife was a friend and collaborator of the Trotskys. So far as I know, however, she never had any affiliation or connection with the SWP. I know I certainly never met her, but only knew of her as the sister of Sara Weber, a party member at the time.

How did "George Novack and Mrs David Dallin" manage "re-integrating him [Zborowski] into the top levels of the Fourth International although he was gravely suspect . . ."? What post exactly was he given? Healy keeps a deafening silence.

Healy says that Zborowski "disrupted Trotsky's campaign to defend himself against the Moscow Trials frame-up."

Zborowski may have tried, but he did not succeed. The SWP was instrumental in setting up what became known as the Dewey Commission which, after exhaustive hearings in Mexico, published its unanimous verdict *Not Guilty*, refuting all of Stalin's frame-up charges. It was published as a book under that title soon after.[4]

Healy says:

> Within a year [after arriving in the United States—S.G.] Zborowski was working as a close confidante of *Sam Gordon*, party name J.B. Stuart, and Jean van Heijanoort [sic], leading members in the international work of the Fourth International; SWP meetings were held in his [Zborowski's] Manhattan apartment.

Healy lies on all counts once more. Healy knows what the relations between the SWP and the Fourth International were after the passage of the Voorhis Act at that time and since. For what purpose is he dragging in this red herring?

As for identifying Zborowski, I must acknowledge a certain gratitude to Healy for publishing the GPU agent's photograph in *Workers Press* in the issues of January 5 and January 10, 1976. I can state categorically that I never laid eyes on the man, let alone visited his apartment.

5. *The case of Sylvia Caldwell*. Healy presents as "evidence" against Sylvia the assertions of Louis Budenz, who wound up as an FBI informer. Before that, on his own testimony he was a *real* accomplice of the GPU. That was in 1950.

In 1960 a federal grand jury included Sylvia's name, along with the names of Beria, Zubilin, Soblen, Miller, and others, in an indictment for

---

2. See "Healy's Frame-up Against Joseph Hansen" in the December 8, 1975, issue of *Intercontinental Press*, p. 1710.

3. See *The Mind of an Assassin* by Isaac Don Levine, p. 30.

4. The book was reprinted in 1972 and is available from pathfinderpress.com.

alleged espionage for the Soviet Union.

An indictment by a grand jury (consisting of twenty-four businessmen or other pillars of capitalist society) is not equivalent to *conviction*. Those named are subject to trial by jury in which twelve "peers" decide on the guilt or innocence of the defendants. But Sylvia was never brought to trial. Evidently the political purposes of the indictment had been served and the government prosecution decided they had no case that would stand up in court.

In any event, the SWP, on Cannon's initiative, carried out a control commission investigation of Sylvia Caldwell's case and found all of Budenz's accusations against her to be groundless.

No *new* charges were brought in 1960. So you have a choice between the federal grand jury indictment, which was never tested in court, and the findings of the SWP control commission, which showed Sylvia to be innocent. Healy chooses to believe the unproved indictment. Anything goes in Healy's "class struggle."

6. *Desecrating the grave of Robert Sheldon Harte*. Healy accuses Hansen of "covering up" for Harte, the guard at Coyoacán who was killed by the GPU gang in the May 24 attack on Trotsky's home. Of Harte, he claims that "a mountain of new evidence has been gathered casting the gravest suspicion on him."

What does the mountain consist of? Healy presents only a mouse—the opinion of Julian Gorkin, leader of the Spanish Workers Party of Marxist Unification (POUM) and a sworn enemy of Trotskyism from the days of the civil war in Spain, that "if it were admitted that Sheldon was a spy, that would place the question of responsibility in the chief Trotskyists in New York, who had sent him to Mexico."

Gorkin, an adversary of Trotsky and the Fourth International, helped General Sanchez Salazar, "Ex-Chief of Secret Service of the Mexican Police," to write a book *Murder in Mexico—The Assassination of Leon Trotsky*. It was from that book that Healy selected his quotation.

The book was published in 1950. Where was Healy then? Did *he* at that time back Gorkin's charge?

Trotsky's own tribute to Harte is well known. It was reprinted in the November 24, 1975, issue of *Intercontinental Press*.

7. Healy seeks to make much of Hansen's conversation with McGregor at the American consulate after the assassination of Trotsky in 1940. Among Hansen's objectives was to secure evidence as to the real identity of the assassin, an effort in which he succeeded. McGregor later reported that Hansen mentioned having been approached by a GPU agent named "John" in the United States in 1938. Healy has seized on this as one of his main "proofs" that Hansen is an "accomplice of the GPU."

He claims that Hansen never told Trotsky about this. As "proof" of this charge, Healy says that there is nothing about the incident in "Trotsky's writings or in the published correspondence of the period."

And as further "proof," Healy says that if Trotsky had been informed, "it could have led to the earlier unmasking of Sylvia Franklin and prevented the sending of the inexperienced and politically suspect *Robert Sheldon Harte* as a guard."

Joe has taken care of the "proof" relating to McGregor's report faultlessly in puncturing Healy's previous series of "exposures."[5] But may I add here a general observation? Why should the "John" case be mentioned in Trotsky's "published correspondence of the period"? How does Healy know there was not *unpublished* correspondence or communication? Healy knows very well that in security cases informality is often the case and the necessity.

And why would publicizing the "John" meeting necessarily lead Trotsky to the "unmasking" of the innocent Sylvia Caldwell or have prevented "the sending of the inexperienced and politically suspect *Robert Sheldon Harte*" as one of the guards? The GPU, like the secret agencies of other governments, does not bandy about the names of real coconspirators and often these do not know the names themselves.[6]

---

5. See "On Healy's 'Investigation'—What the Facts Show" by Joseph Hansen in the November 24, 1975, issue of *Intercontinental Press*, p. 1636.

Intercontinental Press is on the *Index Expurgatorius* of Pope Gerry for all the faithful—except the "experts"—as is indeed every publication supported by the SWP or any left-wing periodical that criticizes, or replies to, his unholiness.

6. In her book *Our Own People*, Elisabeth K. Poretsky reports her last conversation with Zborowski. Note the following

Healy merely lends his support to the desecration of Harte's grave by the enemies of Trotsky and the SWP.

8. The "testimony" of FBI agent Thomas L. Black, which Healy cites, includes absolutely nothing that can even remotely pertain to the alleged crimes of Hansen and Novack. Of course, Black says he was told, when he was working as an agent of the GPU, "to go to Coyoacan, and there would be other Soviet agents in Trotsky's household. . . ."

But was Black given any names? Did he add anything new in his testimony? In any case, what does it all prove? Only that Healy's writers are capable of what is called in Fleet Street journalistic padding.

9. *The Orlov letter.* This was sent directly to Trotsky. Trotsky chose a method of testing its authenticity that was his own. In this instance it did not work because General Orlov would not entrust his information to "Martin," whom Trotsky recommended he see in New York.

Orlov mentioned a "Mark" in his letter as being in Trotsky's entourage. It is just possible that no one in our movement at that time knew that the real name of "Etienne" was Mark and that those most intimately associated with him then thought the letter, because of its anonymity, was a GPU hoax.[7] In any case, apart from providing from its midst someone whom Trotsky told Orlov he could entrust his information to (probably "Martin" was Cannon), the SWP had nothing to do with this matter. If Healy has a point that is different, let him state it clearly—if he can.

10. *Once more on Gordon.* Healy says:

"[Floyd Cleveland] Miller took over from *Sam Gordon*, alias J.B. Stuart, as editor of the Seafarers' International Union newspaper. When Sam Gordon became responsible for the work of the International Secretariat of the Fourth International in New York, he worked closely with *Mark Zborowski* who arrived from occupied France in 1941." (Note Healy's use of the word *alias*.)

Another tissue of prestidigitations. Miller did indeed follow me as editor of that paper, but he did not "take over" from me. I may have *informally* recommended him as a fellow party member, but he had to make his application to the elected officials of the union and be accepted by them as is the case in every trade union. Miller had better professional qualifications for the editorial job than I had then; he was earning money by writing, mostly radio scripts.

As for me, I shipped out as a seaman, an occupation I followed to the end of the war in 1945. My "responsibility" for the International Secretariat of the Fourth International had been terminated with the passage of the Voorhis Act. As I mentioned before, I had on occasion informal meetings with international cothinkers thereafter, but Mark Zborowski was not one of them. Not in 1941, before 1941, or after.

I did meet an Etienne; but he was not Zborowski. The Etienne I met was a leader of the French Parti Communiste Internationaliste *after* the war. A Rumanian by origin, he later emigrated to the United States. There is more than one Etienne in the world, just as there is more than one Steven.

11. When Novack said that the "principal actors were Trotsky and Sedov themselves who trusted Etienne and allowed Jacson entry into the household,"[8] he was simply stating an incontrovertible fact as to their attitude.

Trotsky, let us recall, took Jacson into his study without notifying any of his guards.

As for *the* "Etienne," that is, Zborowski, not one of the SWP leaders (with the possible exception of Albert Goldman, who was in Europe during 1939) had more than a nodding acquaintance with him. Possibly Cannon and Shachtman met him at the time of the world congress of 1938.

Healy turns Novack's statement of fact into "a lie which Novack has taken directly from the GPU." Healy then charges: "This makes Novack the co-conspirator of Hansen."

But Healy could do a similar hat trick with Isaac Deutscher, who takes several pages in his

---

question and reply on page 274: "Then I asked him point-blank: 'Were there other agents than yourself among the Trotskyites?' By now he had regained his composure and answered angrily: 'I don't know, but you ought to know that an agent is never told about another unless they are supposed to work together.'"

7. Deutscher puts it: "Trotsky wondered whether the denunciation was not a G. P. U. hoax. . . ." See *The Prophet Outcast*, p. 409.

8. "Healy's Frame-up Against Joseph Hansen," *Intercontinental Press*, December 8, 1975, p. 1711.

biography of Trotsky to report the facts referred to by Novack.⁹

The question really is, Whose game is *Healy* playing?

12. Deutscher, after examining the Zborowski case and particularly the Orlov letter, drew his conclusions about Trotsky's approach:

> All too many accusations had already been bandied about in the small Trotskyist circle in Paris anyhow; and if all of these were to be taken seriously, there would be no end to the chasing of *agents provocateurs*. He knew all too well what a curse stool-pigeons were in any organization; but he also knew that constant suspicion and witch-hunting could be even worse. He decided not to lend ear to any accusation unless it was unequivocally presented and substantiated. He preferred to take the gravest risks and to expose himself to extreme danger rather than to infect and demoralize his followers with distrust and scares. And so the *agent provocateur* went on acting as his factotum in Paris until the outbreak of the war.¹⁰

You may differ with the great biographer's interpretation of Trotsky's theories, and perhaps incidental facts, but no one has yet challenged him on the key evidence bearing on Trotsky's assassination. Does Healy? Or is he going to include Deutscher among the "accomplices" of the SWP?

13. Healy quotes from a speech made by Cannon on September 28, 1940, at a plenum-conference held by the SWP in Chicago. Cannon was proposing a control commission to

> begin a closer checking up of party responsibility, discipline, and loyalty without permitting any panic in the ranks. [He made the observation]: If we had checked up on such matters a little more carefully we might have prevented some bad things in the days gone by.¹¹

---

9. See *The Prophet Outcast*, pp. 495–504.

10. Ibid., pp. 409–410.

11. See *The Socialist Workers Party in World War II—James P.*

Healy calls this "an obvious reference to the assassination of Trotsky." He demands to know if there was a control commission investigation of Trotsky's death and what its findings were. He continues: "Since no report was ever published, we can only assume that it was blocked. By whom?"

Cannon did not specify what the "bad things" were. So far as the assassination of Trotsky was concerned, the leadership of the SWP was doing its utmost to nail down the responsibility. This work centered on proving Jacson's connections with the GPU murder machine and seeking to establish his real identity. Full publicity was given to this as can easily be verified by consulting the pages of *The Militant* and the *Fourth International* of that time.

As I recall it, setting up a control commission was visualized by Cannon as only one aspect of proletarianizing the party following the defection of the petty-bourgeois opposition headed by Burnham, Shachtman, and Abern. Some of the weaknesses requiring rectification that Cannon had in mind concerned countering agents provocateurs, particularly in the trade unions and other mass organizations. But he also viewed the control commission as a body the ranks could count on to come down hard on false charges.

Is Healy insinuating that *Cannon* blocked the control commission from functioning? Again, an example of the baseless innuendos spread by the sleuths of Clapham High Street.¹²

14. Pierre Frank, too, is dragged in. Why? He explained his views on the American Trotskyists and Zborowski to Georges Vereeken, perennial opponent of Trotsky's politics both inside and outside the Fourth International in Belgium since the 1930s or even earlier. Vereeken said in his book *La guépéou dans le mouvement trotskiste* that he sent a letter dated March 5, 1956, to the International Secretariat concerning Zborowski. On the same page, he reported that Frank replied in a letter dated March 2, 1956, (sic) that the

> American groups (Cannon, Shachtman . . .) ought to get together on it and try to make

---

Cannon Writings and Speeches, 1940–43 (Pathfinder, 1975), p. 99 [2011 printing].

12. The location of the WRP headquarters in London.

this Etienne speak. Unfortunately we get the impression that they are not very keen on the whole business. Perhaps it's only an impression. In any case, they are much more preoccupied with defending themselves against the witch-hunt, and perhaps that explains it.

Healy raps Frank over the knuckles:

> It explains nothing of the kind. The SWP was not facing any witch-hunt; the McCarthyite period had been over for the best part of two years. What was happening to Vereeken's campaign for an investigation was more straight-forward—it was being suppressed.

Suppressed by whom? Healy is not too straightforward. But there is more than a hint that Pierre Frank and his associates might be . . ."accomplices of accomplices of the GPU." For Pierre Frank is billed here by Healy as "a co-editor today of 'Intercontinental Press' with Joseph Hansen." Can others take a hint?

An interesting point is made here in "demolishing" Frank's view on the witch-hunt. ". . . the McCarthyite period had been over for the best part of two years," says Healy. That is, since some time in the "best" part of 1954. This is not some youngster newly come to the WRP talking. This is Healy. He should remember McCarthyism firsthand.

In 1957 he personally knew the case of an American comrade whose passport was still "withdrawn" after having been first taken away by the State Department in 1953, and whose English wife could not get a reentry permit to the United States, not even on compassionate grounds. There must have been others, surely, he knew about. Withdrawal of passports and reentry permits of real or alleged members of radical organizations was one of the hallmarks of McCarthyism.

The whole world was made aware of this aspect of American reaction when it hit even the internationally famous, particularly in the banishment of Charlie Chaplin.

Even fiddling with the span of historic periods is not to be despised, the author of the smear seems to tell us.

It is possible to go on and disprove Healy's lies one by one as they come up. And we can be sure that we have not seen the last lot in his obsessive drive to besmirch the SWP and the Trotskyist movement as a whole. It is certainly our duty to block his foul aim.

It is necessary, however, to pause and take stock. For, involved is not only Healy but many hundreds, perhaps even a thousand, in the WRP who genuinely regard themselves as Trotskyists. To them I would like to address a few words.

> *It is necessary that every member of the Party should study calmly and with the greatest objectivity, first the substance of the differences of opinion, and then the development of the struggles within the Party. Neither the one nor the other can be done unless the documents of both sides are published. He who takes somebody's word for it is a hopeless idiot, who can be disposed of with a simple gesture of the hand.—Lenin.*[13]

How many of you have studied the views of both sides and the course of the struggle? The course of the struggle involves method. In the latest exchange, even Healy says, "A clear method emerges." If you have not just taken his word about it, you are bound to have your doubts at least about what he says of the methods of others. To settle your doubts, you ought to check the replies to his charges.

Ask yourselves: Who was it that accused *all others* who remained alive of Lenin's 1917 Central Committee of being anti-Soviet wreckers and fascist dogs in 1936–38? And even implicated some of them in plots to assassinate Lenin? And who now makes accusations against all the living leaders of the SWP who collaborated with Trotsky of being "accomplices of the GPU" in the assassination of Trotsky? The linking method that emerges here is clear, all right, but it emerges not from the Trotskyist movement but from pristine Stalinism.

Perhaps we can attribute phrases like "covered up for," "took over from," even "alias," etc., etc., to the influence of too many Hollywood gangster movies. But the dragging in of names of other

---

13. As quoted in *The Militant*, Vol. 1, No. 1, November 15, 1928. The quotation is from "The Party Crisis," *Collected Works*, Vol. 32, p. 43. It should be noted that the English translation issued by Moscow is defective. The Russian original can be found in the fifth edition of Lenin's *Complete Works*, Vol. 42, pp. 234–35.

persons, associating them with the alleged crimes of the primary targets, cannot be dismissed as accidental. A political method is involved. The intention is to compel the cooperation of those named, or at least their silence. This use, or attempted use, of political blackmail comes straight from Vishinsky, not from Trotsky.

Compare Stalin's use of frame-up methods to try to incriminate Trotsky with Healy's efforts to incriminate the close American associates of Trotsky. Against the verdict of the control commission of the SWP, Healy accepts the word of the perjurer Budenz and a stacked grand jury. Hasn't Healy presented us with a caricature of the method used by Stalin in the Moscow Frame-up Trials?

The Socialist Workers party and the Young Socialist Alliance are now engaged in a $27 million suit against the U.S. government because of illegal actions taken by the FBI over a period of decades. By coincidence Healy publishes fabricated charges that the party's leaders were "accomplices" of the GPU. Whom can such charges help?

Every conscientious member of the WRP ought to ponder this and try to think where Healy's course against the SWP logically leads—and so, too, ought Gerry Healy, if he is capable of it.

Trotsky once said that if Stalin could have foreseen in 1923 that his course against the Left Opposition would lead him one day to defame all living members of Lenin's Central Committee as Hitler's agents, etc., he would never have embarked on it. Stalin did not set out to be a Thermidorian, a counterrevolutionist. The means Stalin chose brought him to ends he had not anticipated. Means and ends are intertwined. A thought worth mulling over.

The voice in the series of articles against Hansen, Novack, and the SWP, published under the signature "International Committee of the Fourth International," is that of Healy even if the hand that penned the words was trained in the Fleet Street school of yellow journalism. All the gloss and polish does not lessen the big lie or save the WRP from the shame of having peddled it.

> *If a lie can serve for a moment it is inevitably injurious in the long run; the truth, on the other hand, inevitably serves in the end even if it may hurt for the moment.—Diderot.*[14]

---

14. As quoted by Max Shachtman on the title page of *Behind the Moscow Trial.*

More facts on a Stalinist-type frame-up

HEALY CAUGHT IN THE LOGIC OF THE BIG LIE

By Joseph Hansen

The first twenty-six articles

The April 19, 1975, issue of the *Workers Press*[1] carried the first of a series of seven articles signed by the "Political Committee of the Workers Revolutionary Party," the British sect headed by Gerry Healy.[2] The articles purported to deal with "Security and the Fourth International." I was singled out as the main target.

The series evidently did not satisfy the authors. The seven articles had proved to be duds. This ought to have been no surprise. Who is interested in the opinions of a nameless and faceless committee on such subjects as "Pabloism," Hansen's alleged "revisionism," the categorical imperative of constantly combing your own organization for agents provocateurs, and whether the brutal way in which Tim Wohlforth and Nancy Fields were treated proved Healy to be a Leninist rather than a candidate for psychiatric examination?

A second series, intended to be both quantitatively and qualitatively superior, began in the August 14, 1975, issue of *Workers Press*, ending in the September 9 issue. The series consisted this time of nothing less than nineteen articles bearing the impressive signature of the "International Committee of the Fourth International."[3] Healy's American followers republished the nineteen articles as a booklet of 138 pages entitled *Security and the Fourth International—An Inquiry Into the Assassination of Leon Trotsky*.

The central accusation leveled in the series, as formulated in the introduction to the booklet, was as follows:

> The IC [International Committee] charges Joseph Hansen and the Socialist Workers Party to which he belongs, with criminal negligence in relation to the security implications of the death of Trotsky and the tasks of revolutionary security in relation to the defense of the Fourth International.

In an article "On Healy's 'Investigation'—What the Facts Show," published in the November 24, 1975, issue of *Intercontinental Press*, I answered the key allegations made in the two series of twenty-six articles.

For instance, the "International Committee" asserted in the September 9, 1975, issue of *Workers Press* that Max Shachtman had "raised questions about Sylvia Franklin before ex-Stalinist Louis Budenz made public her GPU role in Cannon's office. But although he pressed the leadership to conduct a security commission, his request was pushed aside. Cannon went on with a GPU bug on his phone and a Stalinist agent as his secretarial aide.

"Was this because Hansen was applying his anti-Trotskyist theory that it is better to have a spy in the organization than to take notice of 'personal suspicions'?"

---

1. *Workers Press* folded up, the last issue appearing February 14, 1976. It was replaced by a new publication, the *News Line*, the first issue of which was dated May 1, 1976.

2. In an advertisement for a rally in London, published in the first issue of the *News Line*, Michael Banda is listed as the "General Secretary" of the WRP. Healy is listed as only a member of the Central Committee. The meaning of the shift, however, remains obscure.

3. Whether the "International Committee of the Fourth International" and the "Political Committee of the Workers Revolutionary Party" actually consist of two different bodies is dubious. The "International Committee" may consist of only one person—possibly Cliff Slaughter. The writing style of the two committees is identical.

I *proved* that this was a tissue of lies and slanderous insinuations. In the same issue of *Intercontinental Press* in which my reply appeared, I reprinted an article by James P. Cannon entitled "An Answer to Budenz's Latest Frame-up" that was first published in the August 28, 1950, issue of the *Militant*. In the article, Cannon reports on the inquiry conducted by the Control Commission of the Socialist Workers party in response to a "tip" received in 1947 "purportedly emanating in the first instance from circles close to the FBI."

Among other things, Cannon said:

> The investigation conducted by the Control Commission at that time established that the "information" given to identify the accused comrade as to her biography, her previous occupation, and her personal life, was false. It was evident to us then that the accusation was based either on mistaken identity, or was a deliberately planted story designed to create a spy-scare in the organization.
>
> The Control Commission rejected the accusation and exonerated the accused comrade, who had fully cooperated with the investigation, answered all questions put to her and supplied the Control Commission with all the data relating to her biography and previous occupations, which were subject to verification.

In the same article, Cannon pointed to one of the "established principles of the revolutionary workers' movement"; namely: "A 'spy scare' caused by planted 'disinformation' can do a hundred times more damage than any spies by undermining the confidence of comrades in each other and disrupting the comradely collaboration which is necessary for fruitful work."

Neither Healy, his Political Committee, nor his International Committee has answered this exposure of their lie about Cannon's "silence."

They have compensated for it by shouting all the louder about the "guilt" of Sylvia Caldwell (Franklin), as if what Cannon said about the perjurer Budenz meant nothing. Thus they reveal their hostility toward James P. Cannon, one of their principal targets, and their readiness to accept a slander that first emanated in the FBI and was later spread by Budenz, a former Stalinist who switched to the camp of the American political police.

Again in reply to the gross slander that I had a "familiar relationship" with "an FBI agent who was operating under diplomatic cover at the American Embassy,"[4] I *proved* that if the charge were true, then it could be lodged with greater justice against Trotsky because of his association with the same official (Robert C. McGregor, an aide to the American consul in Mexico City). Thus the FBI smear, while ostensibly aimed at me, actually struck at Leon Trotsky.

On this, too, Healy and his committees have failed to answer up to now. Their need for more time is understandable. After all, they have had only since last November to think it over.

Three cases like the Hotel Bristol

I did more than show that their slanders necessarily involved slandering Trotsky. I *proved* that they had used frame-up methods. I listed three cases that anyone interested in the truth can easily verify by checking the references:

1. A statement that appeared in the December 7, 1953, issue of *Labor Action*, the newspaper of Shachtman's Independent Socialist League, was doctored up to read:

> When it comes to normal polemicizing against opponents there are all sorts of comrades who can undertake this task, but when Cannon wants to sharpen things up, with a real dirty below the belt job, all eyes on the committee turn automatically in the direction of Joe Hansen.

This item, an attempt at character assassination, was a rehash of words written by a bitter enemy of the Socialist Workers party twenty-three years ago. The rehash appeared for the first time in an article by "G. Healy National Secretary of the Socialist Labour League" in the September 10, 1966, issue of the *Newsletter*. Healy said the source of the quotation was "a member" of the "SWP leadership."

The venomous quotation, along with the lie about its source, was repeated in the April 25,

---

4. See *Workers Press*, September 6, 1975, or *Security and the Fourth International*, pp. 93–95.

1975, issue of *Workers Press* in an article ironically entitled "Hansen's Campaign of Slander."

2. In the same 1966 article from which the above quotation and lie about its source were taken, Healy put words in Cannon's mouth that Cannon did not and could not have said:

"'Eventually', said Cannon, 'we cannot avoid discussion so your task Joe is to poison the political atmosphere inside the SWP against the SLL so that when we have to discuss our members will be dead against them.'

"By implication he was saying: 'Never mind about principles and truth. We're pragmatists like President John F. Kennedy, so we do what is "best" to preserve ourselves now.'"

Whatever the final judgment of the literary critics may be concerning the merits of this piece of fiction, it does offer an illuminating insight into the mind of the author. Healy projects his own reasoning onto the devil he has created and accuses this fictional character, "Cannon," of doing what he himself did in poisoning the political atmosphere in the SLL against the SWP.

3. In the April 23, 1975, issue of the *Workers Press*, the Political Committee of the Workers Revolutionary party slandered Bala Tampoe as "associated with the Central Intelligence Agency."

To place me in association with Bala Tampoe, and thus—in accordance with witch-hunt logic—in association with the CIA, Healy's committee said that "Hansen wrote, 'Mr Robert McNamara, president of the World Bank, appeared to be very well briefed on the Ceylon situation,' He was indeed—by, among others, one Bala Tampoe, Hansen's man on the island."

I showed that the quotation about McNamara was taken from the February 14, 1972, issue of *Intercontinental Press*. I proved that I did not write it. The original source was the *Ceylon News*, and that paper ascribed it to a "senior western diplomat" in Colombo.

With the exposure of such frame-up practices, the entire structure of lies and slanders collapsed. For the question at once arose, Why did the authors of the twenty-six articles decide that they had to include outright fabrications? The answer was as obvious as the question: because they felt that their concoction was so implausible that it required falsified "proofs" like these to put it across.

They were correct in their calculation—provided they could get away with it. But they lost the gamble. And while they may have thought that it would not make much difference if a few bits like these were exposed as frauds, they failed to foresee what would happen to the credibility of their "evidence" and argumentation as a whole when it became known that they were using frame-up methods.

For a well-known example of the logic they overlooked, one can point to what happened to the concoctions in Stalin's frame-up trial of Zinoviev-Kamenev in Moscow in August 1936 when a few small details in the "evidence" were shown to be lies. Defendant Holtzman testified that he had met Leon Sedov in 1932 in the lobby of the Hotel Bristol in Copenhagen and had been taken by Sedov to see Trotsky, who gave him "terrorist" instructions.

It was proved that Sedov was not in Copenhagen at the time. It was further proved that the Hotel Bristol, along with its lobby, went out of business in 1917. Small details—but Stalin was never able to overcome the exposure of the fabrications included by the GPU in the script written for Holtzman.

An expert opinion

While I was writing my reply, George Novack, then on a lecture tour that took him to the West Coast, wrote a short piece, stating his opinion of Healy's charges. This was published in the December 8, 1975, issue of *Intercontinental Press* under the title, "Healy's Frame-up Against Joseph Hansen."

> During my political career [Novack said, among other things], I collaborated not only with Trotsky but with Joseph Hansen and Gerry Healy. I have been a close associate and literary partner of Hansen's since we jointly wrote the introduction to Trotsky's last work, *In Defense of Marxism*, in 1942. From 1951 to early 1953 I worked on a daily basis with Healy in England. I know both men well.
>
> From this personal experience and direct knowledge I believe I am as qualified as anyone living on either side of the Atlantic to judge the probity of both men and assay the charges Healy has leveled against his former associate. I may cite a further qualification.

Since the Scottsboro case in 1931 I have been involved in defending civil liberties and labor's rights in a series of cases here and abroad too numerous to itemize. The best known are the Tom Mooney Case, the Moscow Trials, the Minneapolis Case, the Kutcher Case, and currently the SWP suit against the FBI, CIA, etc. As a result I have learned to smell the frame-up of a militant from miles away and have time and again organized movements to defend the victims on a national and international scale. As an expert on frame-ups of all kinds, I feel well equipped to render a verdict on this one. It stinks to the heavens.

Apart from the total absence of a shred of evidence Healy can bring forth, to anyone who has known Hansen at the closest range for decades, it is a psychological impossibility that he could be an agent of the Soviet secret police or the FBI. On the other hand, I know that Healy is quite capable of spreading false reports about his opponents for the sake of factional advantage, especially against those who tread upon his ego.

In my judgment Healy is in this case a shameless liar, an unmitigated rascal, and a political hooligan. I state this, less to exculpate Hansen and Cannon, who do not need my defense, than to characterize Healy for what he has shown himself to be. In all my experience I have rarely seen so odious and flimsy a frame-up as this spicy dish he has concocted.

His stupid calumnies against Hansen and Cannon are as detestable and unfounded as Stalin's accusations against Trotsky and Sedov in the Moscow Trials. Why does he refrain from including Dobbs and Novack, who were equally involved in and responsible for planning Trotsky's security—or are we being reserved for a second round?

Novack's statement was a staggering blow to Healy's frame-up. In the world Trotskyist movement, no one has had as much experience as Novack in exposing frame-ups and defending victims of them. He was a key figure in the efforts that were finally successful in finding asylum for Trotsky in Mexico, and he played a central role in organizing the International Commission of Inquiry into the Charges Made Against Leon Trotsky in the Moscow Trials, which was headed by John Dewey.

In the American radical movement as a whole, Novack is a well-known authority on civil liberties and defense of victims of the class struggle, whose advice and participation are sought in all kinds of cases in the struggle on this front.

Novack's considered statement on the Healyite concoction was thus certain to carry great weight in circles reaching far beyond the Trotskyist movement. Still worse from Healy's narrow factional viewpoint, knowledge of Novack's judgment could spread among the ranks of the WRP and the ranks of sister groups in other countries. The consequences could include fresh questioning and even criticisms. These would have to be met with expulsions that might prove to be even more damaging than those that have affected the Healyite movement in the past couple of years.

Healy's second round

Several alternatives were open to Healy's two committees. They could have held a joint session—even if it meant simply counting the same persons twice—to discuss what to do now that the frame-up practices, for which they were responsible as leaders, had been exposed. If their main concern was the interests of the world Trotskyist movement, which they profess to uphold, here are some possible lines of action they could have considered:

1. They might investigate the ghost-writer, if one had been employed to put the material together in readable form, and try to ascertain what his or her anti-Trotskyist associations or connections might be. An honest public report of the findings could help redress the damage done by the falsifications.

2. In case members of the two top committees were the authors, these members might be investigated to determine who cooked up the fabrications and why. Again, an honest public report of the findings would open an honorable way out.

3. If all of the members of the two committees had participated in forging the material, at least a part of them—possibly a majority—might agree that a frightful mistake had been committed. A

public self-criticism (with due space allotted for minority views on the question) would go far in making amends.

These alternatives were rejected, if they were ever considered. Healy and his lieutenants are not concerned about the interests of the world Trotskyist movement. Their own narrow interests, as they conceive them, come first. In place of seeking a way out that would have helped to rehabilitate the reputation of the WRP in left circles, they decided on a "second round"—as Novack had anticipated.

This course was the same in its logic as the one that engulfed Stalin when he tried to overcome the effect of the exposure of his frame-up in the first big Moscow trial by escalating the lies and staging more monstrous frame-ups.

How making Novack an 'accomplice' further exposed the frame-up

The first of a new series of seven articles by Healy's literary team, the "International Committee of the Fourth International," appeared in the January 5, 1976, issue of *Workers Press*.[5] The members of the committee evidently wanted to demonstrate that they had spent the Christmas holidays in productive labor, for they dated the article "January 1, 1976." By way of season's greetings, they entitled the first of the new series "ACCOMPLICES OF THE GPU."

The title referred to a pair caught by the Healyite network of investigators:

> After painstaking research in Europe and America, the International Committee presents an irrefutable indictment of both men and calls for a public inquiry along the lines of the Dewey Commission of 1937 with a tribunal including worldwide representatives of the Trotskyist movement.

The two "accomplices of the GPU" were unveiled as "Joseph Hansen" and "George Novack."

The opening paragraph of the "irrefutable indictment" reads:

> We accuse Joseph Hansen and leaders of the Socialist Workers Party (USA) of deliberately covering up GPU murder and penetration of the Trotskyist movement for the purposes of spying and disruption.

Thus, in the pattern followed by Stalin in the Moscow trials, Healy sought to cover up the exposure of his frame-up practices by doubling his previous lies and extending them to cover the entire leadership of the Socialist Workers party. The geometrical progression of the big lie was under way.

It is obvious why the frame-up artists decided to elevate George Novack to the position of "accomplice of the GPU." As an expert witness, he was guilty of publicly testifying that the facts showed Healy had concocted a frame-up against Hansen. In accordance with the technique of the big lie, the best way to dispose of that authoritative testimony was to scream in all keys that Novack, too, was an "accomplice of the GPU."

Consequently from January 1, 1976, up to the present time, the Healyites have campaigned in their press, in leaflets, in posters, and in rallies that Novack—like Hansen—has served for "35 years" as an "accomplice of the GPU," his function being to remain "silent" about activities of the GPU in the Trotskyist movement and to block investigation of them.

With two exceptions, the Healyite sleuths cite no new "evidence." They simply add Novack's name to some of the items they had previously charged against me (allegedly preventing a "full-scale inquiry into the security at Coyoacan," defending Cannon's secretary Sylvia Caldwell against her slanderers, defending Trotsky's martyred guard Robert Sheldon Harte), all of which I answered in my article "On Healy's 'Investigation'—What the Facts Show."

The two new "crimes" chalked up against Novack were as follows:

1. In his statement condemning Healy's frame-up, Novack mentioned participating in work to save the lives of socialists in Western Europe from the

---

5. An eighth article, "Open Letter to the SWP," was signed by Harold Robins, bringing the total to thirty-four in the three series. The Healyite press has published additional articles repeating the themes of the three series, plus a parallel series denouncing Alan Thornett of the Workers Socialist League in Britain as a "renegade," and still another series denouncing Tim Wohlforth and Nancy Fields in similar terms because they joined the Socialist Workers party in the United States.

Nazi butchers. The efforts were quite successful. Nonetheless, one of the refugees who received aid, Novack said, was a GPU agent, a fact the committee had no way of knowing at the time. The agent, Zborowski, was later exposed. He was deeply implicated in the assassination of Klement, Sedov, Trotsky, and perhaps others.

Pointing dramatically at Novack, Healy's committee screamed in chorus:

> We accuse George Novack and Mrs David Dallin (Lola Estrine) of admitting the GPU spy MARK ZBOROWSKI into the United States and re-integrating him into the top levels of the Fourth International although he was gravely suspect, and then suppressing this fact for 35 years.

Admitting Zborowski into the United States? Isn't that charge rather wild? Neither the State Department nor Immigration placed Novack in charge of admitting aliens to the United States. That can easily be proved.

As for "re-integrating" Zborowski "into the top levels of the Fourth International," that bit of garbage has been disposed of by Sam Gordon in his article "Healy's Smear Against Trotsky's Last Collaborators."[6]

2. Novack's second "crime" was discovered through "painstaking research." The committee went through the public statement made by Novack condemning Healy's frame-up. A promising paragraph was spotted. It was placed under a microscope and scrutinized in the most detailed way. The paragraph, consisting of only three sentences, was as follows:

> Healy likewise does not see that Hansen and the others are only secondary figures in the drama. The principal actors were Trotsky and Sedov themselves who trusted Etienne and allowed Jacson entry into the household. *By aiming at the American Trotskyists Healy strikes at the victims themselves.*

I added the emphasis to the last sentence because that is the sentence to be watched. Even as you

---
6. See *Intercontinental Press,* May 24, 1976, p. 854.

watch, the sentence will suddenly vanish.

The meaning of the paragraph is clear enough: Healy accuses the secondary characters of being inexcusably lax in their security measures. But the main actors themselves trusted Zborowski and allowed Jacson entry into the household. Therefore, Novack contends, if Healy were consistent, he would have to say that Trotsky and Sedov were themselves inexcusably lax in their own security measures. By aiming at the secondary figures, Healy strikes at Trotsky and Sedov.

A bonanza for Healy! The meaning of Novack's paragraph can be converted into its opposite by the simple operation of slicing off the last sentence and amalgamating the remaining two sentences with a "theory" used by the GPU in 1940. The committee came up with the following "irrefutable indictment":

> *George Novack accuses Leon Trotsky and his son Leon Sedov of responsibility for their own deaths.*
>
> Novack writes: "Healy likewise does not see that Hansen and the others are only secondary figures in the drama. *The principal actors were Trotsky and Sedov themselves who trusted Etienne (Zborowski) and allowed Jacson (Ramon Mercader) entry into the household.*" ('Intercontinental Press', December 8, 1975.) [Emphasis added by Healy's committee.]
>
> This is the most monstrous lie of all—a lie which Novack has taken directly from the GPU.

What miracles can be accomplished with a razor blade and Scotch tape! The paragraph from Novack's statement, its last sentence neatly amputated, is fitted into the "theory of self-assault" advanced by the Mexican Stalinists after the May 24, 1940, machine-gun assault on the Trotsky home in Coyoacán. The "self-assault" theme was a propagandistic ploy of the GPU. In the weeks before the police uncovered the identity of most of the assailants, who were headed by the painter David Alfaro Siqueiros, the Stalinist press in Mexico insinuated that Trotsky himself had staged the raid, machine-gunned his own bedroom, and whisked his guard Robert Sheldon Harte into hiding or out of the country.

When the body of Harte was discovered in a shallow, lime-filled grave, the Stalinists at once dropped the "self-assault" campaign. It remained to Healy to claim that Novack revived it thirty-five years later, taking it "directly from the GPU."

The Healyite team continues:

> Trotsky defended himself indefatigably against this Stalinist lie which was fabricated by the GPU after the unsuccessful assassination attempt of May 24, 1940. The purpose of the GPU's "theory of self-assault" was to cover the tracks of its agents.
>
> "The GPU mobilised with great skill its agents in order to kill me. The attempt failed owing to an accident. The friends of the GPU are compromised. They are now compelled to do everything in their power in order to fix upon me the responsibility for the unsuccessful attempt of their chieftain. In accomplishing this they have not a wide choice of means. They are compelled to operate with the crudest of methods, and to guide themselves by Hitler's aphorism: the bigger the lie the more readily it will be believed."
>
> The words are those of Trotsky, written in 1940. But 35 years later, Novack revives the old GPU slander to shift attention away from its crimes. This makes Novack the co-conspirator of Hansen.

Novack can now truthfully say that he has seen everything. After devoting a lifetime to fighting frame-ups, he himself has become a victim of a frame-up, and one that is about as crude as they come.

Let us consider the Healyite script more closely. It goes as follows:

One year after Trotsky's death and four years after his achievement in organizing the Dewey Commission that found Trotsky and Sedov innocent of the charges leveled against them in the Moscow trials, George Novack went over to the side of Stalinism, and not only Stalinism but the GPU itself. Novack decided, according to the "irrefutable indictment," to devote himself to "deliberately covering up GPU murder" and other crimes of Stalin's political police.

Novack's first act in the new role cast for him by the Healyites was to "admit" GPU agent Zborowski into the United States. His second act was to "reintegrate" Zborowski into the "top levels of the Fourth International."

In the subsequent thirty-five years, Novack perfidiously defended GPU agents in the SWP whenever they were exposed. In addition he was always right there to block any investigation of these agents.

As his latest monstrous act, Novack revived the GPU lie that Trotsky—in a conspiracy with Robert Sheldon Harte—machine-gunned his own bedroom on May 24, 1940. This constitutes the final damning piece of evidence that "makes Novack the co-conspirator of Hansen." (The word "makes" was well chosen by the committee.)

LEON SEDOV

Thus, to believe Healy's committee, Novack has led a double life since 1941, when he allegedly "admitted" Zborowski to the United States.

So far as Novack's public activities are concerned, he has spent full time—and a little extra—as a socialist editor, lecturer, and teacher, writing books, pamphlets, and innumerable articles in which not a single phrase can be found even remotely favoring Stalinism. In fact, in all his published works, Novack has assiduously defended, advocated, and sought in every way possible to advance Trotskyism, from the level of dialectical materialism right down to daily practice in the class struggle.

All this was a "masquerade" as the members of Healy's committee put it.[7] "Fully conscious

---

7. "Both [Hansen and Novack] have conducted a 35-year

of the extremely grave charge we are presenting," they say, "painstaking research in Europe and America" has uncovered evidence proving that since 1941 Novack has actually alternated between being a good Dr. Jekyll and an evil Mr. Hyde. Whenever the moon is high and werewolves are on the prowl, Novack is to be found running with the hellish host, doing his bit as an "accomplice of the GPU."

What motivated Novack? Why did he strive secretly to tear down what he was publicly building up? Healy's committee says not a word about this crucial question. Here the Healyites fall below the level of the organizers of the Moscow trials, who understood that their victims had to have "reasons" for the criminal acts they were forced to confess to before being shot, such as wanting to be on the payroll of the Mikado or hoping for rewards from Hitler if they helped smash the planned economy and restore capitalism in the Soviet Union.

Was it Moscow gold that caused Novack to follow the path charted for him by Healy's committee? It is not visible in his standard of living or in the income tax forms he has filed.

If not Moscow gold, was it the Stalinist politics of betrayal of the world revolution that won Novack over? Or the Stalinist theory of building socialism in one country? Did Novack succumb to the powerful personality of Stalin, say in a secret meeting in the lobby of the Hotel Bristol in Copenhagen?

No doubt we will receive answers to these questions in a "third round" soon to be prepared by the Healyite imitators of Stalin's methods.

Meanwhile, let us note what the inclusion of George Novack's name in the "second round" has done to the frame-up as a whole. The charges leveled by Healy's two committees against me and the rest of the leadership of the SWP are just as flimsy and just as self-contradictory as the charges leveled against Novack. In fact, they are the *same charges* in substance. Since the frame-up against Novack topples of its own weight, the frame-up of all the other intended victims goes down with it.

---

masquerade as 'Trotskyists' living off the legend of their association with the exiled Trotsky in the 1930s until his assassination in Mexico on August 20, 1940." *Workers Press*, January 5, 1976.

A house of cards falls, no matter how high it has been built, if only one card gives way.

Why is Healy silent about his connections with Zborowski?

In a letter to me dated March 14, 1960, Healy revealed that he had met "Etienne" in the 1946 period.

> First of all, Etienne was in Europe after the war and attended the second congress. I personally met him on a number of occasions and in fact he stayed overnight at my place once. If Etienne was an agent of Stalin, then a whole number of things follow from this, the chief of which would be who replaced him in the ranks of the 4th International.

In another letter dated March 28, 1960, Healy added:

> The important story is that this Etienne arrived with a large sum of money in his possession in Paris. We were given to understand that the man had been all the time in a concentration camp or living in illegality and, in fact, when he was in Britain we bought him a pair of shoes because he said he hadn't had a decent pair since before the war. I give you this item in order to show the skilful type of agent which he was.

Let us note, first of all, that in 1946 Healy did not suspect that this "Etienne" was in reality a GPU agent. In 1960, however, Healy thought the "Etienne" he met was Zborowski. This leads to a puzzle. If Healy did not so much as suspect Zborowski in *1946*, how can he assert that in *1941*—five years earlier—that Zborowski was "gravely suspect"? Yet this is the basis on which Healy today condemns Novack!

According to Healy's "irrefutable indictment," Zborowski, despite being "gravely suspect" in 1941, was "admitted" by Novack into the United States and "reintegrated" by him into the top levels of the Fourth International. Healy's committee avers, consequently, that Novack led a double life for thirty-five years.

There are various possible solutions to the puzzle:

1. Healy's committee lied about Zborowski being "gravely suspect" in 1941. That would help explain why Healy did not suspect him in 1946.

But it would also prove that Healy's committee framed up Novak.

2. Healy's committee told the truth about Zborowski being "gravely suspect" in 1941. That would help in framing up Novack.

But it would also prove that Healy lied in 1960 when he said he did not suspect Zborowski in 1946. *Healy then becomes "gravely suspect."*

3. Another possibility is that Healy is mistaken as to the identity of the "Etienne" he met, invited home, and favored with a new pair of shoes. This would strengthen the testimony of Sam Gordon, who has stated that he never met Zborowski, but did know another "Etienne," who was not Zborowski and not a GPU agent.

But Healy claims Gordon is lying on this point. In the June 15, 1976, issue of the *News Line,* Healy's masked members of the "International Committee" say that Gordon's article is "clouded with evasions, double talk and downright lies." Among the "downright lies," they list Gordon's statement "that he had never met Zborowski (Etienne), the GPU mastermind behind the murder of Leon Sedov, Rudolf Klement, Erwin Wolf and Ignace Reiss."

These assertions, of course, do not affect the truthfulness of Sam Gordon's testimony. They only give greater weight to Healy's admission that the person *he* was dealing with was Zborowski. And Healy himself leaves us no choice but to accept the implications.

His letters of 1960 then *prove* that not only was he in close association with GPU agent Zborowski, he remained silent about it all these years. He continued to maintain silence even while purporting to be engaged in "painstaking research" to uncover GPU agents and their accomplices in the Fourth International.

Healy acted precisely as if he were trying to cover up his relations with Zborowski.

If the members of Healy's two committees were consistent, they ought to give their chief an intensive grilling on his highly suspicious relationship with Zborowski. Here are some suggestions:

Where did Healy customarily meet with Zborowski? In Paris cafes? In London pubs? Who said what?

What information did Healy pass on to this GPU agent? How many Trotskyists lost their lives because of what he told this spy?

How long did Healy keep on seeing Zborowski? One year? Two years? Five years? When did he stop seeing him?

Healy admits he invited Zborowski to stay overnight. Did they sleep in the same bed? Or did one of them sleep on the floor? Which one?

Healy admits he bought Zborowski a pair of shoes. What kind of shoes? And only *shoes*? No lunch?

Why did Healy lead a double life for thirty years? What hold does Zborowski have on Healy?

Isn't it the moral duty of Healy's two committees to issue an "irrefutable indictment of Healy's guilt"? Isn't it imperative to brand Healy as one of Hansen's many "co-conspirators"?

Of course, Healy's top lieutenants will consider none of these embarrassing questions. They will issue an authoritative statement, bearing the customary rubber-stamp signature of the "International Committee." The statement will say that Healy's letters constitute one more damning proof that Hansen is an "accomplice of the GPU."

First, because Hansen maintained a deafening silence about the letters for sixteen years. Second, because Hansen had a mysterious hold on Healy, through which he contrived during the same sixteen years to prevent the author of the letters from making them public.

The contribution of 'Captain' Harold Robins

One of the key contentions made by Healy's "International Committee" is that the security at Coyoacán was "criminally lax," that I was responsible for that laxness, and thus acted as an "accomplice of the GPU."

The main evidence offered by the committee is the word of Harold Robins whom they list as "captain of the guard at Trotsky's household-in-exile at Coyoacan in Mexico, in 1939–1940."

Robins does not appear to have bestowed the title of "captain" on himself, but he does say that he was the "last chief guard, selected by Comrade Trotsky after the May 24, 1940, assassination attempt on his life had failed. . . ."

Why Robins says that he was "selected" by

JOSEPH HANSEN

Inside the patio. Jake Cooper, one of Trotsky's guards, is talking with Milt Lesnik, *right*, a visitor. In the lean-to standing to the left, a signal board connected to fine wires strung along the walls made it possible to immediately locate an attempted break-in.

Trotsky, I do not know. The guards themselves elected one of their ranks to act as head guard, generally for periods of three months. Thus Robins's position as "chief guard" would have ended about the time Trotsky was murdered.

The post was equivalent to that of an organizer of a party cell or branch. It was seldom that anyone sought to be head guard, since it involved additional drudgery and routine details such as keeping track of the expenses of the guard. Besides reminding guards of assignments democratically decided on at meetings, it also meant assuming full responsibility in relation to Trotsky for anything that occurred. For instance, if Trotsky saw a fault, he went to the head guard, and that head guard was held responsible. There was no passing the buck or making excuses, even though another guard might have been directly responsible for the error.

Such items, of course, are of no interest to Healy's committee. They are looking for mud. Thus in an interview published as "Part Five"[8] in the series begun January 1, 1976, they report "Captain" Robins as saying:

> Now this may be that this so-called security set-up was a matter of perhaps congenital

---

8. *Workers Press,* January 9, 1976.

stupidity on the part of the comrade who set it up, and of the Political Committee who delegated it to Comrade Hansen; because he was their representative in charge of the guard, that this was all a case of stupidity and incompetence. In that case, a correction is in order.

> The other question that arises is: if one wants to see Comrade Trotsky protected, this is not the way to do it. *This is the way to get the guard knocked off and Comrade Trotsky murdered.* This is the appearance of the thing; the word but not the deed. This is, in other words, a set up: either through stupidity or through *planning.* (Emphasis added.)

If "Captain" Robins actually said this, he was obviously faithfully following the logic of the big lie, but he was a jump ahead of Healy's committee. The charge that I helped *plan* a "set up" to "get the guard knocked off and Comrade Trotsky murdered" fits into the coming "third round" of the frame-up, not the "second round."

To back his assertions, "Captain" Robins cites some details of his experience. Most of these are one-sided impressions, quite biased judgments, half-truths, and mistruths. Since they are typical of the material throughout the articles produced by Healy's two committees, it may be useful to take up at least the worst ones to show what a task it would be to answer all the allegations in the frame-up.

1. "Now let me talk about the security arrangements. And when I say *security*, let's put this in quotations. This was instituted by Hansen, and the comrades accepted it because he was the representative of the Political Committee."

Robins gives me too much credit. When I accepted the invitation to join the Trotsky household in 1937, I was not a member of the Political Committee. And I was not sent by the Political Committee to institute a security system, as he avers. I simply replaced Bernard Wolfe as a secretary to Trotsky. The head guard was Henry Stone, a capable comrade.

The security regulations were the same as those that had been followed in the household in Turkey, France, and Norway. Trotsky's secretary Jan Frankel introduced me to them and gave me some good advice on how to function most effectively in the household.

The danger that Trotsky might be assassinated by the GPU continued to rise. It was clear that among other measures, the guard in the household had to be strengthened. The Socialist Workers party responded to the need in its customary way. Despite its poverty, the SWP managed to get together enough funds to help improve the immediate situation. For instance, the SWP bought a new Dodge sedan for Trotsky, which I drove to Mexico.

The main contribution of the SWP was to make available an additional number of guards to stay in the household on a full-time basis. The strongest contingent came from the Twin Cities. They were experienced union battlers, capable drivers, and familiar with small arms, like most workers in that region at the time.

The guns carried by members of the guard were an odd assortment of makes and calibers brought from Europe. I recommended that they be replaced, and that we select a firearm not easily jammed, powerful enough to be deadly at short range, but not so powerful as to be difficult to handle; and that we settle on one caliber, enabling us to standardize on ammunition. This recommendation was accepted and we were able to buy enough .38 caliber Colt pistols to adequately arm the household.

2. "The guard would sit in a covered house which had no windows . . . and he'd sit there under a reading lamp and he'd read all night long. This was guard duty."

We did not have this problem during the first period when the Trotskys lived in Frida Kahlo's house on Avenida Londres. After the break with Diego Rivera (the husband of Frida Kahlo), a place was found on Avenida Viena.

In the new location a good deal of work had to be done such as heightening the walls and sealing off the windows that opened on the street.

Among the improvements sought by the guards was a lean-to that would give them a clear view of both sides of the patio, which they could step into during the rainy season. (The rain can be chilly at night in Mexico City.)

Jean van Heijenoort duplicated and improved an alarm system first used at the Avenida Londres address. If a break occurred in fine wires strung along the walls, a red light would flash on in the lean-to, indicating the precise section affected. The system was ingenious, but it did not work well because of the number of false alarms caused by things that fly at night—large moths, beetles, and so on. A tendency developed to let it fall into disuse.

Worst of all, some of the guards—*not all*—began to read in the lean-to, presumably keeping an eye on the indicator board, but actually absorbed in a book or document. When I discovered this upon returning to Coyoacán after a stay in New York, I took up the question with the guards. A sharp dispute flared. One of the European comrades, who thought reading did not lessen his alertness or increase his vulnerability to being shot by a sniper, considered my intervention to be impermissible, a typical example of the brutality habitually displayed by Americans.

Robins is right in pointing to the danger of a guard reading while on duty. He lies in implying that I instituted this violation of security and did not oppose it.

3. On the question of the guards' skill in handling guns, "Captain" Robins is quoted as saying:

> That's what Hansen writes in his document and in the introduction to the autobiography of Trotsky. Of course, when he faced the fact that Robins had never fired a gun in his life when he went down there, well, "Robins was a special kind of case".[9]
>
> Now was he? Let me name some names. There were comrades from Czechoslovakia, from Germany, some of whom had fired guns, some of whom hadn't. We had Comrade Munis who was a member of the International, representing the Spanish section.

When I asked him to take a practice test with a revolver at ten yards, he couldn't hit a target. Comrade John, a Czechoslovak comrade whose name isn't mentioned at all, never tried his gun out.

If there had been a rule that only experts in the use of arms would be accepted for Trotsky's guard, it is absolutely certain Robins would never have been selected. Yet, to hear him tell it, the choice was not bad at all—he turned out to be the only competent guard in the household. The truth is that Robins was chosen because we needed a *driver*, one with good enough reflexes to learn—without a serious accident—how to get an automobile down the Mexican roads of those days. It was expected that Robins would eventually prove capable of mastering the trick of holding a gun on target while squeezing the trigger. At close range, as in the patio, that would be sufficient.

Robins does not provide sufficient information for one to judge the marksmanship test to which he submitted Grandizo Munis. Was the target an American dime or an object the size of a GPU agent?

In any case, Munis was not a full-time member of the guard. Like the Mexican comrades, most of whom were excellent guards, he was among those who volunteered for occasional duty. Whatever "Captain" Robins's opinion was of these comrades, Trotsky was deeply appreciative of what they did to help defend him and Natalia Sedoff.

The Czechoslovak comrade mentioned by "Captain" Robins was added to the guard on the recommendation of Trotsky. He was a refugee from the Nazis, and Trotsky felt deep sympathy for him. I met him the first time upon returning from a stay in New York. It was clear to me that it would be a mistake to depend on him as an effective guard. I took up the problem with Trotsky. It was only with the greatest reluctance that Trotsky agreed to let him go—Trotsky understood the comrade and his demoralization as an exile. We managed to find a place for him to stay in Mexico City. He came out to Coyoacán rather regularly to talk with Trotsky and to borrow books from him, which he did not return promptly.

"Captain" Robins tries to score a point by saying that I did not mention this case. On the other hand,

---

9. I did not say "Robins was a special kind of case." What I said was the following: "Marksmanship was not the sole criterion by which guards were selected. Expert drivers were just as badly needed. Robins had had experience as a New York taxi driver. Also Robins had proved his capacity as a union battler, even having served a term in prison for union activities." See my article "On Healy's 'Investigation'—What the Facts Show," *Intercontinental Press,* November 24, 1975, p. 1645.

concentrating on his assignment of grinding an ax for Healy, Robins forgets Hank Schnautz, another comrade—really a sympathizer of the SWP—who came down to Mexico on his own in hope of seeing Trotsky. L.D. was attracted to this comrade, and asked me if it wouldn't be possible to include him in the guard. Unlike the other guards, Trotsky pointed out, Schnautz had a *farm* background. I recognized that Trotsky really wanted to get acquainted with a live American fresh off the farm.

Although a pacifist by conviction, Schnautz happened to be a gun enthusiast. He was a dead shot with a rifle, his preferred firearm. After some troubled thinking, he agreed that if we were attacked, he would not hold the lives of the assailants as something sacred. He would shoot to kill. So we included him among the full-time guards. Besides his handiness with guns, he was a hard worker, who knew a good deal about construction. Schnautz fitted into the household very well.

4. Healy's "International Committee" avers:

> There is still another facet of the events of the Siqueiros raid raised by Robins which calls for further investigation: the jamming of the guards' guns on the evening of May 24 during the raid. Robins raised this occurrence when he described his reaction to the raid:
>
> "Standing behind a eucalyptus tree that was three foot thick or two and a half foot thick, with a machine gun in his hand, was this guard (actually, a member of Siqueiros' raiding party in disguise). And he turns around and starts shooting at my door way. Naturally I had to go back in.
>
> "I picked up a sub-machine gun which was in my room. It was a Thompson .45 calibre and we didn't know lead bullets would jam the gun. When we had fired the shells we refilled them with lead bullets and a powder charge. And Hansen knew it. And the others who all handled guns according to Hansen—who knew how to handle guns—didn't know you needed a steel-jacketed bullet in an automatic weapon.
>
> "Otherwise, the lead on impact will flatten out and the gun will jam. So I had a machine-gun that didn't work. Charlie had a rifle, so again we had a gun handled by men who knew guns and who were used to handling them for a good part of their lives and who only required a small amount of practice—according to Hansen.
>
> "But none of us knew enough about guns to know that you couldn't in an automatic weapon use lead-tipped bullets. Now there's a question of security here, isn't there."

The question arises: When Robins saw the member of Siqueiros's raiding party behind the eucalyptus tree, why didn't he fire at him with his .38 caliber Colt pistol? The target was only a few yards away. It would have been hard to miss. The answer is that Robins thought the man belonged to the police detail. Robins called out, "Bob, Bob." The bogus policeman responded by firing at Robins.

Why didn't Robins then drop to the floor, take a dead rest, and put the gunman out of commission? Did he suddenly lose confidence in the one firearm he had learned to use? There's a clue for Healy's sleuths.

As for the "sub-machine gun" Robins reached for, I have already told how the question of standardizing our equipment had been decided several years earlier. The submachine gun had been fired successfully on outings, and it looked imposing.

After checking it out, my opinion was that it ought to be junked. The barrel was badly pitted. To try to replace it and perhaps secure a couple more would be a mistake in my opinion. Besides the prohibitive cost of practice ammunition, skill in the use of such equipment would tend to narrow down to a couple of persons. It was much easier, in the circumstances we faced, to widen familiarity with the use of guns if we settled on pistols. Besides which, it was easier to carry them.

A couple of the guards argued against junking any of the guns already accumulated. They were certain in particular that the submachine gun could be kept operating smoothly enough so that it would not jam. Moreover, occasionally displaying it would help keep up the image of the place as being well armed. A compromise was eventually reached. In return for relying on pistols, the guards interested in the submachine gun could keep it.

As it turned out, the compromise was a mistake. The dubious piece of equipment ended up in the hands of Robins, who decided, when the test came, to substitute it for the gun he had learned how to handle.

5. Healy's "International Committee" includes the following paragraph in the presentation of the interview with "Captain" Robins:

> Another guard was a comrade from Philadelphia who was known, according to Robins, for his lack of physical courage. Also, another aspect of his behaviour while in Mexico gave rise to the story among the guards, recalls Robins, that *"the day this comrade went back to the United States, they shut down the Quarta Mesine whorehouse district"*.

I do not know to what test Robins submitted the comrade from Philadelphia in order to ascertain his level of physical courage. Perhaps the comrade refused to step into the alley to settle a point of difference with Robins.

As for the sex life of the guards, this was their private concern. Even when the Mexican bourgeois press sought to step up circulation with headlines about Robert Sheldon Harte in this respect, Trotsky said nothing publicly. In a meeting with leading comrades from the Socialist Workers party, including James P. Cannon and Farrell Dobbs, who came to see him in June 1940, Trotsky indicated embarrassment over the scandal-mongering in the press, yet he made no big point of it. He began by saying: "I have never asked that the guards and secretaries live like monks—just the same...."

SIQUEIROS. Headed the May 24, 1940, assault on Trotsky's home.

That Healy's "International Committee" would ape the bourgeois press in searching for scurrilous material reveals more about the regime in the Workers Revolutionary party today than it does about security in Coyoacán thirty-six years ago.

The rule appears to be that in the interest of proper security, members of the WRP must keep the Political Committee duly informed on their sex lives and prove to the same authorities that their physical courage remains up to the level set by the leading plug-ugly.

How Robins met the test

In judging how well Robins himself met the test of the May 24 assault, the details reported by Salazar[10] should be noted. Here is the section:

> I [Salazar] could wait no longer. I had Charles Cornell and Otto Schuessler arrested and brought to the *Pocito*. The former did no more than give a few precise details in his declaration. He was asleep when the attack took place. He was awakened by the noise of a machine-gun, and thought it was his comrades who were repelling an attack. At that moment he heard someone cry out in English:
>
> "Don't move, and nothing will happen to you!"
>
> He looked for his revolver, but could not find it. He then remembered that he had lent it the previous night to Harold Robins: guns were often lent to one another by the guards. He then went towards the door of his room. As soon as Harold saw him, he cried out:
>
> "Put your head down, Charles! Don't let them see you!"
>
> In spite of this command, he looked in the direction of the guard post and saw three individuals, two dressed in dark suits and the other in a light one. He ran to look for his rifle, with the intention of going out into the courtyard. As he was wearing light-coloured pyjamas, he quickly donned a dark coat so as not to present too easy a target to the enemy. Just as he was going out, Harold cried

---

10. General Sanchez Salazar, *Murder in Mexico* (London: Secker & Warburg, 1950), pp. 20–21.

out to him again:

"Don't show yourself, Charles! Keep your head down!"

Without any doubt, this new order saved his life. Harold could see who was firing the machine-gun. He [Cornell] stayed at the door of the room, with his rifle ready to fire. He did not think that the attackers were in control of the whole house. At that moment he saw someone whom he did not know running in the yard. He fired at him with his rifle, but missed him. He saw Otto going down from his own room to Trotsky's, and heard Harold cry out to him:

"Careful, Otto! You are in danger!"

After the firing, they all joined Harold in one of the rooms used by the duty guards.

"Can I go and have a look at the old man's room?" he asked.

"Wait until we've put out the light," replied Harold.

Having done so, they ran to the door leading into Trotsky's study. It was locked. He then went towards the yard. Neither before nor after the firing had he heard the sound of cars running. It was only afterwards that they noticed their disappearance, and also that of Sheldon.

Facts like these do not say much for Robins's capacities as a captain. His concern for his own safety and that of the other guards was high. But what about the safety of Trotsky and Sedoff? Why no counterattack? Why did Robins shout no instructions to the other guards until they showed up of their own volition at their doors? Why did his only instruction consist of passing on the order of the assailant, "Don't move, and nothing will happen to you!"

Why did Robins fail to see the three individuals that Cornell saw? How did it happen that Cornell was the first to fire, although he had to search for a rifle, his pistol having been "borrowed" by Robins, who forgot to use it?

After the firing by the assailants, why did Robins have the guards stop for a meeting in one of their rooms?

Why was it Cornell and not Robins who first pressed to see if the Trotskys had survived? Why did Robins refuse to move until the lights were turned off, giving the assailants still further cover?

Healy's experts in security matters have no difficulty in turning this sad exhibition into its opposite. In the April 19, 1975, issue of *Workers Press*, the Political Committee of the WRP states the following:

> [Hansen] was one of the guards in Trotsky's headquarters-in-exile in Coyoacan, Mexico, when the GPU agent Mercader struck his fatal blow with an ice pick. Hansen goes down in history, in the words of one of the guards, Harold Robins, as "the man who couldn't find his gun," although he had the reputation of being a "crack shot."

I have heard this story about the guards before, but not in relation to me specifically, or in relation to the assassin Mercader (with whom I will deal further on). I heard it, in fact, shortly after the May 24 assault—it may have first appeared in a Stalinist-influenced journal.

Healy's committees know very well that *I was in New York—not Coyoacán—at the time of the May 24 assault.*

To shift the slander to August 20, the day Mercader drove his ax into Trotsky's brain, and to credit Harold Robins as its source is a new wrinkle. It shows the ingenuity of Healy's operators in working out the details of their frame-up.

In his "Open Letter to the SWP,"[11] Robins is more restrained. He makes several points of interest, two of which are worth noting:

1. He does not appear to agree that Healy has proved Robert Sheldon Harte to have been a traitor. He says on this:

> The matter of loyalty of Comrade Sheldon Harte has been raised and discussed in this dispute. An inquiry may possibly bring about much greater clarity than exists now on this score. The various pieces of evidence indicate a serious conflict that is unavoidable in arriving at a decision.
>
> *Comrade Trotsky raised the matter of his surprising Sheldon Harte in Trotsky's bedroom—un-*

---

11. *Workers Press,* January 12, 1976.

invited—and absolutely none of us ever would think of doing that. Nevertheless, although I may turn out to be wrong, I am of the opinion that it was Sheldon Harte who fired his revolver after he was captured—and this awakened me. My calls of "Bob, Bob" brought about the situation where the bogus policeman standing by the big eucalyptus tree near the guards' rooms then turned back to face in my direction firing his sub-machine gun at my doorway and at me in it. This chatter of the sub-machine gun awakened Trotsky and Natalia, saving their lives during the May 24, 1940, assassination attempt. Accident often determines things.

2. Robins mentions that he disagreed quite strongly with Trotsky on a number of issues:

> In the instance described above [Trotsky embracing Colonel Salazar, the chief of the Secret Police of Mexico, after he apologized for having arrested two of Trotsky's secretaries], it was precisely that objective view which distinguished the levels of operation of Comrade Trotsky from our subjective viewpoint of righteous indignation and reaction. Here I must say that despite numerous disputes on issues with Comrade Trotsky, I never, but never, found him difficult to work with. Some of those disputes resulted in sharp emotional reactions on either side or on both sides. They were always settled by one or another of us changing a point of view on an issue.

An account of the disputes that aroused sharp emotional reactions in either Trotsky or Robins or both ought to be of interest. Isn't it time to describe these charged exchanges? If they have already been written up, shouldn't they be published? Surely the Healyites, if no one else, would welcome the opportunity to publish Robins's account of his brushes with Trotsky in the field of ideas.

Taken altogether, what do the allegations, insinuations, and sensationalistic rumor-mongering of "Captain" Robins prove? Merely that the Trotsky household was not always smooth-running and that with our limited resources many difficulties confronted us in organizing even a small force of guards on an effective basis within the high walls of what Trotsky called a "prison." Not the least of the difficulties were personal weaknesses that showed up under the strain, including antagonisms that were hard to reduce. The role of Robins in helping to solve these problems, it must be said, was not exactly brilliant.

Plain Harold Robins tells it like it was

Among our difficulties was Trotsky's dislike of having a guard present in his study when he talked with a visitor whom we had come to trust. Of course, in the case of reporters, tourists of various kinds, prominent persons from afar who wanted to talk with Trotsky as the basis for a possible article, Trotsky made sure to have a guard or secretary present. One reason for this was to have a witness to the conversation in case Trotsky was badly misquoted. But Trotsky balked at making this a rule applying to all who were invited into his study.

Trotsky also opposed searching everyone who came to visit him. To him, this was intolerable.

Moreover, Trotsky was insistent on our maintaining confidence in each other—of not engaging in spy-hunting, and above all of not permitting disinformation planted by the GPU or other police to sow suspicion and disruption among our own ranks. Trotsky followed this rule himself. For instance, in the absence of convincing proof that "Etienne" (Zborowski) was guilty of disloyalty or of being an agent, Trotsky and Sedov maintained their confidence in him.[12] Trotsky even invited Jacson into his study alone although the agent's

---

12. See Isaac Deutscher's discussion of this question in *The Prophet Outcast*, pp. 390–410. Deutscher, who had access to the closed section of Trotsky's archives at Harvard, shows that there was rising suspicion in 1937 that an agent provocateur was operating in Leon Sedov's circle. But just who? Suspicion fell on "Etienne" (p. 390), but also Victor Serge (p. 391), and even Sedov himself (p. 392). "Etienne" asked Trotsky what he should do about the suspicion of him voiced by Sneevliet and Serge. Trotsky advised him to ask for an investigation and a chance to clear his honor.

A letter was received by Trotsky from a GPU officer, who had defected and found refuge in the United States, warning Trotsky to beware of a dangerous stool pigeon in Paris. The letter described "Mark" so accurately that there could be no doubt that it was "Etienne." But the author hid his own identity and failed to respond to Trotsky's request to get in touch with his followers in New York.

actions there caused Trotsky to think something was wrong about him.

When George Novack referred to these well-known facts, Healy's "International Committee"—as we have seen—charged Novack with reviving the GPU "theory of self-assault," which in their words meant accusing "Leon Trotsky and his son Leon Sedov of responsibility for their own deaths." Novack did nothing to the kind, as I proved earlier.

Yet it is a fact that it was on the basis of Trotsky's feelings in the matter that Harold Robins, the guard on duty the afternoon of August 20, 1940, did not search Jacson's raincoat upon receiving the assassin in the patio.

About twenty-six years ago, Robins—who was just plain Harold Robins then—put down some of his recollections as one of the guards in Coyoacán. Among other things, he said the following:

> Comrades often ask how did we permit Stalin's assassin entry into the house without search? Was the guard lax? Or of questionable loyalty?
>
> I can only answer that every living member of the 1940 guard was completely devoted to the "Old Man" and proved it on every occasion. Trotsky refused to permit us to search everyone in spite of persistent urging on the part of the guard. He would not permit any of us to be present when he met with strangers unless he specifically invited us. He maintained this policy despite Natalia's and Hansen's opposition during a period of several years.[13]

The apparent lack of response on the correspondent's part and the strange form of his warning made Trotsky doubt his trustworthiness. Nevertheless, a small commission was formed at Coyoacan to investigate the matter; but it found no substance in the charges against Étienne. Trotsky wondered whether the denunciation was not a G.P.U. hoax, designed to discredit the man who appeared to be the most efficient and devoted of his assistants, who spoke and wrote Russian, was thoroughly versed in Soviet affairs, and edited the *Bulletin*. (p. 409.)

13. Cited from a copy of the manuscript in the archives of the Socialist Workers party.

According to the logic applied by Healy's committee to George Novack, doesn't this account by plain Harold Robins show that he was reviving the "most monstrous lie of all," a lie he had "taken directly from the GPU"?

Doesn't it prove that Robins was a "co-conspirator" of Hansen and therefore "an accomplice of the GPU" perhaps as long ago as 1940?

Why isn't his name included in the "indictment" worked up by Healy and his crew of frame-up artists "after painstaking research in Europe and America"?

Or is some unidentified person in the top circles of the WRP covering up for Robins? For what reasons?

Natalia Sedoff's testimony

To bolster their frame-up of Novack and me, the members of Healy's "International Committee" write as follows in the January 5, 1976, issue of *Workers Press*:

> Nor had Trotsky "trusted" Jacson. Isaac Deutscher described Trotsky's reaction to Jacson on August 17, 1940, three days before the assassination:
>
> "Reluctantly but dutifully, Trotsky invited 'Jacson' to come with him to the study. There they remained alone and discussed the article. After only ten minutes Trotsky came out disturbed and worried. His suspicion was suddenly heightened; he told Natalya that he had no wish to see 'Jacson' any more . . . He had the feeling that the man was an imposter. He remarked to Natalya that in his behaviour 'Jacson' was quite unlike a Frenchman—yet he presented himself as a Belgian brought up in France. Who was he really? They should find this out . . . These questions must have been on Trotsky's mind, for two days later he repeated his observations to Hansen, as if to ascertain whether similar misgivings had occurred to anyone beside himself . . . it was on the day before the attempt on his life that Trotsky confided his vague suspicions to Hansen." ('The Prophet Outcast', Oxford University Press, pp. 498–499.)
>
> Despite the warnings, Jacson passed through the gates into the villa the next day.

Hansen was the guard on duty.[14]

In the above quotation from Deutscher, it will be noticed that ellipses (. . .) occur in three places. The deleted sentences are not without interest. They show that Trotsky had noted something qualitatively different about Jacson, but that Trotsky did not draw the proper conclusions fast enough.

Here are the sentences that should be replaced where the first ellipses appears:

> What upset him was not what the man had written—a few clumsy and muddled clichés—but his behaviour. While they were at the writing table and Trotsky was looking through the article, "Jacson" seated himself on the table and there, placed above his host's head, he remained to the end of the interview! And all the time he had his hat on and clutched his coat to himself! Trotsky was not only irritated by the visitor's discourtesy; he sensed a fraud again.

The second set reads as follows:

NATALIA SEDOFF

> Natalya was taken aback; it seemed to her that Trotsky "had perceived something new about 'Jacson', but had not yet reached, or rather was in no hurry, to reach, any conclusions". Yet the implication of what he had said was alarming: if "Jacson" was deceiving them about his nationality, why was he doing it? And was he not deceiving them about other things as well? About what?

The third one is a single sentence:

> However, the assassin moved faster than the victim's intuition and instinct of self-preservation:

What are we to say about such dexterous handling of texts? It's at least up to the level of a cutting

---

14. "Hansen was the guard on duty." This is a good example of the calculation that goes into the lies presented in the "indictment." Robins was the guard on duty. I was on the roof working with Melquiades Benitez and Charlie Cornell on the alarm system.

room in a Hollywood film factory, isn't it?

Now we come to the reference to Hansen—"it was on the day before the attempt on his life that Trotsky confided his vague suspicions to Hansen"—which is what the indicters wanted to weave into their exhibits.

When Deutscher showed me the page proofs of the chapter on the Mexican period, "The 'Hellblack Night,'" in the final volume of his biography of Trotsky, I mentioned several facts that were new to him, and also pointed to a few errors. He made notations on these and was able to make some changes.

Among these points, I told Deutscher I could not recall Trotsky telling me he had developed suspicions about Jacson.[15] In previous weeks Trotsky had been of the opinion that we should try to win over this "sympathizer," the husband of Sylvia Ageloff. As Deutscher points out, three days before the assassination, Trotsky was still only vaguely disturbed about Jacson. If Trotsky had told me, for instance, what had happened in that interview, I think the attitude of the entire guard would have changed at once. But Trotsky did not even tell us he had made an appointment to see Jacson on August 20.

Deutscher said he was sure that there was a documentary basis for this part of the chapter but that he would check.

Three sources are cited by Deutscher for the passage quoted above: Natalya Sedova in Victor Serge's *Vie et Mort de Trotsky*, p. 319; the *Biulleten Oppozitsii*, no. 85, 1941; and *Fourth International*, May 1941.

I will begin with the third reference, "How It Happened," written by Natalia Sedov Trotsky, which was published in the May 1941 issue of *Fourth International*. There is not a word in it about Trotsky having communicated suspicions to me about Jacson the day before the assassination. In other respects, the account confirms Deutscher's summary, and further shows with what deliberation Healy's committee distorted the facts and even suppressed crucial items.

Deutscher's second reference is to the *Biulleten Oppozitsii*, no. 85, 1941. But this is merely the Russian original of Natalia's article "How It Happened."

Deutscher's first reference is to Victor Serge's *Vie et Mort de Trotsky*.[16] The passage is by Natalia Sedoff. Her recollections here are virtually the same as those in "How It Happened." However, it contains some additional details that help bring out aspects of the security problem that have been challenged by Healy. I am including more pages than Deutscher referred to:

> On another occasion, he [Jacson-Mornard] took some of our American friends from Minneapolis on a drive to Toluca. On the way back, he pretended he was going to drive the car over a precipice. "Then it would all be over!" he said to our friend Anna Konikova, who attached no particular importance to his sudden fit of depression. His visit to the States had completely changed him—the somewhat vulgar *bon vivant*, who had been content to lead an easy and leisurely life, was suddenly in a terrible state of nerves . . . He called on us seven or eight times and we would speak to him for a few minutes in the garden and on two occasions in the house. "Sylvia's husband" seemed neither interested in politics nor particularly likeable as a person. Leon Davidovich would see him out of politeness during breaks from his work, while feeding the rabbits . . . Mornard, who was extremely discreet about his business affairs, even with Sylvia, kept speaking to Leon Davidovich about his "boss", a "brilliant businessman" whose speculations had apparently earned him a fortune. Knowing of our financial difficulties, his employers had no doubt advised him to hint how useful he could be to us in that sphere. Leon Davidovich, who was utterly indifferent to all this talk, replied with vague remarks about commercial ability and similar things. These short conversations used to irritate me, and Leon Davidovich disliked them as well. "Who is this fabulously rich boss?" he asked me. "We should find out. After all, he

---

15. See Deutscher, *The Prophet Outcast*, pp. 498

16. Victor Serge, *Vie et Mort de Trotsky* (Paris: Amiot-Dumont, 1951), pp. 318–20 An English translation of the book was released in November 1975. See *The Life and Death of Leon Trotsky* by Victor Serge and Natalia Sedova Trotsky (New York: Basic Books, Inc.), pp. 264–66.

might be some profiteer with Fascist tendencies and it might be best to stop seeing Sylvia's husband altogether . . ." Mornard used to call on the most trifling pretexts; he would bring me a box of chocolates from Sylvia; he was leaving for New York and insisted on lending us his car; his boss was winding up some important business and he was going to leave Mexico with him . . .

When he returned from the States in about the middle of August, he looked awful. His complexion had gone pale and grey. "Are you ill?" I asked him. "What is the matter with you?" He said that he had been ill in Monterrey. I mentioned a mountain walk I had taken with Leon Davidovich. I was struck by his sudden interest. How had we got there? Why had we not taken him up on his offer to drive us? . . . At the time, I failed to understand why he was so anxious to accompany Leon Davidovich to the mountains . . .

During his breaks from work, Leon Davidovich avoided serious subjects—those who sought political discussions with him had to make a special appointment. Leon Davidovich would receive them in his study, listen attentively, his head slightly inclined, his hands often clasped on the table, while he carefully weighed his answers . . . A week before the black day, Sylvia and her husband had tea with us for the first time; Sylvia passionately defended the minority standpoint in the [American Trotskyist] Party. Jacson Mornard said hardly anything; it appeared that the arguments ranged so widely as to exclude him altogether. But a few days later, he asked if he could show Leon Davidovich a draft of an article he had written.

Leon Davidovich saw him in his study for ten minutes . . . He seemed worried after the interview. "He showed me a paper devoid of any interest. It's confused and full of banal phrases. He says he can produce some interesting French statistics." Leon Davidovich looked uneasy. "I don't like him. What sort of a fellow is he? We ought to make a few enquiries . . ." Jacson Mornard, instead of taking a chair, had sat down on a corner of the large table, wearing a hat and carrying his raincoat over his arm . . . It had obviously been a sort of rehearsal of his crime. We were so far from suspecting the man who, for two years, had been the companion of an unaffected and agreeable young comrade, that when one of our American friends suggested we search him, Leon Davidovich exclaimed, "Come, come! What are you thinking of?" But he did not want to see him again. Despite his long and unhappy experience of people, Leon Davidovich was not in the least suspicious. On the contrary, having spent the best part of his life among the revolutionary masses, he had great confidence, both reasoned and emotional, in the average man in the street. There was so much ability, so much potential and idealism in a crowd at a meeting or in a small group of labourers. He had so often devoted long hours to discussions with American workers, or with Spanish refugees . . .

Note especially Natalia Sedoff's report of L.D.'s reaction to the suggestion from "one of our American friends" that Jacson ought to be searched when he was received at the entrance. "Come, come! What are you thinking of?"

According to Healy's logic, that attitude surely proves in retrospect that Trotsky was a "co-conspirator" with Hansen and therefore was an "accomplice of the GPU." Why isn't Trotsky's name included in the indictment?

In her account, "How It Happened," Natalia cries out against the length to which security measures were being taken.

> After the failure suffered by our enemies in the May 24 attack, we were absolutely certain that Stalin would not halt, and we were making preparations. We also knew that a different form of attack would be used by the G.P.U. Nor did we exclude a blow on the part of a "solitary individual" sent secretly and paid by the G.P.U. But neither the bullet-proof vest [a gift sent by Los Angeles well-wishers] nor a helmet could have served as safeguards. To apply these methods of defense from day to day was impossible. It was impossible to convert one's life solely into self-defense—*for in that case life loses all its value.* (Emphasis in original.)

In Healy's two committees does Natalia Sedoff pass "security" scrutiny? Or, in accordance with the logic followed by these inquisitors, is she to be branded as Hansen's "co-conspirator" and therefore an "accomplice of the GPU"?

What was the source of Deutscher's error? I do not know. Perhaps it was a mere slip of the pen. Nor do I know whether he intended to correct this error in a subsequent edition of the biography. In any case the error was minor and does not affect his delineation of how the assassin wormed his way into the confidence of the household and why Trotsky did not sense something "new" about Jacson until just three days before the assassination (two days by Natalia's account), communicating his feelings to Natalia the following day in such a way as to indicate that he had not yet come to any definite conclusion.

Natalia's testimony in turn, both substantiates Deutscher's account while providing nothing to indicate that her words constituted the source of the detail about Trotsky's having communicated suspicion of Jacson to me on August 19.

The role of President Cárdenas

> The IC charges Joseph Hansen and the Socialist Workers Party to which he belongs, with criminal negligence in relation to the security implications of the death of Trotsky and the tasks of revolutionary security in relation to the defense of the Fourth International.[17]

If we leave aside the frame-up, of which this concoction is a central part, Healy's concept of the defense at Coyoacán does not correspond at all with the reality. As he (and others of the same cast of mind) conceive it, everything depended on the handful of guards that could be assembled; and this in turn, according to his argumentation, was the responsibility of the Socialist Workers party. (At that time Healy, as an opponent of Trotsky and Cannon—but not as an "accomplice of the GPU," contributed nothing.)

Robins goes even further. To read his criticisms and reconstruction of events, the main thing was skill in handling a pistol or Thompson submachine gun, a skill that he found especially difficult to master. So that to choose as a guard someone like him, who had never stepped inside a shooting gallery, was to demonstrate "criminal negligence in relation to the security implications of the death of Trotsky."

PRESIDENT CARDENAS

However, the most essential element in the defense was the interest displayed by President Cárdenas in providing protection for the hounded revolutionist to whom he had granted asylum.

Cárdenas provided a police detail at the entrance to Trotsky's home on a twenty-four-hour schedule. Besides this, the Mexican government kept up a certain watch. For example, in 1939, the Stalinists held a big rally in which Trotsky was made the main target. It appeared that the Mexican CP was trying to organize a raid by a crowd of ostensibly outraged, honest workers. Shortly after midnight, two busloads of police arrived to beef up the detail. V.T. O'Brien, then the head guard, remembers the incident well, as he met them at the door to find out what their mission was.

After the May 24 assault, the Mexican government tripled the size of the police detail to help guard Trotsky.

On excursions, or on trips for a few days of relaxation at Taxco or elsewhere, Jesús Rodríguez Casas, the head of the police detail, usually accompanied us. Often one or two more police in uniform went along as guards.

It is true that the government was permeated with members of the Communist party or fellow travelers, who sought to undermine the efforts of Cárdenas to protect Trotsky. Thus, according to Salazar, they succeeded in getting the original detail of thirty-three men cut to eight, a compromise

---

17. Introduction to *Security and the Fourth International*, p. vi.

finally being set at ten. (The ten were divided into two squads of five men, the squads alternating on duty every twenty-four hours.)[18]

Some interesting theoretical questions arise concerning the relation of the defense of Trotsky and the Cárdenas government. On this not a word has been said by either the philosophical pundits or the frame-up artists of the WRP. (They may be the same individuals.) For instance, was it principled of Trotsky to:

1. Accept asylum from a bourgeois government?
2. Accept protection by the police of a bourgeois government?
3. Collaborate with the secret police of a bourgeois government against the secret police of a workers state?
4. Press the bourgeois secret police to stop being diverted by red herrings dragged across the trail by the secret police of a workers state?
5. Demonstratively embrace the head of the Secret Police of Mexico when he apologized for arresting Charlie Cornell and Otto Schuessler?

Two more related questions demand answers: If a line is to be drawn somewhere, just where should it be drawn? Precisely what is the basic principle that was observed by Trotsky in his actions?

While Healy's staff wrestles with the problem of whether to indict Trotsky as an "accomplice of the Secret Police of Mexico," let us return to the role of Cárdenas.

First of all, it is obvious that without the asylum granted by the Mexican government, the Norwegian government might well have turned Trotsky over to the Moscow executioners at the end of 1936 or early 1937.

Second, without the police protection provided by the Mexican government, Trotsky's personal guards could not have saved him very long from Stalin's murder machine, which had a powerful state apparatus and the resources of a number of Communist parties at its disposal. The attitude of Cárdenas, who was abiding by the principles of bourgeois democracy in this instance, placed serious obstacles in the way of the GPU.

To have gunmen, easily identifiable as agents of the Kremlin, kill Trotsky could prove costly to Stalin, since it would cast a glaring light on his arrogant violation of the sovereignty of Mexico. If one or two members of the Mexican police were killed in the process, the cost would be still higher.

The GPU's first efforts were therefore directed at making it appear that a sector of the populace was highly opposed to Trotsky's presence on Mexican soil and that their anger was rising. The objective was to stage a mass raid on the Trotsky household. The leaders of the Mexican CP and figures in the labor movement were assigned to whip up the public atmosphere required to put across the tactic.

This line of action failed because the virulent propaganda directed against Trotsky did not catch on, partly because of the efforts of Trotsky and his followers to expose the true reasons for the Stalinist campaign, partly because of the friendliness of the masses toward Trotsky, and most importantly because Cárdenas demonstrated his readiness to step up his government's defense of Trotsky's right to asylum.

The GPU therefore shifted to a different course. With the advent of World War II, Stalin plotted an attack that would depend on a few GPU agents at the head of a squad of especially selected members of the Mexican Communist party. The calculation was that the tragic onrushing international events would help turn public attention away from the crime of murdering the Soviet Union's most able defender.

One of the obstacles to carrying out this operation was the police detail at the entrance to Trotsky's home. Special planning went into overcoming this difficulty. Hence the elaborate measures of seducing some of the police to gain inside information on their routine, and of securing police uniforms as disguises for the assailants in the May 24 attack.

A close study of that attack shows that the main scheming went into overcoming the possible resistance of the police, who were well armed and knew how to use their guns. Careful attention was also paid to the problem of breaching the armed defense inside the walls. If the assailants did not succeed in getting Harte to open the doors, they had other means of getting inside. They brought a scaling ladder, evidently intending to place it against the wall on the patio opposite Harte's station; that is, the wall running parallel to the Churubusco River, which had been recognized by

---

18. *Murder in Mexico*, pp. 17–18.

the guards from the beginning as a weak spot in the layout of the place. The assailants also brought an electric saw and an iron bar, which Salazar describes as used by Mexican malefactors "to open doors or to stun their victims with."[19]

That L.D. and Natalia were not killed in this attack was accidental. Harte did die, executed by the GPU after being kidnapped.

The capture of most of the Communist party members who had participated in the attack was a setback for Stalin. He was left with the damaging political costs of the attempt without achieving the goal he sought. It was under the *direct orders of President Cárdenas himself* that the Secret Police of Mexico succeeded in arresting most of the participants in the crime, including David Alfaro Siqueiros, and in locating the body of Robert Sheldon Harte. Cárdenas's action was decisive in solving the crime. Before he intervened—in response to an appeal from Trotsky—the Secret Police had been diverted by the Stalinists into adopting the "theory" that Trotsky and his guards had staged an assault on themselves.

Stalin was thus compelled to resort to the most hazardous and easily exposed means of murdering Trotsky; that is, a blow struck by a single individual—the one who had used Sylvia Ageloff to gain the confidence of the household. Even here, in case Jacson were killed in the attempt, the GPU planted false evidence making out that the assassin was a member of the Fourth International who had turned against Trotsky.

To leave out the role played by Cárdenas and the Mexican government in the defense of Trotsky—as Healy and sectarians like him do—totally distorts the reality. It, of course, helps Healy in constructing his frame-up, particularly in presenting any relations Trotsky's secretaries had with a bourgeois government or its police as a betrayal of revolutionary Marxism, even though such relations solely concerned upholding the bourgeois-democratic right of not being murdered.

The assassin—the main exhibit

In proving Moscow's linkage to the assassination of Trotsky, the world Trotskyist movement as a whole sought to keep the spotlight on the killer.

"Jacson" thus lived for almost twenty years in a Mexican prison as a constant public reminder of Stalin's guilt in the murder of Trotsky. Writers far removed from the Trotskyist movement wrote articles about him and his Kremlin ties that received wide distribution. Interest in the details of the assassination of Trotsky kept up for two decades because of the possibility that this proven agent of the GPU might talk.

Immediately after Jacson's arrest, we established his identity as a GPU agent so thoroughly that the proof was accepted as irrefutable by all circles except those completely taken in by the propaganda of the GPU. This was done through analyzing the Moscow trials-style "confession" he had typed up and put in his pocket, and through exposing the contradictory nature of the statements he made to the police.

Albert Goldman, Trotsky's attorney before the Dewey Commission and one of the leaders of the Socialist Workers party, was permitted by Judge Raúl Carranca y Trujillo to cross-examine Jacson, which led to further confirmation of Jacson's identity as a GPU agent.

Through the American consulate, which I visited, material was obtained of decisive importance concerning Jacson's identity—he had used an altered passport that once belonged to a Canadian, Tony Babich. Babich enlisted in the International Brigade to fight against Franco in the civil war in Spain, where he died. His passport fell into the hands of the GPU, as did the passports of others who were in the Stalinist-controlled International Brigade.

Because Jacson applied to the American consulate June 12, 1940, for a transit visa to Canada (he went only to the United States), the American authorities were able to check out the false passport even though Jacson had burned it.

All this material was reported and analyzed by Goldman in a booklet dated October 11, 1940, *The Assassination of Leon Trotsky—the Proofs of Stalin's Guilt*, which was widely circulated by the Socialist Workers party at the time. It still remains a valuable source of material on the case.

During subsequent years, we noted such things as Jacson's reliance on Stalinist attorneys in his legal moves, the reports that he was well supplied with funds, and his shift to open support of the

---

19. Ibid., p. 14.

Stalinist line during the war.

Proof of Jacson's personal identity, however, remained at a standstill until Julian Gorkin, who collaborated with Salazar in writing *Murder in Mexico,* said in that book (which appeared in Mexico in 1948) that he had received convincing information from Catalonian refugees who once held responsible positions in the Catalan Stalinist organization that they knew both the assassin and his mother, Caridad Mercader.

When Salazar's book appeared, I took the position that Gorkin's evidence was inconclusive. It rested on the word of unidentified persons.

In 1959 Isaac Don Levine in his book *The Mind of an Assassin* proved beyond doubt who "Jacson" was. His fingerprints matched those of Jaime Ramón Mercader del Rio, taken when he was arrested in Barcelona on June 12, 1935, on the charge of secret membership in a Communist youth organization.[20] From the family album in Barcelona, Levine was also able to get photographs of Mercader, his mother, sister, and two brothers.[21]

Although it was superfluous, the final proof that the assassin was a GPU agent came when he was released from prison in 1960. The *Militant,* of which I was editor, published a full account in the May 16, 1960, issue under the headline, "Prague Accepts Trotsky's Killer—Natalia Trotsky Predicts His Reward Will Be Liquidation by Stalin's Heirs."

To illustrate the attitude of the *Militant* toward "Jacson," the prime exhibit among the GPU agents who have been exposed, here are some excerpts from the account:

JOSEPH HANSEN

An outing in the mountains. Trotsky asked that a photograph be taken of him and two members of the police assigned by the Cárdenas government to help guard him.

On May 6 the Mexican authorities announced that they had released the assassin of Leon Trotsky from prison, some four months before completing his 20-year sentence, ordered him deported as an "undesirable alien," and had placed him on a plane bound for Havana where he would remain one week before departing for Prague, Czechoslovakia, his eventual destination. . . .

He was taken from the prison just before noon, driven in a prison van for about a mile and transferred to a government limousine. The automobile drove onto the ramp where the plane of Cubana's Flight 465 was warming its engines. There the prisoner was met by two Czechoslovak diplomats, Oldrich Novicky and Edward Foulches. They made the flight with him. . . .

The Czechoslovak government provided "Jacson" with a diplomatic passport for his exit from Mexico. Made out in the name of "Jacques Mornard Van Dendreschd," it did not list his place of birth or the names of his parents. But it was good for a transit visa through Cuba; and Mexican officials said that on his arrival in Prague he would assume Czechoslovak citizenship. They did not explain why the Czech government felt impelled to extend

---

20. See *The Mind of an Assassin* (New York: Farrar, Straus and Cudahy, 1959), pp. 209–10.

21. See reproductions; ibid., pp. 12–13.

this honor to Trotsky's murderer. . . .

The ones who have most to gain from committing Mercader to the silence of the grave are Moscow's secret political police and those at the very top of the Soviet government who inspired Prague's department of foreign affairs to make Mercader a Czech citizen.

Trotsky's widow, Natalia, now nearing 80, expressed this in a few vigorous words when she told the Mexican press May 7: "Mornard goes now to his reward of elimination. He was just an instrument. We knew that from the beginning. If he had not succeeded in his task, some other Kremlin hatchet man would have taken his place."

In two editorials (May 8 and May 9) the New York Times sought to utilize the murder of Trotsky by Stalin's secret police as an argument to defend American provocations against the Soviet Union. Trotsky, however, was too powerful a defender of the workers state which he helped create to be easily utilized in imperialist propaganda and it does not seem likely that this twist will be followed up.

A more objective attitude was taken by the St. Louis Post Dispatch which expressed regret at the pending disappearance of "Stalin's best-known triggerman." For "unless the man was an ignorant tool, blindly obedient to others, how much he could tell of what led to the end of Leon Trotsky!"

That is exactly why Stalin's heirs were so interested in getting Trotsky's assassin in their hands. They want to end once and for all the danger that this professional butcher might finally speak and reveal to the world their share of the guilt in one of the most unspeakable crimes in all history.

In Prague, the assassin vanished from public view. Rumors circulated that he had continued on to Moscow where he was given the medal said to have been awarded him by Stalin for his success in murdering Trotsky. Possibly the GPU gave him a sinecure. More likely he was punished for not having committed suicide in Trotsky's study and for having lent himself for twenty years to the production of publicity highly embarrassing to Stalin and his heirs. Was his last walk along a corridor of the Lubyanka prison?

The revelation, fifteen years after Trotsky's death, of Zborowski's role in feeding information to the GPU was important. It added fresh evidence confirming the accuracy of the analysis made by Trotsky in 1938 showing the responsibility of the GPU in the deaths of Sedov and Klement and in plotting his own assassination.

A book assembling this evidence with what was already established in relation to Mercader could prove useful as a condensed account of the way Stalin mobilized the forces at his disposal to kill Trotsky.

A survey of that kind ought to include a résumé of the Moscow trials, the work of the Dewey Commission, a summary of the pressures Stalin exerted to deny asylum to Trotsky anywhere on the planet, and an account of the blows struck by the fascists against Trotsky and his followers.

However, Healy's committees are not at all interested in an objective work of that kind. For reasons I will take up further on, their sudden preoccupation with this material is based on the possibility of turning it to account in framing up the leaders of the SWP. Consequently the selection fitted together by Healy's lieutenants is shot through with inaccuracies, untruths, half-truths, distortions, omissions, poisonous interjections— whatever might help advance the main lie. Healy has gone out of his way, it seems, to prove once again that the end determines the means.

For this reason the series remains silent about the role played by the SWP in exposing "Jacson" so thoroughly that during his entire term in prison he could not escape functioning as a public reminder of Stalin's guilt in the assassination of Trotsky.

Healy's silence is understandable, if hardly commendable. To acknowledge the role of the SWP in exposing "Jacson" would be difficult—if not impossible—to fit into his frame-up of Hansen, Novack, Gordon, Cannon, and others still to be named in his big lie.

Healy's singular confidence in Thomas L. Black

The testimony of Thomas L. Black is without doubt the most damaging piece of evidence dug up by Healy's sleuths in their "painstaking research in Europe and America." Upon studying Black's revelations, Healy—despite his well-known reluctance to speak evil of the SWP—obviously felt convinced that he had no choice but to issue an "irrefutable indictment" naming George Novack and me as "accomplices of the GPU."

Black is cited in the *Workers Press* of January 5, 1976, as having testified "before the United States Senate judiciary committee on May 17, 1956," that he was told by a Soviet espionage agent to proceed to Coyoacán where "there would be other Soviet agents in Trotsky's household." Black's mission would be to work out the details of assassinating Trotsky.

According to Healy's committee, "Hansen and Novack have completely betrayed [these] responsibilities [of maintaining security and safeguarding Trotsky] by suppressing vital evidence of Stalinist GPU penetration of Trotsky's household itself" as revealed in Black's "sworn testimony."

The quotations in the *Workers Press* are not the same as the official Senate transcript. They have been touched up (presumably to make them more readable), and five lines have been dropped without this being indicated in any way. Black's "vital evidence," it is true, is reported as he gave it; the small alterations, however, serve to remind one of the notorious unreliability of the Healyite press. For the sake of accuracy, I will quote the passage as it appeared in the record, including the bit about the spelling of Coyoacán, which Healy left out.

MR. MORRIS: Did he give you an assignment?
MR. BLACK: Yes, sir; when I was released from the hospital. He told me that he wanted me to quit my job and make arrangements to go to Coyoacan.

MR. MORRIS: Would you spell that for us, please?
MR. BLACK: I am sorry. I can't spell it.
MR. MANDEL: That is C-o-y-o-a-c-a-n.

MR. MORRIS: He wanted you to go down there?
MR. BLACK: That is right.

MR. MORRIS: Did he state for what purpose?
MR. BLACK: Not specifically. He said that he wanted me to go down and join Trotsky's household.

MR. MORRIS: In other words, he wanted you to join the household itself?
MR. BLACK: That is correct.

MR. MORRIS: And keep contact with him.
MR. BLACK: That is right.

MR. MORRIS: Did you learn what Rabinowitz's plan was at that particular time?
MR. BLACK: No; not at that time. I asked some questions, and he told me that the questions the nature of which I was asking did not need to concern me then. I would get instructions later.

First I was to go to Coyoacan, and there would be other Soviet agents in Trotsky's household, and I asked him who they would be.

He said I would find out that when the time came.

I asked him what I was supposed to do, and he said I would be told when the time came. He refused to answer any questions about what the nature of the work was.

MR. MORRIS: Did you subsequently find out what the nature of that assignment was?
MR. BLACK: Yes, sir.

MR. MORRIS: What was the nature of that assignment?
MR. BLACK: To arrange for the assassination of Trotsky.

This is the end of the quotation in *Workers Press*. It is taken from pages 1119–20 of the U.S. government publication *Scope of Soviet Activity in the United States*. Having quoted this much, we might as well add a few more lines—those immediately following the place where Healy's trimmers cut off the interrogation:

MR. MORRIS: Did you take that assignment?
MR. BLACK: No, sir.

MR. MORRIS: Why did you not take that assignment?
MR. BLACK: Because, as I stated previously, in

1936 I had lost complete sympathy with the Communist movement, and the Soviet Union, and I was trying to break away from these Soviet agents. Incorrectly, but I was still trying to make a break.

MR. MORRIS: Will you tell us why it is that you appear here today and tell us that you were disassociated ideologically with the Communists, and yet you kept accepting these assignments?
MR. BLACK: I did it because of fear.

A few lines further down on page 1120, the interrogation continues as follows:

MR. MORRIS: Now, what reason did you give Rabinowitz for not going to Coyoacan?
MR. BLACK: I told him that it would look very suspicious if I were to suddenly leave the country without appearing before the workmen's compensation court which was to settle my accident case. He accepted that.

When did Rabinowitz make his proposals to Black? Elsewhere in his testimony, Black said that his previous contact, "Paul Peterson," broke off "probably the latter part of 1937, or the early part of 1938." Peterson was followed by "Semon Semonov" for "a very short period" and then "Gregor Rabinowitz." The date of the latter shift is not specified.

We now come to an astonishing revelation in the very next lines of Black's testimony:

MR. MORRIS: I see. Now, what was your next assignment after that?
MR. BLACK: After that, after the assassination of Trotsky, I didn't see any more of Rabinowitz. But I was contacted by another agent, the one I believed I knew as Jack.

Note that parenthetical clarification: *after the assassination of Trotsky*. That occurred in August 1940. So, to believe Black, in 1937 or possibly 1938 Rabinowitz breezed into the hospital where Black was laid up from an industrial accident and introduced himself. When Black was released from the hospital, Rabinowitz proposed that Black quit his job, go to join Trotsky's household in Coyoacán, and meet other Soviet agents there. Subsequently Rabinowitz told him his job would be to arrange for the assassination of Trotsky.

Black couldn't leave right then—it would look suspicious if he failed to appear at a hearing for workmen's compensation for injuries suffered in the accident. Rabinowitz accepted that, and left the scene as vaporously as he had appeared.

Black was not contacted by any more GPU agents until after August 1940; that is, perhaps three years later, when "Jack Katz" gave him a buzz on the phone.

A few lines further on we come to a revelation that seems to belong to science fiction—the timing of the assignment given Black by "Jack Katz":

MR. MORRIS: What assignment did he give you?
MR. BLACK: Well, a period of some months had elapsed. Then he finally contacted me by a method which had been prearranged by other agents.

We seem to have suddenly slipped back to 1937 or so—*a period of some months had elapsed*. But, no, as many as three years have slipped by, not just "some months":

MR. MORRIS: What year is this?
MR. BLACK: I believe that this must have been about 1940. The reason I believe that, is that, in checking some dates this morning with Mr. Mandel, he pointed out that Trotsky had been assassinated in 1940. This was after the assassination of Trotsky, I am almost certain.

In coaching Black, Mr. Mandel may have done his best to stress the difference between 1937–38 and 1940 and how overlooking this could prove fatal to the internal consistency of the story he was about to tell under oath. No doubt Black did his best with a tough assignment.

There are other curious items in Black's testimony that Healy's committee, for reasons best known to themselves, chose not to report. For example, at one point Black's relations with "Paul Peterson" became strained:

MR. MORRIS: Through what period did you work with Peterson?
MR. BLACK: Until about 1938–1937 or 1938.

MR. MORRIS: From 1934 to 1938.[22] During that period, the time was consumed principally in training you for espionage work?
MR. BLACK: That is correct.

MR. MORRIS: No specific assignments were given to you at that time, were they?
MR. BLACK: Yes; but they were not in connection with espionage.

MR. MORRIS: I see. What was the nature of those assignments?
MR. BLACK: In 1936, at the time of the first Moscow trials, I lost sympathy with the Communist movement, and I told Peterson that if this terror was going to continue in Moscow, I would become a Trotskyite.

MR. MORRIS: How did he react to that disclosure by you?
MR. BLACK: He became violently angry, and we parted on very bad terms.

Black's revulsion over the first Moscow frame-up trial in 1936 was deep enough to lead him to tell "Paul Peterson" that he was considering joining the Trotskyists. Nevertheless, to believe Black, within a year or so, Rabinowitz, who took over from "Paul Peterson" and "Semon Semenov," thought highly enough of Black to assume that he would jump at the proposal to rush down to Coyoacán, join Trotsky's household, and arrange for the assassination of Trotsky.

What led Rabinowitz to be so sure of Black's responsiveness to the bid? The way he responded at his next meeting with "Paul Peterson"? Let us read on:

MR. MORRIS: Now, did he ever drop you as a contact?
MR. BLACK: No, sir.

---

22. Like Black, Mr. Morris has difficulty keeping his dates straight. "Paul Peterson" was in charge of Black "from 1934 to 1938." But Mr. Morris also specifies that Semenov replaced Peterson in 1937. Rabinowitz took over at an unspecified date. He was followed by "Jack Katz" in 1940. Why is it so difficult to fix the date Rabinowitz took over command of Black and the length of time he stayed before taking the tubes back to New York?

MR. MORRIS: What happened?
MR. BLACK: A period of time elapsed—I don't recall just how long. Possibly a few months. Then I got a phone call from him, and in the telephone conversation he seemed rather friendly. He asked me to meet him. I kept that appointment.

MR. MORRIS: Did you meet him in New York?
MR. BLACK: Yes, sir.

MR. MORRIS: Did he give you another assignment?
MR. BLACK: Yes; he did. He told me that he had been thinking over what I had told him about becoming a Trotskyite, and he thought that was a very good idea. So he instructed me to join the Socialist Party, the Trotskyist faction.

In carrying out this assignment, did Black become so thoroughly indoctrinated in favor of Stalin that his GPU superiors came to the conclusion that he—more than any other agent in the world—would leap at the chance to sink an ax in Trotsky's brain? If so, Black does not report it. On the contrary, he says that he was trying to break from the clutches of his contacts.

Moreover, the duties assigned him under the command of "Paul Peterson" do not seem to have run along the line of intensive indoctrination and preparation for the job of hatchet man. "I was instructed to be a good party member and to ingratiate myself with the leadership of the party," Black says.

Thus we come to another revelation that ought to cause even Healy's eyebrows to lift:

MR. MORRIS: Now, will you tell us the nature of your assignment with the Trotskyist party?
MR. BLACK: The only definite assignment I had was to become friendly with the leading Trotskyists.

MR. MORRIS: And to report back to Peterson?
MR. BLACK: Just to keep contact with him. Not to report anything specific to him. As a matter of fact, he was not interested in what was going on in the Trotskyist movement.

Of course, it is possible that Black lied about this. Perhaps "Paul Peterson" actually hounded him for information about what the Newark Trotskyists were doing. In that case, however, none of Black's testimony can be accepted as truthful.

As a matter of fact, it can be established that Black did not speak as he was required to under oath. He told Mr. Morris:

> Carlo Tresca was an anti-Communist radical who had been active for a great many years. I don't know what his political philosophy was. I believe he was an anarchist, but I am not sure.

George Breitman, a leading Trotskyist in Newark at the time, recalls that Black

> told us, as he did not tell the committee, that he was an anarchist at heart, with a lower-case *a*, and that he hoped the Soviet Union, regenerated, would lead to an anarchist-type society. When he told the committee that he thought Carlo Tresca was an anarchist, but he was "not sure," pp. 1121–22, he was lying; he knew very well what Tresca was.

Carlo Tresca, a renowned figure, was gunned down on a New York sidewalk on January 11, 1943. He had participated for almost forty years in labor struggles and in defense of victims of the class struggle. He battled Italian fascism from the beginning, condemned Stalinism, and among other things, was a member of the Dewey Commission. The motives for assassinating him were generally assumed to be political.

The murder was never solved. While the GPU was under suspicion, it seemed more likely that Mussolini had ordered his death. As the case developed, the leads pointed to local Italian fascists in New York. The New York police exhibited exceptional reluctance to follow up these clues.

Black, however, had something to say about the case—this was probably why it came up in his testimony. His GPU contact at the time, "Jack Katz," had decided to reveal to him in a "conversation" who it was that killed Tresca:

MR. MORRIS: What did Katz say about Carlo Tresca?

MR. BLACK: Carlo Tresca was murdered in New York as he was leaving an office building.

MR. MORRIS: Was that in January 1943?
MR. BLACK: I think so. The Trotskyists accused the Communists of the murder. In the press, of course. So I asked Katz what the story was there. I told him that it was my opinion that that sort of thing gave communism a very bad name, and I didn't approve of it.

MR. MORRIS: What did he tell you about Tresca?
MR. BLACK: He told me that Tresca was an enemy of the working class, and that as such he had received a fair trial in Moscow.

MR. MORRIS: He had been tried in Moscow?
MR. BLACK: He had been tried in Moscow in absentia, and this was not a murder; it was an execution.

MR. MORRIS: He said that he had been tried and found to be an enemy of the working class; is that it?
MR. BLACK: That is correct.

Sensational as the revelation appears to be, it is so vague as to prove nothing. Its vagueness, in fact, is on a par with the unlikelihood that Black's GPU overseer would ever pass that kind of information on to an agent as insignificant and uncertain in loyalty as Black.

Black's assertion that a Soviet spy had admitted that the job was done by gunmen of the GPU was well calculated to help the New York police, who were under fire from civil libertarians and the left for their resistance to following up the known leads pointing to local ultrarightists as the killers of Carlo Tresca.

The gaps, sensationalistic inclusions, and contradictions that jut out in Black's testimony may become less of a mystery if we take a closer look at the committee before which he testified.

According to Healy's research experts, it was the "United States Senate judiciary committee." At best this is a half-truth. The testimony was taken by a subcommittee of the Judiciary Committee. The name of that body, as shown on the title page of the document cited by the Healyites, was "Subcommittee To Investigate the Administration of the Internal Security Act and Other Internal Security Laws." This infamous crew of witch-hunters was headed by Senator William E. Jenner, a Republican of Indiana and one of Senator Joseph R. McCarthy's closest and most vicious collaborators.

The Committee still exists. It is now headed by Senator James Eastland, a Democrat of Mississippi. Recently it published a 472-page report entitled "Trotskyite Terrorist International."[23]

In 1956, Jenner held a powerful position among the McCarthyites after McCarthy himself had suffered a setback—a censure by the Senate on December 2, 1954.

Jenner's main purpose in interrogating Black was to gain headlines on Soviet espionage in the United States through a confession by Black that Moscow spies had tried to get him to deliver industrial secrets (his deliveries did not satisfy his Soviet contacts). The bit about Tresca being secretly sentenced in Moscow, and the sentence being carried out by Soviet executioners, appears to have been inserted to help gain publicity (and help the New York police). The same bid for headlines appears to apply to the story about Black being commandeered to proceed to Coyoacán and arrange for the assassination of Trotsky.

To fill out the picture, one more piece of information is required—Black's attitude toward Jenner's notorious body of witch-hunters. Here it is on page 1124 of the transcript:

MR. MORRIS: How long have you been cooperating with the FBI?
MR. BLACK: Since 1950.

MR. MORRIS: You have made, to the best of your knowledge, full disclosure to them?
MR. BLACK: That is correct.

MR. MORRIS: In view of the witness' very responsive attitude to the questions that have been asked him, and because of his voluntarily testifying about other things he was not asked about, I would like the record to show that the committee should commend him for his testimony before the committee.

SENATOR JENNER: The committee does commend you, Mr. Black, and furthermore, let me state that it is unusual for this committee to get a man who has had past affiliations with the Communist Party such as you have had to come out openly and help this committee in their effort to stop this Communist conspiracy.

This particular phase of our study is to look into Communist tactics, how they operate in our country. We know they are operating today. We know the method of operation continues to change.

It is our duty as a subcommittee of the Judiciary Committee, a Subcommittee on Internal Security, to try to keep abreast of their machinations.

I want to commend you, and I want to thank you for your cooperation here, and I do believe that the fact that you have come forward will give you more protection from the fears you have expressed in the past. Furthermore, you may encourage others to do the same.

Thank you very much.

MR. BLACK: Thank you.

Let us summarize the facts. Thomas L. Black, who had been working as a stool pigeon for the FBI for six years, appeared before the witch-hunting committee headed by McCarthy's good right arm, William E. Jenner. The senator, after listening to the FBI agent's well-prompted recital of his lines, issued an official commendation for services rendered. Jenner's praise was equivalent to a pat on the back from McCarthy himself.

Bearing this situation in mind, we should now be able to judge the credibility of Black's claim that one of his Soviet espionage contacts was Rabinowitz and that, among other sensational items, this Soviet spy said "there would be other Soviet agents in Trotsky's household."

What conclusion should we draw? One thing can be said for sure. Stalin must not have had much confidence in the competence or intelligence of the "other Soviet agents in Trotsky's household" if he thought they could not "arrange for the assassination of Trotsky" on their own without Black's expertise and personal participation. But why did Stalin have such high confidence in *Black*? Why

---

23. See "SWP answers 'terrorist' smear," *Militant*, March 12, 1976, p. 5.

did Stalin consider Black so important that he decided to send "Rabinowitz" as an emissary to enlist his aid?

The conclusion that best fits the facts is that Black's testimony regarding a mission to Coyoacán was intended by Jenner and J. Edgar Hoover to create a furor among the Trotskyists. Perhaps it would sow enough distrust to embroil them in a disruptive "investigation" as to the identity of these "other Soviet agents in Trotsky's household." It is *disinformation* of the kind regularly produced and disseminated by the FBI in the Cointelpro (Counterintelligence Program) set up by J. Edgar Hoover.[24]

The gullible Healy has the utmost confidence in the credibility of the testimony FBI agent Black gave before the witch-hunting Jenner committee.

> We say, every single member of Trotsky's household who is still alive should be investigated to clear the stains of suspicion in the Senate record and to unmask the GPU agents Rabinowitz referred to.[25]

Had we reacted that way to the disruptive ploys of the McCarthyites and the FBI, the SWP would have ceased to exist long ago.

If an investigation is called for "to clear the stains of suspicion," it should be centered on those who decided to dig through the refuse of the Jenner committee. They obviously knew what they were doing. The lying testimony of an *avowed* agent of the GPU and of the FBI, they decided, could be used to perfection to "prove" that Hansen and Novack were "accomplices of the GPU"—the fraudulent Black thus being pressed into Healy's service to smear Hansen and Novack as frauds.

What Healy's garbage collectors failed to see was that exposure of the "proof" would by itself blow their frame-up sky-high. Healy now stands so discredited by his use of the lies of an FBI stool pigeon that he will never be able to live it down.

---

24. For an extensive and accurate account of the FBI's program of disruption, plus photographs of a number of poison-pen letters and other incriminating documents written by the FBI, see *COINTELPRO: The FBI's Secret War on Political Freedom*. (New York: Pathfinder Press, 1975, 1988)

25. *Workers Press*, January 5, 1976.

Not retreating, just twisting

If he did not have such an overpowering urge to do in the SWP, Healy might prove capable of taking a more critical attitude toward testimony offered by agents of the FBI. It was simply owing to his factional obsessions that he combed through the "findings" of the Jenner committee.

Healy's readiness to turn to the FBI in search of material with which to smear the SWP was shown in the article "The Role of Joseph Hansen and Pabloite Revisionism" published in the September 6, 1975, issue of *Workers Press*.

My attempt to secure information on the identity of "Jacson" from the American consulate was given the most invidious interpretation. Healy's "International Committee" flatly asserted that Robert G. McGregor, the aide to the American consul whom I saw, was "an FBI agent who was operating under diplomatic cover at the American Embassy in Mexico City."

The insinuation was pursued:

> Until the International Committee discovered the existence of a statement he gave to the FBI agent at the US Embassy in Mexico on August 31, the movement knew nothing of it. Why?

To make their associating me with the FBI still more plausible, Healy's committee pictured me as almost an intimate of the alleged FBI agent:

> The tone of the opening sentence of the US Consul McGregor's report hints at a familiar relationship with Hansen. Perhaps this is why they made a Saturday morning rendezvous. It raises the question whether Hansen had met McGregor before. How many times? What had they discussed?

To this and similar slanders by Healy's committee, I pointed out in the November 24, 1975, issue of *Intercontinental Press* that their real target was Trotsky inasmuch as Trotsky himself had initiated relations with the American consulate, had invited the supposed FBI agent to visit him, and had been "most polite," according to McGregor.

In a scathing analysis of Healy's frame-up, Betty

Hamilton and Pierre Lambert began their article with the following sentence:

> We have read the indescribable articles written at the orders of G. Healy attempting to prove that Joseph Hansen and George Novack are agents of the CIA and the NKVD.[26]

This was the only point on which Healy's committee felt capable of offering a concrete rebuttal. In the June 15, 1976, issue of the *News Line*, they responded:

"No such charge was ever made. The International Committee's indictment charged them with being accomplices of the GPU."

Does this mean that Healy has begun to retreat? That he has given up his attempt to frame me up with the lie that as a secretary to Leon Trotsky I had a "familiar relationship" with an FBI agent in Mexico City?

Not at all. Healy is simply twisting. While trying to save the frame-up by adding fresh lies, such as labeling Novack an "accomplice of the GPU," he is also trying to cover up some of the earlier fabrications, which as he now may be able to see only served to immediately expose what he was up to.

Should I have gone to the French Consulate instead?

Healy's "International Committee" has presented as its chief finding against me a report sent by McGregor to the State Department on my visit to the American consulate in Mexico City shortly after the assassination of Trotsky. McGregor's report clearly shows that my purpose in seeing him was to seek information concerning the identity of "Mornard" which the consulate, through its resources, might be able to supply. I also inquired about the possibility of visas for Natalia Sedoff and Trotsky's grandson to enter the United States. McGregor did not mention this, at least in any material I have seen.

Naturally I sought to stress the American base used by the GPU in organizing the assassination.

---

26. See "A Statement on Healy's Frame-up of Hansen and Novack" by Betty Hamilton and Pierre Lambert, *Intercontinental Press*, March 15, 1976, p. 397.

In the September 6, 1975, issue of *Workers Press*, Healy's committee jeered at this:

> Hansen makes another puzzling statement to the man from the embassy. He says that he believed that the Stalinist murder plot originated in the United States. But all the evidence demonstrates that the center was in Paris. This was easily deductible by even the most amateur observer. It is surprising that it wasn't deduced by Hansen, who was the head of security in Mexico.

But I did not say that the murder plot "originated" in the United States. McGregor does not attribute that word to me; he attributes to me the assertion that the plot was "engineered" from the United States. I, of course, take no responsibility whatsoever for McGregor's report or its formulations. If the "origin" of the murder plot had come up I would probably have said "Moscow," not Paris or New York.

As for the fact that a base of GPU operations did exist in the United States, I called attention, among other things, to "Mornard's" trip to the United States after May 24.

What point is Healy trying to make? Is he implying that I went to the American consulate to divert McGregor from instituting inquiries in Paris? Is he implying that the GPU did not operate out of New York? Since he is hardly an "amateur observer," just whom is Healy trying to cover up?

One of the striking contradictions in the frame-up perpetrated by Healy's "International Committee" is that one of their main charges is based on the lying testimony of Thomas L. Black, a resident of Newark, New Jersey, and not of Paris, France. And Black's tale about being told to go to Coyoacán, where "there would be other Soviet agents in Trotsky's household," involved Rabinowitz of the GPU base in New York, not Paris.

By their emphasis on the importance of Black's "sworn testimony," Healy's committee acknowledges the importance of the GPU's base of operations in the United States. In contradiction to this they say that it was "easily deductible by even the most amateur observer" that the "center was in Paris."

Clearly one of the advantages of a frame-up is

that you can keep your cake while you eat it. Or sit in a Paris cafe while you walk the streets of Newark. Observe this remarkable feature of frame-ups as Healy's committee continues:

> The American Stalinists played a role, but it was secondary to that of the Paris GPU network. . . .
>
> Everyone [that included me—J.H.] at Coyoacan knew that Miss Ageloff met Mercader, alias Jacques Mornard, in Paris and it was to Paris that most of them naturally turned their attention. But not Hansen. The chief of Trotsky's security told McGregor that the operation was conducted from the United States.
>
> If Hansen's wrong advice was followed, it must have pleased Zborowski and every GPU agent. Because in a year's time Zborowski was to travel to New York to resume his counterrevolutionary activities in the Fourth International and the Socialist Workers Party.

1. According to Healy, then, I should have gone to the French consulate, not the American.

2. What leads Healy to think that the puppet government of Marshal Pétain, which was set up to meet the conditions laid down by the Nazi conquerors of France, would cooperate in uncovering the identity of the assassin of Trotsky? Or is Healy, after all, only an "amateur observer" who has forgotten that Trotsky was assassinated during the period of the Stalin-Hitler pact when the Gestapo and its counterpart in the French government were collaborating with the GPU?

3. How does Healy account for our success—despite our "wrong advice"—in establishing that Mornard had used a false passport originally belonging to a participant in the Spanish Civil War?

4. How does Healy explain that the false passport was traced through the American—not the French—consulate? Who does he think supplied the necessary clues? (We knew the exact date "Jacson" went to the United States and the name he used.)

5. Why would Zborowski, or any other GPU agent, be "pleased," as Healy's mind readers put it, because of the exposure of the nature of "Jacson's" passport?

Was "Jacson" pleased? Did he think that I was acting as an "accomplice of the GPU" in going to the American consulate in search of substantive evidence as to his real identity?

HEALY: Caught in logic of big lie.

The fact is I was working in a close team with Albert Goldman, Evelyn Reed, and others, to expose the assassin and his master in the Kremlin—not to cover up his identity as Healy insinuates. That is the truth. The only one this does not "please" is Healy. Whose interests is he serving with his frame-up?

6. What did my going to the American consulate in Mexico have to do with Zborowski's coming to New York a year later? Did it not have even less connection than Healy's gift to him of a pair of weatherproof British shoes?

In all this, Healy's target again is really Trotsky. On September 14, 1938, Diego Rivera, acting on behalf of Trotsky, issued a statement to the press that began as follows:[27]

> On September 8, the well-known Chicago attorney, Albert Goldman, informed the press of a GPU plot in connection with the congresses in Mexico. The heart of the plot, according to Goldman, was New York, where the leader of the Mexican Stalinist party, Hernan Laborde, was summoned under greatest secrecy. In order better to hide his participation in the plot against Trotsky and his friends, Hernan Laborde spread the rumor that he was leaving for several months in the USSR.
>
> In reality, however, he remained during

---

27. For the full text, see *Writings of Leon Trotsky (1937–38)* (New York: Pathfinder Press, 1970, 1976), pp. 584–85 [2012 printing].

this entire time in New York in close contact with the most important representatives of the GPU in the United States. Under their direction Laborde worked out a campaign of persecution and slander against Trotsky and his friends. The practical aim of this campaign was either to achieve the expulsion of Trotsky from Mexico—that is, his actual deliverance into the hands of the hangmen of the GPU— or the creation of a favorable atmosphere for doing away with him in Mexico itself. This was Moscow's order.

As a curiosity that may be of interest to students of blind spots, in the very quotation used by Healy to beat the drums about the idiocy of going to the American instead of the French consulate, McGregor writes the following:[28]

> Hansen declared that he shared the opinion expressed to me personally by the late Mr. Trotsky that Mr. Harry Block, an American citizen residing in the Federal District, is the direct agent here for Mr. Oumansky, Soviet Ambassador in Washington. Oumansky, Hansen said, is a police officer whom Trotsky knew personally when in authority in Russia and that Trotsky always felt apprehensive of Oumansky's presence in Washington.

In an earlier article,[29] Healy's "International Committee" quoted from the report made by McGregor on his June 25, 1940, conversation with Leon Trotsky:

> In a strictly confidential and private manner Mr. Trotsky told me that he suspected the orders for this attempt on his life came through the Soviet Ambassador in Washington, Mr. Oumanski, who according to Trotsky is a GPU agent. Trotsky stated that lacking a diplomatic legation in Mexico the Soviet officials in Washington maintain an agent here, who is none other than American citizen Harry Bloch.

---

28. *Workers Press*, September 6, 1975.

29. *Workers Press*, August 21, 1975.

This would show that up to the end, Trotsky kept in mind the GPU base of operations in the United States. Moreover, he expressed his awareness of the danger from that source to the very same American consular official whom I went to see on the same subject.

In claiming that I gave the "wrong advice" to McGregor about the GPU base in the United States, why doesn't Healy put Trotsky on the spit? Doesn't Trotsky's "wrong advice" to McGregor show that he was a "co-conspirator" with Hansen and therefore "an accomplice of the GPU"? Why does Healy insist on maintaining a "deafening silence" about Trotsky's conclusions in this matter? Is he afraid of being exposed as an imposter in claiming to uphold Trotsky's positions in the struggle against the GPU?

'If Hansen had told Trotsky . . .'

The following passage in McGregor's report to the State Department, as cited in the September 6, 1975, issue of *Workers Press*, appears to the Healyites to be at least one item in their frame-up that is truly irrefutable:

> Hansen stated that when in New York in 1938 he was himself approached by an agent of the GPU and asked to desert the Fourth International and join the Third. He referred the matter to Trotsky who asked him to go as far with the matter as possible. For three months Hansen had relations with a man who merely identified himself as "John," and did not otherwise reveal his real identity.

On the basis of this passage (for which I once again disclaim any responsibility), the unidentified members of Healy's "International Committee" make a series of assertions in which lack of proof is counterbalanced by a brazenness remindful of Vyshinsky, the prosecutor in the Moscow Frame-up Trials. They have repeated the litany several times; the version in the January 5, 1976, *Workers Press* is typical:

> We state categorically that Hansen is lying when he says that Trotsky told him to consort with the GPU agent "John" Rabinowitz. It is inconceivable that the Bolshevik leader would

instruct the head of his security arrangements at Coyoacán to meet a GPU agent over a period of three months.

If Trotsky knew that Hansen had been approached by "John", he would have exposed it at once. He would have unmasked the GPU's attempt to suborn one of his secretaries as a warning to the New York organisation as well as the Trotskyist movement elsewhere.

Trotsky's custom and practice would have led him to take a statement from Hansen about the GPU encounter and publish it along the lines of *"Stalin Seeks My Death"*.

As Trotsky wrote on November 2, 1937:

"We must tirelessly gather printed material, documents, *testimonials of witnesses* (our emphasis) concerning the criminal work of the agents of the GPU-Comintern. We must periodically publish in the Press rigorously substantiated conclusions drawn from these materials." ('It is High Time to Launch a World Offensive against Stalinism—An Open Letter to all Workers' Organisations'. *Writings of Leon Trotsky, 1937–1938*, Pathfinder Press.)

Although this was Trotsky's firmly-held policy, there is not a solitary mention of Hansen's meeting with "John" in Trotsky's writings or in the published correspondence of the period. For this reason we are convinced that Hansen never told Trotsky anything about it.

If Hansen had told Trotsky about his contact with the GPU agent, Trotsky's attention would have immediately been drawn to attempted penetration of the SWP at national level in New York. He would have instituted the most extreme precautions regarding the selection of his guard.

It could have led to the earlier unmasking of Sylvia Franklin and prevented the sending of the inexperienced and politically suspect *Robert Sheldon Harte* as a guard.

Hansen's deliberate concealment of his meetings with the GPU agent "John" until the International Committee unearthed official documents in 1975 sabotaged the security vigilance of the Trotskyist movement in the days leading up to Trotsky's assassination and until the present day.

This "indictment" should not be dismissed as mere garbage. While it is that, it is also an unusually good example of "subjective idealist" reasoning, the dangers of which have been stressed in many a sermon by Healy's experts in philosophy.

Note with what admirable conciseness the committee of subjective idealists demonstrate how they project onto the world what is in their own minds, or the mind of Healy. Note how powerful is the conviction that the reality conforms to the specious line of reasoning. Note the complacency—even satisfaction—over the complete absence of proofs!

And note especially the following sentences by Trotsky, which appear elsewhere in the very article quoted by Healy:

> Only windbags and dilettantes but not serious revolutionists can confine themselves to pathetic outbursts of indignation. It is necessary to have a plan and an organization. It is urgent to create special commissions which would follow the maneuvers, intrigues, and crimes of the Stalinists, warn the labor organizations of danger in store, and elaborate the best methods of parrying and resisting the Moscow gangsters.[30]

A hitherto unpublished letter by Trotsky

McGregor's report to the State Department on my visit to the American consulate includes among other discrepancies the statement that in 1938 I met an agent of the GPU in New York. But I was in Coyoacán throughout 1938.[31] Upon leaving there, I went to New York, arriving about the first of February 1939. The date is of importance, since it shows the relevance of the following letter to me from Trotsky, which is dated March 8, 1939; that is, a little more than a month after I reached New York.

March 8, 1939

Dear Joe:

I see again from your letter, as from my discussion with two women comrades who came here

---

30. *Writings of Leon Trotsky (1937–38)*, p. 39.

31. I arrived in Coyoacán September 28, 1937, and met L.D. and Natalia the following day.

from New York, that there exists a very poor state of affairs as regards the work of our party inside the Communist Party. There are no connections at all and there is a certain fatalism in this respect. "We are too weak. We do not have enough manpower to begin a systematic action. Etc."

I find it absolutely false, dangerous, almost to say, criminal. It is my opinion that we must register all the comrades who came from the Communist Party within the last two or three years, those who have personal connections with the Stalinists, and so on. Organize small discussions with them, not of a general, but of a practical, even an individual character. Elaborate some very concrete plans and rediscuss the matter after a week or so. On the basis of such a preparatory work a commission can be crystallized for this purpose.

The end of the Spanish tragedy, the truth about the activities of the Stalinists in Spain and such articles as the excellent correspondence from Terence Phelan in Paris, will inevitably create some disintegration in the Stalinist ranks. We must be present to observe these processes and to utilize the opportunities presented. It is the most important party task of this period.

As you can imagine, it is with the greatest impatience that I await your ultimate information about the manuscript. Your procedure is not clear to me, but I am inclined to suppose that it is good. We will see the results.

We are glad to hear that your and Reba's personal situation is more or less OK and that you have the full possibility of devoting yourself entirely to the Socialist Appeal.

We learn from the Socialist Appeal that our friend Andrews has been arrested. We saw the photos in which he was participating in the "bull fight," not of the Mexican, but of the Yankee "breed." We should be very glad to have some personal lines from Chris himself.

Friendliest greetings from Natalia and myself to you both.

Comradely,

L.T.

Coyoacan, D.F.
LT:L
1–17

PS: I see no reason for writing to Malamuth. He happened to be a poor translator. I did everything in my power to smooth the matter over and not to offend him. He sent me a very appreciative letter. Then, against all my warnings, he permitted himself a condemnable indiscretion with my manuscript. I protested. His elementary duty should have been to apologize for his mistake and everything would have been in order again. I also find that Comrades Burnham and Shachtman committed an error in entering into a discussion with him about the quality of the manuscript without asking him whether or not he had my authorization to give them the manuscript. The best thing would be for Comrades Burnham and Shachtman, on their own initiative, to explain that they, together with Malamuth, committed something of an indiscretion and that it was best to recognize it as such and let it go at that.

Malamuth seems to have at least three qualities: he does not know Russian; he does not know English; and he is tremendously pretentious. I doubt that he is the best of translators . . .

L.T.

For the sake of completeness, I have included the entire letter. A few points require clarification:

1. Photographs of the Yankee-type "bull fight." On February 20, 1939, the fascist movement, which was rapidly expanding at the time, staged a meeting in New York at Madison Square Garden. It was attended by about 18,000 people.

In response to a call by the Socialist Workers party for a counterdemonstration, about 50,000 people assembled in the adjoining streets. In addition, there were about 50,000 "spectators," according to the police estimate. The police sought to cordon off and split up the demonstrators. However, as the fascists left the rally, fighting broke out at various points. Chris Andrews, who had served as one of the guards at Coyoacán, was among those who appeared in press photographs of the scuffling. A week later he was arrested for something entirely different—passing out leaflets at a Stalinist meeting.

2. In the fourth paragraph, Trotsky says he awaits "with the greatest impatience . . . your ultimate information about the manuscript." This is

Trotsky standing at the side of a campfire on a slope of Ixtacihuatl.

the way we had agreed to write about my contact with a GPU agent in New York. That Trotsky approved the way I was following through is indicated by the words, "Your procedure is not clear to me, but I am inclined to suppose that it is good. We will see the results."

3. The postscript deals with the manuscript of Trotsky's biography of Stalin. Malamuth had showed parts of his translation to others. Carelessness of this kind could lead to its falling into the hands of the GPU, which would interfere with my assignment.

4. The parts dealing with the "work of our party inside the Communist Party" relate in particular to Trotsky's views on the "best methods of parrying and resisting the Moscow gangsters."

The dynamic policy advocated by Trotsky

Trotsky's views on how best to combat the Stalinist machine are well worth studying for what they reveal about his politics in general. The caricature of Trotsky offered by the leaders of the Workers Revolutionary party bears no resemblance to the founder of the Red Army and his incessant probing for openings by which the initiative might be seized.

Just as Trotsky made a fundamental distinction between the conquests of the October revolution and Stalin's totalitarian regime, so he distinguished between the ranks of the Communist parties and their bureaucratic leaders. He considered it imperative to reach the ranks—a task calling for actions far more vigorous than simply distributing leaflets at their meetings.

Accordingly, he proposed some practical moves, one of which was to establish pro-Trotskyist groupings inside the Communist party. The first task of such groupings, he held, was to obtain information. To penetrate the wall of prejudice erected by the CP leadership required accurate knowledge of what was happening among the ranks, the impact of events among them, possible lines of differentiation, critical moods that were certain to appear from time to time among the leaders, and so on.

Such work would not only coincide with "parrying and resisting" the GPU; it would facilitate it. Consequently, Trotsky pressed for action along this line. Tactical maneuvers to advance the process interested him to a high degree. If steps had already been taken, he sought for more. This was quite characteristic of him.

In the discussion held in Coyoacán June 12–15, 1940,[32] Trotsky's approach emerges quite clearly. The combination of his train of reasoning, as stated in his arguments, and his proposed line of action is all the more interesting in that the central subject was what attitude to adopt toward the American Communist party, a much smaller formation than the Communist parties in Western Europe and one renowned for its belly-crawling performances in following the twists and turns of the Kremlin.

James P. Cannon posed the problem. The American CP, as its part in supporting the Stalin-Hitler pact, had adopted an antiwar stance that placed it objectively in political opposition to the Roosevelt administration. For the SWP, this created a difficulty. In opposing Roosevelt's preparations to plunge the United States into the Second World War, the SWP had to clearly differentiate itself from the Stalinists. Just how to do this most effectively still remained to be worked out.

"We need a more effective counterattack against the Stalinists," Cannon said. (p. 346.)

Trotsky rapidly went through the possibilities. Did the SWP have its own presidential candidate? No. The smallness of the party and the antidemocratic provisions of the electoral laws made it very difficult to get on the ballot. Was there a labor candidate to whom the SWP could offer critical support? No. The labor bureaucracy as a whole was supporting Roosevelt.

No alternative was left then, Trotsky reasoned, but to offer critical support to Earl Browder, the antiwar candidate of the Communist party running against Roosevelt. That is, there was no other alternative if the SWP were to follow a dynamic policy and not simply abstain in the presidential elections.

In the ensuing discussion, the American delegation and Trotsky disagreed on the advisability of the tactic.

Cannon based his position on the general orientation followed by the American Trotskyists since 1933; that is, toward the militant layers in the trade unions. He saw few cadres left in the American CP who could be won to Trotskyism. Moreover, an electoral maneuver such as Trotsky proposed could create unnecessary obstacles in winning anti-Stalinist militants, among whom the SWP had been successfully recruiting in the years of the big strike waves and the rise of the CIO.

Cannon's opinion was weighty. As one of the founding members, he knew the American Communist party in and out. After founding the Trotskyist movement in the United States in 1928, he had adhered rigorously for five years to a policy of concentrating on trying to win cadres from the CP. In addition, Cannon knew the American labor movement probably better than any other Trotskyist—and there were others who knew it very well.

Trotsky had no disagreement with the general proletarian orientation of the SWP—quite the contrary. Nonetheless, he pressed his point, utilizing *political* arguments that the American delegation pondered and found difficult to answer.

These arguments centered on the political gains that could accrue from the tactic of offering critical support to Browder even if the tactic were but of short duration. Greater receptivity could be expected among the ranks of the CP to Trotskyist ideas. The possible costs among anti-Stalinist workers would in all likelihood not be high, particularly if they were against Roosevelt and his war preparations.

Besides arguing for this "daring" tactic, Trotsky also pressed his view on the broader problem of engaging the Stalinist foe at closer range. Thus he brought up some points that deserve separate

---

32. *Writings of Leon Trotsky (1939–40)*, pp. 335–82.

consideration even though they are meshed with his arguments in favor of a dynamic approach to Browder's candidacy:

❧

"The Stalinists are clearly the most important for us." (p. 348.)

❧

"Imagine the CP without holding a specific hatred toward it. Could we enter it as we did the SP? I see no reason why not—theoretically. Physically it would be impossible but not in principle. After entrance into the SP there is nothing that would prevent our entrance into the CP. But that is excluded. We can't enter. They won't let us."[33]

❧

"TROTSKY: . . . Do we have a nucleus among them?
"CANNON: We have a small nucleus in New York and in one or two other places.
"TROTSKY: Sent in?
"DOBBS: No. They came to us and we advised them to stay and work within.
"CANNON: We got some with our campaign against the fascists." (p. 349.)

❧

"If the results of our conversation were nothing more than more precise investigation in relation to the Stalinists it would be very fruitful." (p. 353.)

❧

"It [critical support of Browder] is a short maneuver, not hinging on the main question of the war. But it is necessary to know incomparably better the Stalinists and their place in the trade unions, their reaction to our party." (p. 354.)

❧

"But we must have contact and information. I don't insist on this plan, understand, but we must have a plan. What plan do you propose?" (p. 354.)

❧

"It is a very daring undertaking. But the cohesion of our party is such that we could succeed. But if we reject this plan, then we must find another policy. I repeat then we must find another policy. What is it?" (p. 355.)

❧

"Shall we follow negative or dynamic politics? I must say that during the conversation I have become still more convinced that we must follow the dynamic course." (p. 357.)

❧

"Our aim is to oppose the Stalinist worker to the machine. How accomplish this? By leaving them alone? We will never do it. By postponing? That is not a policy." (p. 363.)

❧

"Of course we consider the terror of the GPU control differently; we fight with all means, even bourgeois police." (p. 373.)

❧

"It is not just to write a manifesto, but to turn our political face to the Stalinist workers. What is bad about that? We begin an action against the Stalinists; what is wrong with that?" (p. 365.)

To summarize: Trotsky proposed a small, short, political maneuver of a daring type—to support Browder as a presidential candidate, but very critically, insisting that he stick to his antiwar position while predicting that he would surely betray.

In the course of the discussion, Trotsky indicated his preoccupation over setting up nuclei in the Communist party to gain information and so on. Even an entry into the CP would be permissible if it could actually be carried out—but, of course, the Stalinists would never acquiesce.

Trotsky, Cannon, Shachtman fully informed

Trotsky, of course, had been thinking along these lines before Browder found himself temporarily in opposition to Roosevelt and his onrushing prepa-

---

33. The American Trotskyists entered as a group into the Socialist party in 1936. The entry was carried out openly, and in fact upon invitation of the Socialist party leadership who were under pressure from a growing left wing. For details see *The History of American Trotskyism* by James P. Cannon (New York: Pathfinder Press, 1944, 2002), pp. 264–308 [2014 printing].

rations for war.

For instance, in a discussion held in Coyoacán March 20, 1939, Trotsky outlined even more specifically his views on this question.

> By and by, an organization can be established, which must do work of two kinds: one, very delicate and illegal work which must be organized only from the top, locally and nationally, working closely with the rank and file; and another, a general penetration in the Stalinist ranks.

The March 20 discussion is of additional interest in that Trotsky quotes from his letter of March 8 to me and also from a letter I wrote him on the same topic.[34] The letter from me also proves that I discussed the question of fraction work in the CP with the top leaders of the SWP. "I proposed work on a national scale be instituted of an organizational nature, and one of the higher comrades wondered how I would like to do that kind of work." I displayed interest, I can add, and was awarded the assignment.

As can be surmised, it was rather natural for me to accept an assignment in this field. It was part of the struggle to defend Trotsky against Stalin's decision to kill him. Moreover, it was not just a passive defense but part of an effort—however limited—to mount a counteroffensive.

I felt no special aptitude for the task. Nonetheless, under Trotsky's direct influence and the encouragement of Cannon and Shachtman, I was willing at that age to tackle anything that would help advance the Fourth International and speed the victory of socialism. To take on a GPU agent from whom something might be milked would no doubt seem to some to be an unusual and even a "daring undertaking." In Trotsky's battle against Stalinism, it was only a very small maneuver.

I kept Trotsky informed of what I was doing in the assignment, having arranged this with V.T. O'Brien, an American secretary-guard, before leaving Coyoacán. For security reasons, we followed the rule of keeping the number of persons involved to a minimum. For instance, in communicating to O'Brien on this topic, I was to use invisible ink, writing between double-spaced typewritten lines of letters on other subjects.

The response to my first communication was the March 8, 1939, letter from Trotsky. However, because of an error that O'Brien "still finds embarrassing,"[35] the response was unusually delayed.

> A couple of weeks after your departure, [O'Brien continues] I received a long letter from you, full of news from New York and of our friends there and around the country. I read it gratefully but never thought to give it the heat test. I don't remember whether you finally flashed a signal to me or L.D., but I very well recall bringing in the letter with the real message showing plainly. L.D., this man with whom I had a most warm and friendly relationship, said quite seriously and without anger, "Thomas, in time of war you would be shot."

Trotsky and O'Brien then read the letter together, as they did with most letters from the United States, O'Brien recalls, "with my 'translation' of difficult or idiomatic phrases. After apologies for the unconscionable delay, I relayed L.D.'s advice to continue the contact."

Trotsky advised me to ask the comrades in the SWP under whom I had been working in this field to be sure to draw up a memorandum for future reference.

Max Shachtman drew up the memorandum in the form of a report to the Political Committee. (It was actually made known to only some of the members at the time, those with an incorrigible inclination to gossip about matters taken up in the Political Committee being bypassed.) Cannon went over the draft, making a few changes. They thought I ought to sign it, too, although I was not a member of the National Committee, still less the Political Committee, at the time. Here is the text:

---

34. See "Our Work in the Communist Party," *Writings of Leon Trotsky (1938–39)* (New York: Pathfinder Press, 1969, 1974), pp. 308–19 [2012 printing].

35. The quotations are from a letter by O'Brien to me dated June 8, 1976.

April 7, 1939

To the Political Committee
of the Socialist Workers Party
Comrades:

Upon his return to the United States from Mexico, Comrade Joe Hansen chanced to meet an agent of the G.P.U. This agent introduced Hansen to a superior in the G.P.U., a man apparently the head or one of the heads of the American division of the G.P.U. This man whose real name Hansen does not know but who may be called "Y" sounded out the possibilities of converting Hansen into an agent of the G.P.U. Hansen immediately informed Comrades Trotsky, Cannon, and Shachtman. Under their direction and with their full approval he conducted for purposes of reconnaisance in the American G.P.U. organization a series of conversations with "Y" upon the Stalin book which Comrade Trotsky is now writing, the internal status of the S.W.P., and the internal conditions at Mexico, in all cases giving equivocal, mis-leading answers to "Y's" questions or telling him things that are semi-public knowledge, reporting in detail after each meeting to Comrades Trotsky, Cannon, and Shachtman. Through these conversations valuable information has been gained for the Fourth International. Hansen is disinclined—for fear that the story might leak out and because the reconnaisance is not yet completed—that the entire P.C. should be made aware of this affair at present without full guarantees that his personal safety and the further political gains which might accrue be safe-guarded by complete silence on the part of P.C. members with their friends, political associates, and correspondents regarding this affair. Even the most guarded allusions or hints might cause the failure of further work in this respect.

J.P. Cannon
Max Shachtman
Joe Hansen

I returned to Coyoacán the first part of October 1939. When Trotsky reviewed the small maneuver with me, he thought it best not to publicize it. But he did say, "I think you may not have heard the last of it."

Healy's fakery in calling for a 'Commission of Inquiry'

In the June 12, 1976, issue of the *News Line*, Healy's shadowy "International Committee" repeats the litany of their January 1 declaration:

> Joseph Hansen and George Novack of the Socialist Workers Party (USA) have kept a five-month silence since the International Committee of the Fourth International indicted them as accomplices of the GPU.
>
> They cannot reply to our indictment. Only one conclusion can be drawn from this silence. *Until they answer before an international commission of inquiry, our charges are proved and they are guilty as charged.* [Emphasis added.]
>
> The International Committee of the Fourth International has called upon them to submit to an international commission of inquiry along the lines of the Dewey Commission which Trotsky set up to repudiate the frame-up charges of the Moscow Trials.
>
> The International Committee is prepared to appear before such a body and present its evidence. But Hansen and Novack are not. They have shown that they have not the slightest intention of accounting for the 30 years they have masqueraded as "Trotskyists".

"*Until they answer before an international commission of inquiry, our charges are proved and they are guilty as charged.*" Why did Healy feel compelled to take such an antidemocratic position? Must we conclude that it is part of his reformism? That he wants to reform the British juridical system so that it comes closer to the system followed by Stalin and Vyshinsky? The answer is probably, no. Healy took this position because he does not have a particle of evidence, and thus he feels the difficulty of making his charges stick. His proclamation of "guilty until proved innocent" is a way of solving the problem.

How convenient for Healy—he merely spits epithets, and unless his targets answer in the way he prescribes, his epithets are proved. Thus if his victims choose to ignore his slanders, as is their right, they automatically become "guilty as charged."

Let us turn to his proposed "international commission of inquiry."

Concretely, what would be the composition of the commission? For chairman, does Healy have in mind a pragmatist as eminent as John Dewey was in the field of philosophy? Would this person of international stature as a liberal and a civil libertarian accept the ground rule laid down by Healy's nameless and faceless committee that Hansen and Novack are guilty of all charges cooked up by Healy until they prove their innocence?

Just who would organize and finance the commission and its hearings? George Novack with his experience in that side of setting up the Dewey Commission is an indicated candidate; but then Healy charges him with being an "accomplice of the GPU"—guilty beyond a peradventure of a doubt until he proves his innocence to Healy's satisfaction.

Everything has been turned into its opposite in Healy's fake call. It was Stalin in the Moscow Frame-up Trials—not John Dewey—who followed the principle, which Healy has now made his own: *Until they prove their innocence, they are guilty as charged.*

In the hearings before the Dewey Commission, Trotsky set out to prove his innocence, although this was not required under the rules followed by the commission.[36] He set out to do still more—to prove that Stalin was guilty of perpetrating a monstrous frame-up, not only against him and his son Leon Sedov, but against all the defendants in the Moscow trials.

Healy calls for an "international commission of inquiry" as if he were the victim of the frame-up and not its perpetrator. Meanwhile, under the auspices of his "Political Committee of the Workers Revolutionary Party" and his "International Committee of the Fourth International"—both of which he keeps shrouded—he publicizes his lies and defamations in his press in the style of Vyshinsky.

Trotsky, as the major target in those trials, called for an international commission of inquiry because of reasons of much greater import than Stalin's foul slanders. Moreover, his first move was not for a commission of inquiry but a demand that the Soviet government apply for his extradition, which would have thrown the case into the courts where he could appeal to bourgeois justice. The commission of inquiry was a substitute for the stronger and more dynamic procedure.

Let me repeat—it was not merely the slanders directed against him personally that led Trotsky to call Stalin to account, whether in the bourgeois courts or in a commission of inquiry. Stalin held state power, which he had usurped. The lives of an entire generation of revolutionists, including Lenin's top staff of Bolsheviks, were at stake. The Dewey Commission offered Trotsky a platform, even if a limited one, to appeal to world public opinion against Stalin's purges and his international network of killers.

Even more important, the Dewey Commission made it possible for Trotsky to amplify his voice in explaining what had happened in the first workers state; and how best to combat the Stalinist degeneration, defend the remaining conquests of the October revolution, and advance the struggle for a socialist world.

In the case of George Novack and me, the situation is quite different. We are faced with nothing but the miserable slanders of the head of a tiny, ossified sect, a tin-pot despot who cannot extend his purges beyond his own ranks. No lives are at stake.

While our reputation is involved, we feel this requires but little defense. An issue of more general concern is Healy's use of frame-up methods. On that, a quarantine notice should serve for the time being as sufficient prophylaxis.

If it were necessary, we would, of course, call for an investigation of Healy's frame-up; and we would make some specific proposals. The exposure of the frame-up, however, has already been completed.

Healy's International Committee states that it is "prepared to appear" before an international commission of inquiry "and present its evidence." This, obviously, is the "evidence" already published and circulated wherever a hypnotized Healyite is able to function. If Healy has more of such "evidence," let him publish it.

And if the International Committee is prepared to appear before an international commission, let

---

36. On the reasons for Trotsky's decision, see *The Case of Leon Trotsky* (New York: Pathfinder Press, 1968).

this mysterious body begin by publishing the names of its members. Let them come out of the woodwork and into the light. What is the reason for such strenuous efforts to maintain the anonymity of these addicts of the poison pen, who are doing their utmost to destroy the reputations of cadres that have been in the forefront of the struggle for Trotskyism for four decades and more?

Had Healy actually run across evidence strong enough to arouse suspicions of us, his proper procedure would have been to place his findings before the Political Committee of the SWP for its consideration. Instead, he opened a lurid, internationally orchestrated publicity campaign, thereby betraying that his motives were purely factional.

We answered him publicly. Thus the evidence and the arguments of both sides were placed before a broad audience that in this case served as a competent "commission." The decision has been coming in from many countries. The verdict is virtually unanimous—condemnation of Healy for perpetrating a frame-up and denunciation of the use of such methods in the labor movement.

The politics of desperation

In conclusion, a few words should be said about Healy's political motives. For the past couple of years, his grouping has been in a state of crisis. Several substantial splits have occurred, and his press continually features denunciations of "renegades"; that is, cadres who have reached the conclusion that something is decidedly wrong with Healy's leadership. As a result, these cadres are reading material that was previously verboten. Some have opened lines of communication with the Socialist Workers party and with sections of the Fourth International adhering to the United Secretariat.

Healy's number one problem is to stop the disintegration of his forces and to seal them off from the influence of those who became critical of his politics. He is particularly concerned about the attraction of the SWP.

Novack was selected as a target because of his appeal on the philosophical level as a defender, advocate, and user of dialectical materialism; and because Novack spoke out against the frame-up directed against me.

I was selected as a kind of chief target because of criticisms I have made of Healy's politics and practices and because of my editorship of *Intercontinental Press*, a weekly voice of international Trotskyism that gets around in Britain, as it does in various countries where members of Healy's grouping are to be found.

Other SWP leaders, including James P. Cannon and now Jack Barnes, have been singled out for attention because of the influence of the SWP as a whole and because of the contrast it offers to Healy's sectarianism and stifling regime.

Healy was once a promising Trotskyist leader who received strong backing from the SWP in the arduous task of building a mass revolutionary-socialist party in Britain. The opportunities to advance this work in the late 1950s and early 1960s were truly brilliant. However, precisely when the political and organizational problems were becoming acute, going beyond Healy's limited experience, he veered sharply toward sectarianism and the blind alley of ultraleftism. Instead of continuing to collaborate politically with James P. Cannon and other leaders of the SWP for whom the new set of problems was not so new, Healy terminated this fruitful relation, averring that the SWP was capitulating to "Pabloism." Healy's turn cut off the possibility of swift advances in Britain and doomed him to isolation.

Healy is still trying to justify his course, mainly by heaping opprobrium on his former friends and comrades. This way of seeking justification for a tragic departure from Trotskyism accounts on the political level for Healy finding himself compelled finally to resort to the use of frame-up methods.

At this point we hardly need to analyze the bizarreness of his assumption that he could get away indefinitely with such methods if he just used them more and more forcefully. These malicious methods are as self-defeating as were Stalin's deadly frame-ups.

JULY 10, 1976

THE VERDICT: 'A SHAMELESS FRAME-UP'
A Statement on the Slanders Circulated by the Healy Group Against Hansen, Novack, and the Socialist Workers Party

The signers of the following statement represent a rather wide range of tendencies in the left. Some belong to no organized formation but are strong advocates of free and honest dialogue among working-class organizations and are veteran battlers against the introduction of frame-up methods. Others represent groups or organizations holding similar views on this question whatever their special political points of view may be. All of them are familiar with the Trotskyist movement; many are acquainted personally with Joseph Hansen and George Novack, and know the record of the Socialist Workers party, although they may disagree with its positions on a number of issues.

Among the signers are five former secretaries or guards to Leon Trotsky: Chris Andrews, Jake Cooper, Raya Dunayevskaya, Sara (Weber) Jacobs, and V.T. O'Brien. Another secretary, Jean van Heijenoort, who was with Trotsky in Turkey, France, Norway, and Mexico, made a separate statement, which is published below.

Vsevolod Volkov, the grandson of Leon Trotsky, is among the signers. Also Marguerite Bonnet, a close friend of Natalia Sedoff, who was named European executor of Trotsky's literary estate.

Internationally known Trotskyists of various tendencies and affiliations who signed the statement include Tariq Ali, Pierre Frank, Alain Krivine, Livio Maitan, Ernest Mandel, Nahuel Moreno, Jack Barnes, Hugo Blanco, Connie Harris, Peng Shu-tse, Mary-Alice Waters, Arlette Laguiller, Michel Rodinson, Pierre Lambert, Betty Hamilton, and James Robertson.

A number of veteran leaders and militants of the SWP going back to the thirties and earlier signed the statement, including Milton Alvin, George Breitman, Anne Chester, Harry de Boer, Farrell Dobbs, Max Geldman, Karolyn Kerry, Tom Kerry, Marvel Scholl, Art Sharon, and Augusta Trainor.

Arne Swabeck, one of the founders of the American Communist party and of the Trotskyist movement, added his signature, as did Jack (Weber) Jacobs, Morris Stein, Murry Weiss and Myra Tanner Weiss. Charles Curtiss, another old timer, who worked with Trotsky in Mexico, submitted a statement of his own.

Also to be noted among the signers is Ken Coates of the Bertrand Russell Peace Foundation, Tamara Deutscher, Daniel Guérin, and Ralph Schoenman.

C.L.R. James submitted an individual statement.

Statements by the Tendance Marxiste Révolutionnaire Internationale (TMRI—International Revolutionary Marxist Tendency) and the Bulletin Group are also printed.

For almost a year the Workers Revolutionary party, the British group headed by Gerry Healy, has conducted a vicious slander campaign against the Socialist Workers party of the United States and two of its veteran leaders, Joseph Hansen and George Novack. Healy and his followers in various countries have published articles and pamphlets, held public meetings, and distributed leaflets and posters accusing both men of "criminal negligence" in Trotsky's assassination and of being "accomplices of the GPU," alleging that they have covered up crimes of the Soviet secret police and shielded its agents.

They also insinuate that Hansen colluded with the FBI. By implication their charges likewise dishonor James P. Cannon, founder of the American Trotskyist movement, as well as Trotsky himself and his son Sedov.

Healy and his associates have not brought forward the slightest probative evidence, documents, or testimony to substantiate their libelous accusations against Hansen and Novack, the nominal targets of the attacks. The script of their polemics is fabricated out of baseless innuendoes, gratuitous suppositions and outright lies that do not have any political content or foundation in fact. They constitute a shameless frame-up.

The specific allegations have been exposed and refuted point by point in articles by various organizations and individuals printed in *Intercontinental Press* which can be consulted for extensive information.

The records of Hansen and Novack as political figures, writers, and editors are well known to us and many others the world over. Both have been continuously active for more than forty years as prominent members of the American Trotskyist movement and supporters of the Fourth International. It is especially odious that they have been singled out and falsely accused of aiding Stalin's assassins, since they devoted themselves to protecting Trotsky's life during his last exile in Mexico.

The signers of this statement feel obliged to speak out in defense of Hansen and Novack and the Socialist Workers party against the smear campaign impugning their integrity.

But there is more to the matter than that. We are concerned about the practice of such disruptive methods in the workers movement. They are not new. The Mensheviks maintained that Lenin was a paid agent of the Kaiser. Later Stalin accused Trotsky of being an agent of the Gestapo. Marxists and civil libertarians have from the first repudiated these frame-up techniques employed by the Stalinists against their political opponents and critics. Anyone else who resorts to them must be opposed. Otherwise the struggle for socialism, which includes the honest presentation of conflicting views, becomes discredited.

We call upon the leaders of the Workers Revolutionary party and their followers to cease their scurrilous attacks. They discredit the authors, not the accused. We further ask others who share our position that frame-ups have no place in the socialist movement to add their voice of protest and public condemnation to ours.

Argentina
Mario González (Partido Socialista de los Trabajadores)
D. Marcelo (Manifiesto Obrero)
Nahuel Moreno (Partido Socialista de los Trabajadores)

Australia
Phil Griffiths (International Socialists)
Dave Holmes (Socialist Workers party)
Juanita Keig (Socialist Workers party)
Bill Logan (Spartacist League)
Jim McIlroy (Socialist Workers party)
James Percy (Socialist Workers party)
John Percy (Socialist Workers party)
Ted Tripp
John Tully (Socialist Workers party)

Austria
Hermann Dworczak (Gruppe Revolutionäre Marxisten)

Belgium
Eddy Labeau (Ligue Révolutionnaire des Travailleurs/Revolutionaire Arbeiders Liga)
Ernest Mandel (Ligue Révolutionnaire des Travailleurs/Revolutionaire Arbeiders Liga)

Britain
Tariq Ali (International Marxist Group)
John Archer
Mary Archer
Robin Blackburn (International Marxist Group)
Kate Blakeney
Robin Blick
Ken Coates
Tamara Deutscher
Charlie van Gelderen (International Marxist Group)
Sam Gordon
Brian Grogan (International Marxist Group)
Betty Hamilton
Alan Harris (International Marxist Group)
Connie Harris (International Marxist Group)
Quintin Hoare (International Marxist Group)
Mark Jenkins
Margaret Johns
Alan Jones (International Marxist Group)
Pat Jordan (International Marxist Group)
Michael Kidron (International Socialists)
Jim Peck
Bob Pennington (International Marxist Group)
Louis Sinclair
Harry Wicks
David Yaffe (for the Political Committee of the Revolutionary Communist Group)

Canada
Reg Bullock (League for Socialist Action/Ligue Socialiste Ouvrière)
Ruth Bullock (League for Socialist Action/Ligue Socialiste Ouvrière)
François Cyr (Groupe Marxiste Révolutionnaire)
Rene Denis (for the Central Committee of the Groupe Socialiste des Travailleurs du Québec)
Ross Dowson (Socialist League)
Colleen Levis (League for Socialist Action/Ligue Socialiste Ouvrière)
Joyce Meissenheimer
Joe Meslin
Vernal Olson

John Riddell (League for Socialist Action/League Socialiste Ouvrière)
Bret Smiley (Revolutionary Marxist Group)
Ernest Tate (League for Socialist Action/Ligue Socialiste Ouvrière)
William White
Art Young (League for Socialist Action/Ligue Socialiste Ouvrière)

Chile
Luis Vitale (Partido Socialista Revolucionario)

China
Chen Pi-lan (Revolutionary Communist party)
Jerry Chow
Li Fu-jen
Peng Shu-tse (Revolutionary Communist party)
F.H. Wang

Colombia
A. Otto (Grupo Marxista Internacionalista)
Freddy Téllez (Grupo La Internacional)

Costa Rica
Fausto Amador (Organizacion Socialista de los Trabajadores)

Denmark
Gunnar Jensen (Revolutionaere Socialisters Forbund)
Vagn Rasmussen (Revolutionary Marxist Group in the Left Socialist party)

France
Marguerite Bonnet
Pierre Broué (Organisation Communiste Internationaliste)
Pierre Frank (Ligue Communiste Révolutionnaire)
Daniel Guérin
Alain Krivine (Ligue Communiste Révolutionnaire)
Arlette Laguiller (Lutte Ouvrière)
Pierre Lambert (Organisation Communiste Internationaliste)
Michel Rodinson (Lutte Ouvrière)
Pierre Rousset (Ligue Communiste Révolutionnaire)
Gérard Vergeat (Ligue Communiste Révolutionnaire)

Germany
Herwart Achterberg (Gruppe Internationale Marxisten)
Jakob Moneta
Winfried Wolf (Gruppe Internationale Marxisten)

Greece
Giannis Felekis (Organization of Communist Internationalists)

Iceland
Már Gudmundsson (Fylking Byltingarsinnadra Kommúnista)

MARY JO HENDRICKSON/MILITANT
JOSEPH HANSEN

India
Dr. A.R. Desai
Magan Desai (Communist League)

Iran
Javad Sadeeg
Cyrus Paydar (Sattar League)

Ireland
Dermot Whelan

Israel
J. Taut (League of Revolutionary Communists)

Italy
Livio Maitan (Gruppi Comunisti Rivoluzionari)

Luxembourg
Robert Mertzig (Ligue Communiste Révolutionnaire)

Mexico
Manuel Aguilar Mora (Liga Comunista Internacionalista)
Luciano Galicia S.
Jaime González (Liga Socialista [Fracción Bolchevique-Leninista])
Roberto Martínez Aveleira
César Nicolás Molina
Cristina Rivas (Liga Socialista [Fracción Bolchevique-Leninista])
Vsevolod Volkof

New Zealand
George Fyson (Socialist Action League)
Russell Johnson (Socialist Action League)
Keith Locke (Socialist Action League)

Peru
Hugo Blanco (Partido Socialista de los Trabajadores)

Portugal
Paulo Mendes (Partido Revolucionário dos Trabalhadores)
António Sá Leal (Partido Revolucionário dos Trabalhadores)
José Sintra (Grupos de Acção Socialista)

Spain
Manuel (for the Political Bureau, Liga Comunista Revolucionaria/Euzkadi ta Azkatasuna-VI)
Mélan (for the Political Bureau, Liga Comunista)

Sri Lanka
Edmund Samarakkody (Revolutionary Workers party)
Bala Tampoe (Revolutionary Marxist party)

Sweden
Kjell Östberg (Kommunistiska Arbetarförbundet)

Switzerland
Charles-André Udry (Ligue Marxiste Révolutionnaire)

United States
Milton Alvin (Socialist Workers party)
Charles Andrews (Trotskyist Organizing Committee)
Chris Andrews
Jack Barnes (Socialist Workers party)
George Breitman (Socialist Workers party)
Peter Camejo (Socialist Workers party)
Anne Chester (Socialist Workers party)
Jake Cooper (Socialist Workers party)
Lillian Curtiss (Socialist Workers party)
Clifton DeBerry (Socialist Workers party)
Harry de Boer (Socialist Workers party)
Farrell Dobbs (Socialist Workers party)
Margaret R. Dullea
Robert D. Dullea
Raya Dunayevskaya (National Chairwoman, News & Letters Committees)
V. Raymond Dunne
Nancy Fields (Socialist Workers party)
Hugh Fredricks (Trotskyist Organizing Committee)
Max Geldman (Socialist Workers party)
Albert Glotzer
Fred Halstead (Socialist Workers party)
Allan Hansen (Socialist Workers party)
Reba Hansen (Socialist Workers party)
Gus Horowitz (Socialist Workers party)
Jack (Weber) Jacobs
Sara (Weber) Jacobs
Karolyn Kerry (Socialist Workers party)
Tom Kerry (Socialist Workers party)
Bruce Landau (Revolutionary Marxist Committee)
Frank Lovell (Socialist Workers party)
V.T. O'Brien
Earl Owens (Trotskyist Organizing Committee)
Evelyn Reed (Socialist Workers party)
James Robertson (for the International Executive Committee of the international Spartacist tendency)
Grace Saunders
Ralph Schoenman
Marvel Scholl (Socialist Workers party)
Art Sharon (Socialist Workers party)
Ed Shaw (Socialist Workers party)
Barry Sheppard (Socialist Workers party)
Paul N. Siegel
Morris Stein
Elizabeth Stone (Socialist Workers party)
Arne Swabeck
Tony Thomas (Socialist Workers party)
Augusta M. Trainor (Socialist Workers party)
Harry Turner (Trotskyist Organizing Committee)
Mary-Alice Waters (Socialist Workers party)
Murry Weiss
Myra Tanner Weiss
Tim Wohlforth (Socialist Workers party)
Milton Zaslow (Revolutionary Marxist Organizing Committee)

Venezuela
Andrés (Liga Socialista)
Antonio (Liga Socialista)
Carlos (Liga Socialista)
Daniel (Liga Socialista)
Eva (Liga Socialista)
Juan (Liga Socialista)
Orieta (Liga Socialista)
Ulises (Liga Socialista)

CHARLES OSTROFSKY/MILITANT
GEORGE NOVACK

Sara (Weber) Jacobs Recalls A Conversation With Trotsky

Sara (Weber) Jacobs served as a Russian-language secretary to Leon Trotsky during his exile in Turkey, and again in Mexico, and was a close friend of Natalia Sedoff. Jack (Weber) Jacobs was an old-timer in the American Trotskyist movement.

We are naturally outraged by the venomous, malicious attacks against Joseph Hansen and George Novack, both in leading positions in the SWP, of involvement with the GPU,—and all that thirty six years *after* the assassination of Leon Trotsky by a GPU assassin.

It is almost impossible to untangle the web of lies, prevarication and confusion which the "accusation" contains. It so happens that Sara personally can offer testimony on an occurrence which would have seemed impossible of proof. It concerns Joseph Hansen's meetings with the so-called "John" of the GPU.

One evening, L.D., Natalia Sedova and Sara were in a car being driven by Hansen through a crowded section of Mexico City. In lowered voice, apparently pursuing a previous conversation, L.D. told Hansen (I do not recall the exact words, but I recall the sense vividly) that he thought that Joe should pursue his "contact" with the GPU man who had approached him (later identified as "John") to see what would develop further.

Sara and Jack (Weber) Jacobs

Charles Curtiss Condemns Frame-up

April 22, 1976

More than four decades have passed since I first met Joe and Reba Hansen, originally in Salt Lake City, they as recent adherents to the Trotskyist sector of the socialist movement, and I as a footloose organizer, a "veteran" of several years of activism. I spent days under their hospitable roof, I shared meals with them, they provided me with a bed. I came to know Joe's family and Joe and Reba's circle of friends. Joe and Reba won his teenage brothers to Trotskyism, and convinced many of their friends to take places in the Trotskyist ranks. By events through more than 40 years, years that tested the firmness and dedication of socialists, I was able to appraise these two persons, we then young and now gray. My original estimate has not changed, despite divergences in our paths: they were and are dedicated and incorruptible socialists. One is embarrassed to even have to make this testimonial and sickened to have to refute the gross charge or despicable insinuation that Joe was an agent of the KGB or FBI—or both!

I can personally testify to the confidence that Trotsky placed in Joe. As is known, Trotsky lived day by day; each dawn marked one more day of reprieve from Stalin's, or reaction's, inexorable sentence of death. Given Trotsky's trust in Joe, given Joe's innumerable opportunities, were he a KGB agent, to execute the death sentence swiftly and safely, and given, in contrast, the manner and circumstance in which the death-dealing pickaxe descended, any of those days in which Trotsky survived could have been Trotsky's day of death, were Joe in the service of the KGB, long before the actual murder. The charge against Joe is as illogical as it is repulsive.

My knowledge of George Novack is as long if not quite so close as my knowledge of Joe and Reba Hansen, but all I have witnessed and observed of Novack would lead me to hold the same opinion of him as of Joe and Reba.

The bringing to an end the entire history of class exploitation and bureaucratic totalitarianism is a formidable endeavor, as is the construction of a new socialist world, the fostering of compassionate, free and thoughtful men and women, out of the debris of the old. In this effort there have been and will continue to be great debates and differences as to course, program and means. This is inevitable and salutary. We are striving for an entirely new, clean, classless epoch, and to accomplish that requires all the clarity we can receive from debate. But to inject into these differences calumnies and other methods reeking of the most desperate and degenerate of the defenders and beneficiaries of the societies of exploitation and privilege is destructive. Such means do not educate, slanders and lies do not clarify and invigorate but obscure and dishearten; such methods can cripple and destroy people by suspicion, above all precious "seed" people, so needed for motivating and enthusing the great majority for international socialism.

Charles Curtiss

Ready to Participate in Jury of Honor

The following letter and resolution state the position taken by the Tendance Marxiste Révolutionnaire Internationale. The leading figure in the TMRI is Michel Pablo.

Paris, April 7, 1976

Socialist Workers Party
Dear Comrades,

The International Secretariat, at its meeting of March 27–28, 1976, voted unanimously, with the exception of Comrade Vereeken, for the following resolution, which we are enclosing.

*With our revolutionary greetings,
Bureau of the International Secretariat of the TMRI*

Resolution

The International Secretariat of the Tendance Marxiste Révolutionnaire Internationale [TMRI—International Revolutionary Marxist Tendency], at its meeting of March 27–28, 1976, rejected the irresponsible accusations launched by the Healy tendency against Comrades Hansen and Novack of the Socialist Workers party.

It states that in case these comrades ask that a Jury of Honor be set up on this affair, the TMRI is ready to participate in it.

It thus considers it likewise necessary to express its disagreement with the public position taken on this question by its Belgian section.

Jean van Heijenoort's Opinion

The following interview with Jean van Heijenoort was obtained by George Weissman on June 15, 1976.

Van Heijenoort served as a secretary to Trotsky in Turkey, France, Norway, and Mexico.

QUESTION: You have seen some of the material published by the Healyite press attacking the SWP and in particular Joseph Hansen and George Novack; for example, the booklet *Security and the Fourth International*. Have you formed any opinion about the accuracy or merit of the contents of these charges?

ANSWER: I would like to talk first about things which concern me directly and which I know very well and which are alluded to in the booklet, namely the coming of Zborowski to the United States. As a matter of fact, I did not help Zborowski to come to the United States, on the question of a visa and so forth. But I might have very well, if the occasion had arisen.

He was considered a comrade in the organization. He had been trusted by Sedov and Trotsky. Even when these two were alive, they dismissed the charges against him, and nothing more concrete had been presented since then.

So, as a matter of fact, I didn't do anything to bring him to the States, but if I had had the occasion, I would have done it very well as for any other comrade in the organization.

Now, as for the relations between Zborowski and the SWP, there were none practically. There was a small group of European émigrés, French and other nationalities, in New York. We were perhaps eight or ten, and Zborowski was one of them. I was acting as a kind of secretary for that group. And I would maintain the connection with the SWP. I would very often meet SWP members, but the other members of the group, on the whole, did not have contact with the SWP. I saw somewhere in the booklet that there were SWP meetings in Zborowski's apartment on the West Side. That's absurd. It just does not correspond at all to the actual situation.

Then some point is made that I was International Secretary of the Fourth International at that time and that Zborowski had access to a lot of information. Well, that's false too. It's true that I was International

Secretary at that time. But my work as International Secretary was kept quite separate from my work as secretary, or organizer, of that small émigré group. These were two entirely different things.

Q: Since the publication of that booklet by the American Healyites, their press has begun another series of articles on the same subject strongly attacking, among other things, George Novack because he was on a committee during the war years which helped political refugees in France to come to the United States; and among those so helped was the GPU agent Etienne (Zborowski). What is your opinion of the merit of this charge against Novack?

A: First of all I don't consider that a charge. I don't have any recollection one way or another whether Novack had anything to do with the visa and affidavits for Etienne. But in a sense, it was his duty, namely Novack's duty, to get refugees out of France.

And let us imagine, for instance, the following hypothetical situation—that Trotsky had been alive after the fall of France and I had been with him in Mexico. Then I can very well imagine that Trotsky would have asked me to approach the Mexican authorities and get a visa for Zborowski out of Europe. It's the kind of thing I did in 1938 and 1939 for Czech refugees and that would have been totally in place at that time. So I really don't see that a fact like that, if it is a fact, can be brought against Novack. The whole story is absurd.

Q: I understand that you have written, or are just now completing, a book of memoirs about your years with Natalia and Leon Trotsky. In it do you give any description or evaluation of the character and trustworthiness of Joseph Hansen and George Novack?

A: Yes. I have a few months more of work. I hope by the end of the year the writing will be over. Of course I speak about many things in that book, but one of them is the relationship between Trotsky and the secretaries and other people around him, and one of these people is Joe Hansen.

I must say that the relations between Trotsky and Hansen were the best, and with time, they always improved. Trotsky had respect and affection for Joe Hansen, for his firmness and stable character, and I don't recall any incident that would reflect against Joe in any way. The relations were really the best that one could imagine, which was not the case with everybody else. I think Joe was one of those which were most successful as a secretary with Trotsky.

Q: What would be your reaction, then, to the charges by Healy that Joe Hansen was criminally negligent in the events surrounding the assassination of Leon Trotsky and that he is in some way to be considered an accomplice of the GPU and a possible accomplice of the FBI?

A: As to the motivations of Healy I don't know anything at all. From what I have seen so far and from what I know, of course, there is no content at all. It is a huge hue and cry about nothing.

A number of authentic and interesting documents are reproduced. And there they are. And then after that comes some kind of wild commentaries, unconnected with the documents. The whole thing is absurd to me. If Healy has some specific facts, he should present them. But so far I have not seen any such facts.

Q: On the security of the Trotsky household, do you think that greater vigilance or preparation on the part just of the secretaries and guards could have saved Trotsky's life? Didn't a great deal depend on the attitude of the Mexican government and its police in addition to what the guards could do? And in general what is your opinion of the responsibility of the guards in this assassination?

A: Of course when we look back we can always say, "Ah, well, if we had known . . ." or "If we had done this or that . . ." But one must realize what the situation was. It was a few people, which could

STATEMENT BY BALA TAMPOE

We are of the view that the allegation that comrades Hansen and Novack were or are "accomplices of the GPU" is not merely due to "some obsession" or "madness" or "paranoia" on the part of Healy. We are strongly of the view that the slanders are deliberately intended to serve a political purpose, just as in the case of the Stalinist slanders of Trotsky and Trotskyists.

be counted on the fingers of one hand, trying to protect the life of one man against attacks coming from the government of a big country which had at its disposal an unlimited supply of men, money, and technical means.

And I remember very well, in those sleepless nights of watch on Prinkipo, that I did not have illusions in the effectiveness of our guard. We gave our time, our attention, our efforts, but without much illusion as to their effectiveness. If one attempt could not succeed one way, the next would be tried in another way. The means against us were unlimited.

Of course we can always regret—and I'm sure Natalia regretted not to have seen more in Mercader—and Trotsky himself, for that matter. We can always regret that more was not done. But that's not the same thing as accusing specific persons of specific negligence.

Q: In regard to the accuracy of the booklet *Security and the Fourth International,* you had a comment to make about the photograph that appears on page 66.

A: Yes. With all the accumulation of documents by Healy (not *written* by him; he just put them together), some are interesting, of course, and it is nice to read them. But I feel there is not a deep understanding by Healy himself of what he is doing. For instance, on page 66 there is a picture which according to the caption is supposed to represent Mercader with his Mexican lawyer.

Now, "Mercader" is not Mercader in that picture; it's really the French lawyer for Trotsky, Gérard Rosenthal. And the person in the center which is supposed to be the Mexican lawyer of Mercader is in fact Leon Sedov. The whole thing is absurd. And it betrays a complete lack of understanding of what is being done.

Statement of 'Bulletin Group'

The "Bulletin Group", which consists of the supporters in Britain of the Organising Committee for the Re-Construction of the Fourth International, condemns the dishonest campaign in which the Workers' Revolutionary Party, under the inspiration of G. Healy, on the pretext of "investigating" the murder of Trotsky by the G.P.U. in 1940, is devoting substantial resources to an attempt to represent Comrades Joe Hansen and George Novack, of the Socialist Workers Party (U.S.A.) as "accomplices of the G.P.U."

This campaign has been eagerly seized upon by the bourgeoisie and its press, to which the W.R.P. took it, to discredit Trotskyism.

The "Bulletin Group" expresses its solidarity with Comrades Hansen and Novack, and rejects the demagogic proposal of the Healy-ites for an "enquiry" into the conduct of these comrades, who have already conclusively dealt with the content of Healy's attempts to frame them up. The "Bulletin Group" declares that this campaign is a manifestation of the degeneration of the W.R.P., which, having broken from Trotskyism, comes into ever-sharper conflict with the historic movement towards the re-construction of the Fourth International, and increasingly endangers that movement.

The "Bulletin Group" declares that the W.R.P. finds itself obliged deliberately to undertake this dishonest campaign, because it feels the necessity for yet more desperate efforts to divert any militants whom it may be able to influence, whether inside or outside its ranks, from studying objectively the historical and theoretical questions which confront them, questions which the W.R.P. has shown itself unable to answer and to the discussion of which it has shown that it has nothing useful to contribute.

AUGUST 21, 1976

Opinion of C.L.R. James

C.L.R. James is the author of *The Black Jacobins*, *World Revolution*, and other works.

I want to say that I knew and worked with Joseph Hansen and George Novack for a length of time during which I had every opportunity of forming an opinion of their political and personal conduct. The idea that they have at any time been in contact with or in any way associated with the G.P.U. is utterly false and a dangerous political fabrication. I am most certain of that because of the reputation of the leaders of the organization which accuses them.

C.L.R. James

Escalates slander campaign against Joseph Hansen and George Novack

WRP HOLDS FRAME-UP STYLE RALLIES

By Jim Atkinson and Skip Ball

LONDON—The Workers Revolutionary party, the British ultraleft sect headed by Gerry Healy, has stepped up its slander campaign against the veteran Trotskyists Joseph Hansen and George Novack.

The WRP press has been pouring out vitriolic abuse at Hansen and Novack, two central leaders of the American Socialist Workers party (SWP), accusing them of acting for almost forty years as "accomplices of the GPU," the Kremlin's secret police.

Now the WRP leaders have escalated their venomous witch-hunt by scheduling five public rallies on the issue in cities across the country and by attempting to enlist the aid of the bourgeois press in spreading their slanders.

The "Get Hansen and Novack" campaign has evidently become an all-absorbing affair for the sect's dwindling number of adherents. At the same time, the "Trotskyist" WRP's campaign is being utilized by the capitalist press to discredit Trotskyism.

On August 16, the WRP leaders held an anti-Hansen press conference at the London Press Centre.

The dead-end factional character of the Healyite slander campaign was what the press played up. The affair, commented columnist Martin Walker in the *Guardian* on August 17, would seem like an "internal witchhunt" among the "eternally squabbling" Trotskyist groups. In like manner, the August 17 issue of the London *Times*, Britain's leading capitalist daily, commented that "the core of the undertaking is simply another of these interminable factional disputes."

Matthew Blair wrote in the August 20 issue of the prestigious pro-Labour party weekly *New Statesman* that the WRP's antics give "some clue to the repeated failures of Trotsky's movement to develop beyond small groups and factions."

The August 20 issue of the left Social Democratic weekly *Tribune* went on in the same vein.

> Was there anything about Leon Trotsky which would have led one to believe that, 36 years after his most dreadful murder, there would be such a proliferation of sectarian organisations each claiming to be the sole repository of his wisdom? Clearly the battle to the death (literally) which followed his break with Stalin has left an indelible mark on his followers. They fight out their sectarian battles in a fever of accusations about each other's honesty, loyalty and associations.
>
> The most frequent charge which is made between the various groups is that they have been "penetrated" by secret police or other such organisations, or that they involve themselves with shady political characters.

Referring to Healy's call for an "international commission of inquiry" into Hansen's "role" in Trotsky's assassination in 1940, Blair noted in his *New Statesman* article:

> International commissions of inquiry are portentously called for, and some of the witnesses are accused of complicity in the assassination before the membership of the commission has even been announced. Sectarian accusations fly to and fro, with secret spies and agents detected or assumed to be everywhere. Vanessa Redgrave[1] stumbles through a public speech

---

1. Vanessa Redgrave, the well-known actress, was recently promoted by Healy to membership of the WRP's Central Committee.

in which she apologises for once having been a sponsor of the revisionist Bertrand Russell Peace Foundation.

Behind all the "farce and bitterness," suggested Blair, were some interesting implications.

> ... the *New York Times* recently reported that the FBI has admitted 94 burglaries of the offices of the Socialist Workers Party between 1960 and 1966. Many other violations are being cited in a lawsuit brought by the party—Trotskyism's largest single group—against the White House, the FBI and the CIA.
>
> For Vanessa Redgrave and her cothinkers to accuse the SWP of being penetrated by the Russian secret police is thus, to say the least of it, inopportune for the party and the lawsuit. Her friend Harold Robins[2] told me that when a crime is committed you should always ask who benefits. This is a crude method of proceeding (though Trotsky himself did employ it in deciding that Stalin ordered the assassination of Kirov). But if we apply it to the latest round of internecine accusations, then it is the FBI who stand to gain. Who is penetrating whom? The point here is not to make accusations, but to illustrate the importance of paranoia.

The *Tribune* picked up on another aspect of the "Get Hansen" campaign: Healy's use of Stalinist-type methods, although implying that these are the methods of Trotskyists.

> Gerry Healy is a walking encyclopaedia of sectarianism [the *Tribune* columnist wrote, contrasting Healy's latest anti-Hansen outpourings with an article written by Healy for *Tribune* in the mid-fifties]. It was just after the Khrushchev revelations about Stalin and one of Gerry's main targets was Harry Pollitt, the leader of the British Communist Party. Gerry Healy had dug up this devastating quote from Pollitt: "Now after the Rajk trial (Lazlo Rajk was a former secretary of the Hungarian Communists tried for 'deviationism') we know that some of the leading figures around Tito were themselves trained among the Trotskyites and have for many years been agents of British and American imperialism. In fact, Titoism represents the revival of Trotskyism in new and more dangerous form."
>
> Healy went on to dismiss Pollitt's statement for the twaddle that it was. And, some time later, even the British CP fell into line with his view! But what I find surprising is that the Trotskyites who were so persecuted in the past by statements of this sort from the orthodox CP should use exactly the same method as the Stalinists used against them.

Meanwhile, the WRP is holding a series of public meetings (in London, Glasgow, Newcastle, Sheffield, and Liverpool) devoted almost exclusively to promoting their anti-Hansen smear campaign. The first meeting, held in a London dance-ballroom on August 15, gave a flavour of the hysterical factionalism that is now the sect's hallmark.

Ostensibly called to commemorate the thirty-sixth anniversary of Trotsky's death, the five meetings appear to have no purpose other than to help the WRP leaders indoctrinate the sect's ranks into swallowing Healy's bizarre frame-up against Hansen. At the London meeting, the Healyite orators pursued this objective with undivided attention—to the virtual exclusion of reference to the class struggle, either in Britain or anywhere else.

"Three thousand trade unionists, housewives and young people," claimed the *News Line* in its August 16 issue, "packed" the Hammersmith Palais to attend the rally. The *News Line*, which reflects the views of the WRP, is well-known on the British left for its unreliability. In fact, the Palais was far from full. There was a liberal sprinkling of empty seats and, after doing a seat-count, we put the total attendance at about 900.

This was small by WRP standards and is a reflection of the group's declining strength. The point is the more important insofar as the rally was the central focus of the group's "work" for some weeks.

---

2. Harold Robins, an old-timer in the American Trotskyist movement, was selected to go to Coyoacan to join the guard in the Trotsky household, primarily as a driver. See "Healy Caught in the Logic of the Big Lie," by Joseph Hansen, *Intercontinental Press*, August 9, 1976.

The audience was overwhelmingly young. Most seemed new to politics and few knew the words of the "Internationale" when it was sung at the rally's conclusion. In this respect they were probably fairly typical of the many radical-minded youth who have been recruited and then rapidly disillusioned by the WRP's "Young Socialists" over the past few years.

The speakers harangued the crowd for about three hours. There seemed to be little enthusiasm among the audience, which sat passively, somewhat mesmerized by the theatrical delivery of the orators. Some were obviously bored (which is not surprising since the speakers scarcely mentioned such burning issues as the Labour government's wage controls or the British occupation of Ireland) while the Palais's bar carried on a flourishing trade at one end of the auditorium.

Only a tiny minority—the top Healyite cadres—are at all familiar with Hansen's detailed rebuttal of Healy's slanders (see *Intercontinental Press*, August 9, 1976), since the WRP ranks are actively discouraged from reading the papers published by other left-wing groups.

The audience was clearly considered to be sufficiently inexperienced, misinformed, or gullible to accept without question a leaflet, bearing the signature of the WRP Political Committee, with the incredible heading "Hansen Admits the Charges!".

The leaflet began:

> Joseph Hansen's latest article in *Intercontinental Press* (August 9, 1976) shows that after nearly eight months, he has been forced to confirm the major accusations contained in the indictment of the International Committee of the Fourth International. He has acted as an accomplice of the Stalinist GPU.

From Healy's point of view, there was little risk of his indoctrination session sparking embarrassing questions from the audience. In fact, the fanatical tenor of the meeting—one speaker, Georges Vereeken, warned his listeners that "there's an agent of the KGB in this room now"—was enough to intimidate any critical-minded young socialist into keeping his thoughts to himself until he reached the exit.

Only two people raised their hands against a resolution—erroneously reported by the *News Line* as being "unanimous"—which pledged "full support for the call by the International Committee of the Fourth International for a committee of inquiry into the crimes of the GPU in the Trotskyist movement." The inquiry, the resolution stated, "must investigate the conduct of Joseph Hansen and George Novack, leaders of the Socialist Workers Party of the United States, who the International Committee of the Fourth International has indicted as accomplices of the GPU."

Establishment of this "kangaroo court" body is presumably to be the next step in Healy's slander campaign.

Chairing the meeting was Mike Banda, who recently replaced Healy as the WRP's general secretary. In his opening speech, Banda (making a rare reference to the class struggle) launched off with an impassioned plea to "bring down the Labour government." To replace it with what? The WRP? Today, when revolutionary socialists are a small minority in the labour movement, the only real alternative to a Labour government is a Tory administration.

Banda then proceeded to the meeting's main purpose: the WRP's "indictment" against Hansen. This "crushing indictment against the revisionists," the general secretary said, made the meeting "an historic and inspiring occasion." Indeed, the "indictment" was deemed so important that "if the International Committee had done nothing else in its history but publish this testimony, its existence would have been justified," he said.

Banda then introduced the "veteran Belgian Trotskyist" Georges Vereeken.[3] Vereeken said that he had been "isolated" from the Trotskyist movement for the past forty years by the leadership of the Fourth International. But New Park Publica-

---

3. Georges Vereeken, author of *The GPU in the Trotskyist Movement*, is a member of the Tendance Marxiste Révolutionnaire Internationale [TMRI—International Revolutionary Marxist Tendency]. The leading figure in the TMRI is Michel Pablo. The International Secretariat of the TMRI issued a statement March 27–28, 1976, rejecting the "irresponsible accusations launched by the Healy tendency against Comrades Hansen and Novack of the Socialist Workers Party," and disassociated the TMRI from the position taken by Vereeken (*Intercontinental Press*, September 6, 1976).

tions, the publishing house of the WRP, had now ended this isolation by deciding to publish his book, *The GPU in the Trotskyist Movement*. Vereeken, who in his rambling speech reduced everything to GPU conspiracies, was presented to the bourgeois media at the WRP's press conference the next day.

Next came Vanessa Redgrave, who gave a fiery performance.

> Stalinist and revisionist worms are coming out from under the stone to attack the Workers Revolutionary party. Every effort is being made to sow dissension and incite people to abandon the WRP.

This revealed the main motives behind Healy's anti-Trotskyist witch-hunt. By denouncing leaders of the Fourth International as "agents" and "spies," Healy hopes that he can stop the disintegration of his "International Committee," which has experienced several major splits in recent years. The point was noted by one of the more astute commentators in the bourgeois press, Martin Walker. In his August 17 *Guardian* feature, Walker (noting Healy's new bloc with Robins and Vereecken) commented:

> the inroads Mr Hansen's SWP has made into the WRP-linked Workers' League in the US, and the stagnant membership and morale of the British WRP suggest that some kind of dramatic recruiting drive is now overdue.

Redgrave had especially harsh words for Ken Coates, a founder of the Bertrand Russell Peace Foundation, who (she explained) had written her several letters to dissuade her from endorsing Healy's campaign. Behind Ken Coates's "tears," she said, "is the knife." Moreover, "what Ken Coates does is just the other side of what the capitalists do; it is an attack from the other side."

Redgrave assured her audience that the "WRP would expose everyone of these scoundrels right through to the end."

Harold Robins, the "veteran American Trotskyist," followed Redgrave to the microphone. Robins dwelt at length on the revolt of the Levellers, a radical movement of artisans and small propertyowners, in 1649 during the English revolution. According to Robins, there was a revealing analogy between the "treachery" of the guards at the Levellers' rebel camp in May 1649 (when Oliver Cromwell finally succeeded in crushing the Leveller revolt) and the role of Joseph Hansen at Coyoacan, Trotsky's last place of exile in Mexico. The analogy seemed to be lost on the bulk of the audience.

Ironically, Robins—in a passing reference to the Moscow trials of the thirties—noted that Stalin employed bourgeois methods of "justice": "As we say in America, 'Give them a fair trial and hang them.'" Isn't this the very method now being employed by Healy's "International Committee" to frame up Hansen and Novack?

The evening's star was Healy, introduced by Banda as "in charge of cadre training in the party." The WRP's "indictment," Healy suggested, should be thrashed out in the bourgeois courts. "Let the SWP take me to court for slander and libel," he said. "I say Hansen's an agent."

The issue was important, Healy said, because the bourgeoisie was preparing to assassinate revolutionaries on a scale never before seen. The Tories, through the Privy Council, are planning to stage a Fraser-style coup,[4] he said. Then, Healy went on, there will be a general election with a Carter-type candidate to win over the middle class. To ensure victory, emergency laws will be passed and revolutionaries will be arrested. This arbitrary schema was strung together with all seriousness to justify the tissue of lies that constituted the bulk of this "Marxist educator's" speech.

The escalation of Healy's slander campaign brought protests from several left-wing groups here—and indications are that Healy's course will only lead him further into disrepute and contempt on the British left.

The August 19 issue of *Red Weekly*, the paper of the International Marxist Group, British section of the Fourth International, noted:

> As Healy tries to prop up the crumbling edifice of the WRP with the organisational meth-

---

4. This refers to the ousting of the Australian Labor government of Gough Whitlam in November 1975 by Governor General Sir John Kerr after a budget deadlock in the Senate. Conservative Malcolm Fraser was subsequently elected prime minister.

ods of Stalin, branding every political opponent as conspirators of the Special Branch or CIA, one can only wonder how long this not very amusing farce will continue to run.

In a leaflet entitled "The W.R.P. Leadership's Conspiracy Against Trotskyism" (handed out to those attending the WRP's London rally), the International Communist League, a grouping which considers itself Trotskyist, said:

> Today the WRP is "celebrating" the 36th anniversary of Trotsky's death—with an exhibition of the same Stalinist methods of slander and falsification against which Trotsky fought. The slander campaign against Joseph Hansen and George Novack waged by the WRP leadership is unparalleled in its vileness and unscrupulousness since the days of the Moscow Trials and the Stalinist campaign against Trotsky.

The August 9 issue of *Intercontinental Press* containing Hansen's article "Healy Caught in the Logic of the Big Lie" was sold outside the WRP rally by members of the International Marxist Group and by comrades selling the journal *Marxist Bulletin*.

With the help of G. Vereeken
VYSHINSKY RIDES AGAIN
By Charles van Gelderen

The following article appeared in the September 9 issue of *Red Weekly*, newspaper of the International Marxist Group, British section of the Fourth International. Charles van Gelderen has been a Trotskyist activist for forty years.

Since April of last year, the Workers Revolutionary Party headed by Gerry Healy has devoted a great deal of its time and apparently abundant financial resources to a campaign purporting to deal with "Security and the Fourth International." Altogether 26 articles on this subject appeared in the late *Workers Press*. Now the campaign has been reopened with the arrival in this country of Harold Robins, one of Trotsky's guards in Mexico, and George Vereeken from Belgium.

Nineteen of the articles which appeared in *Workers Press* between 14 August and 9 September have been re-published in a luxury paperback under the title *How the GPU murdered Trotsky—Security and the Fourth International*. At £3 per copy, the 1½ million unemployed workers of this country must be making a bee-line for the bookshops to purchase this masterpiece of lies and innuendoes.

Hardly anyone today doubts that Trotsky was murdered on the orders of Stalin, and that "Jacques Mornard" (Mercader) was a GPU agent. So the purpose of this campaign is not to prove the guilt of the Kremlin masters. What then lies behind this prodigious expenditure of time, effort and money? The real reason is to launch a ferocious attack on the Fourth International and its leadership.

Politically bankrupt, organisationally stagnant, Healy has seen his "International Committee" split, with first the return of the American Socialist Workers Party to a sympathetic relationship with the Fourth International headed by the United Secretariat, and the rupture with the Lambert group in France. This has left him almost completely isolated in his Clapham lair, with only a few stooges here and there, propped up by financial aid from the London centre.

Meanwhile, the Fourth International has continued to grow and now has sections or sympathising organisations in more than 42 countries. Its international leadership meets regularly, is elected by International Conferences (not appointed from "above") and are known, unlike the anonymous members of the "International Committee." In Britain, Healy lost his working class base with the expulsion of Thornett and his supporters, and there is an increasing turnover of members in the WRP as more and more of its adherents come up against its harsh and monolithic bureaucratic regime. It is here, in the political field, that we must look for the real motives of the Healy campaign.

While the campaign is aimed at the Fourth International as a whole, its principal targets have been Joseph Hansen and George Novack of the American SWP. This is no accident. For years they were Healy's closest associates. After the split in the International in 1953, Hansen and Novack devoted a great deal of their time and talents to helping Healy to build the Trotskyist movement in this country. In fact, one can state quite categorically that they materially assisted Healy's theoretical development.

In the May/August 1952 issue of *Labour Review* (Vol. 1, No. 2) there appeared an article by Gerry Healy. It was an in-depth review of Aneurin Bevan's *In Place of Fear*. Some of us, when we first read the article (subsequently published as a pamphlet), were not only impressed by its theoretical clarity but also surprised—we were not accustomed to think of Healy as a theoretician of any stature, but rather as a very competent conveyor-belt of other people's ideas.

Also, a second and more thorough reading revealed quite clearly that the article was written in the American rather than the British idiom. Careless editing left in words like "railroad" instead of "railways," "labour" was spelt in the American way without the "u" and so on. It therefore came as no great surprise when John Lawrence (at the time a member of the Political Committee and a staunch supporter of Healy) informed me that the article was, in fact, written by George Novack, and that Healy himself had proposed that it should be published under his name.

Perhaps there should be a Commission set up to enquire how many of Healy's articles were written by him or ghosted by comrades whom he now accuses of being GPU accomplices?

It is precisely because Healy was so close to comrades Hansen and Novack that he never forgave them for "deserting" him and his "International Committee," which is why he is carrying on this vile campaign against them.

Far from running away from Healy's charges, Hansen has met them head-on, and replied to them point-by-point in a number of articles in *Intercontinental Press*. Comrades of the WRP who are really interested in getting at the truth should not accept the garbled "quotations" appearing in *News Line* but should read for themselves what Hansen and Novack have written. We commend to their attention especially *Intercontinental Press* of 24 November 1975 in which Hansen answers the key allegations; the article by George Novack in the *Intercontinental Press* of December 1975—"Healy's Frame-up Against Joseph Hansen," and, above all, the full-length repudiation of Healy's facts in the issue of 9 August 1976—"Healy Caught in the Logic of the Big Lie," where Hansen completely demolishes Healy's fabrications.

In his frenzied attempt to destroy the Fourth International, Healy has found himself some strange allies, among them George Vereeken of Belgium, described in *News Line* of 16 August 1976 as a "veteran Trotskyist." This is interesting, as we are well acquainted with Vereeken's history as a "Trotskyist."

On 20 January 1938, Leon Trotsky wrote to his secretary Van:

> As for Cde. Ver, who unfortunately increasingly takes his distance from Marxism, it is extremely characteristic that he finds it possible to support Sneevliet in his totally opportunist struggle, now open, against the Fourth International and at the same time to conduct against us his ultra-leftist intransigence. . . . (*Bulletin Intérieur International*, édité par le Secrétariat International pour la Quatrième Internationale No. 3, début mai 1938, p. 10).

This "veteran Trotskyist" has, in fact, been a veteran opponent of the Fourth International since its inception. The following is an extract from the minutes of the first EC of the FI after the 1938 Founding Conference:

> Report of the Ver affair by Cde. L. (Belgium): He traced the history of Ver's drift away from us up to his recent resignation from the Belgian Party. Ver violently opposed the "French turn" in 1934 [entry of our French section into the SFIO[1]—CvG] and when in 1935 the Belgian section entered the Labour Party, he and his followers split. Later, the comrades who had entered the LP split away from that party . . . and re-united with V's organisation to form an independent party in Belgium. But V had not forgotten the old differences and regarded all those who supported the "French turn" (i.e. the overwhelming majority of our international organisation) as traitors. Friction speedily developed inside the new party and V began to develop differences with our international organisation on a whole variety of questions, Holland, Spain etc. *On nearly every issue that came up he allied himself with the most backward elements in the International.* [My emphasis—CvG.]
>
> Nevertheless, L. (Trotsky) did not immediately launch a campaign against him. . . . He waited until Ver. saw the Transitional Programme and realised he would have to take up a position on this practical question instead of spending time in fruitless polemics.

---

1. SFIO (Section Française de l'Internationale Ouvrière) French section of the Labor (Socialist) International, formal name of the Socialist Party of France.—*IP*

He was not prepared to take the step towards the masses indicated by the programme and gave in his resignation . . . it appears that he has been working for some time with Sneevliet and Molinier against our international organisation.

The general opinion was that Ver's resignation had removed a persistent obstructionist and confirmed sectarian from our ranks. . . .

But perhaps, after all, it is not so strange that Healy should find himself in close alliance with this veteran of anti-Trotskyism, for this is not the first time that they have worked in double harness.

In 1938 Healy was a leading member of the WIL[2] which rejected the efforts of an International Commission (Cannon, Shactman, Gould) to unite the various Trotskyist groupings in Britain into a single organisation prior to the Founding Conference. The WIL preferred to pursue its own sectarian path and linked itself with Vereeken, the Molinier group in France, and other sectarians who considered themselves more Trotskyist than Trotsky. These organisations published a "Draft Resolution for an International Conference" (*La Verité*, August 1939, No. 2)[3] which contained the following:

> The organisations condemn the bureaucratic system *by means of which Trotsky* [my emphasis—CvG] through the agency of the International Secretariat manoeuvres the B-L Groups,[4] renewing the system of the first years of the CI, a system which favoured the triumph of the bureaucracy over the Left Opposition.[5]

---

2. WIL—Workers International League, a group in Britain that claimed adherence to the Fourth International in 1938, but refused to merge with the Militant Labour League, official British section of the Fourth International.—IP

3. Can also be found in the Vereeken Archives at Harvard.

4. Groups that supported the Movement for the Fourth International, led by Trotsky, frequently called themselves Bolshevik-Leninists.—IP

5. Note the document's references to "the first years of the CI," i.e., when the Comintern was headed by Lenin and Trotsky, thus giving support to the mythology that Leninism fostered Stalinism.

> **LSA ADDS SIGNATURE TO STATEMENT**
>
> The following statement was issued by the League for Socialist Action in London September 10.
>
>
>
> We would like to add our names to those printed in ICP (September 6, 1976) protesting the slanderous campaign launched by the Workers Revolutionary Party against comrades Joe Hansen and George Novack.
>
> We consider this campaign—as we have already stated in *Socialist Action*—to be a frame-up in the Stalinist tradition against leading and tested revolutionary socialists.
>
> *Tony Roberts*

The same EC which rejected Vereeken also considered an application for "sympathetic affiliation" from the WIL. The EC declared itself as not opposed to sympathetic affiliation "in cases where an organisation is moving towards us, but in this case the WIL has shown by its actions that it is moving away from us. . . ."

In an interview in *News Line* (19 August 1976), Vereeken states: "My respect for him [Trotsky] increases as years go by. Trotsky's clear-sightedness about social, political and scientific development was unmatched." What a pity that he should have spent so many years, while Trotsky was alive and trying to build the Fourth International, opposing Trotsky on nearly every important issue; and that now, once again, we find him in the camp of those who are trying to destroy Trotsky's International.

Vereeken also bemoans the fact that Trotsky was "misled" about him by agents of the GPU. This probably refers to the rumour, which was rife at the time, that Vereeken had implicated Trotsky's son, Sedov, in the assassination by the GPU of Ignace Reiss.[6] Who were these GPU agents who so easily pulled the wool over Trotsky's eyes?

Vereeken denied these imputations in *Bulletin Intérieur*, No. 14, May 1938 (page 17), where he stated:

---

6. Ignace Reiss was a GPU agent who broke with Stalin in the summer of 1937 and joined the Fourth Internationalists. He was murdered by GPU agents near Lausanne, Switzerland, on September 4, 1937.—IP

"As a militant revolutionary, I have always opposed false accusations brought deliberately or otherwise against militant revolutionaries of whatever tendency." (Healy, please take note.) But in the same bulletin there is a statement signed "Cami 18.iii.38" which quotes Vereeken as having said: "*Si* le Vieux critique Sneevliet, il devrait avec beaucoup de raisons critiquer son propre fils." (*If* the Old Man [Trotsky] criticises Sneevliet, he should for many [good] reasons criticise his own son.)[7]

If Vereeken does not directly accuse Sedov, it seems he was given to loose talk. He does not seem to have learned anything from his own history.

We must now pose a question. Healy accuses Hansen of concealing his association (sic) with known GPU agents for 37 years. We must now ask Healy why he concealed his own connections with "Etienne" (Zborowski) from his followers. Healy revealed this association in a letter to this very same Joseph Hansen whom he now accuses, in true Vyshinsky style, of the foulest misdeeds, dated 14 March 1960.

Not only did Healy meet "Etienne" on several occasions (how often?), but this GPU agent actually stayed a night at Healy's house. In the kindness of his heart Healy even bought the poor man a pair of shoes. All this took place in 1946. Should there not now be an enquiry as to why Healy kept silent about this for 14 years?

Finally, I offer Healy a little bonus. The writer of these lines actually knew Trotsky's murderer "Jacson" and Sylvia Ageloff in Paris in 1938. The photo in *How the GPU Murdered Trotsky* of these two with Maria Craipeau was taken by me and is my copyright. Perhaps I will now be indicted as an accomplice of Joseph Hansen, George Novack, James P. Cannon, *et al!*

For a suitable donation to the Red Weekly Fighting Fund, I am prepared to let him have a whole list of people who were in Paris at that time and must have met Mornard. Then, like his infamous predecessor in the Kremlin, he can now stage a whole series of "Moscow Trials" and keep the pages of *News Line* filled with the sensational rubbish, thus avoiding the necessity of dealing with the real issues of the class struggle in Britain and the world.

London, 2 September 1976

---

7. Camille was one of the pseudonyms of Rudolf Klement, Secretary of the International Bolshevik-Leninists, murdered by Stalinist agents just before the 1938 Founding Conference. Trotsky was of the opinion that Sneevliet had mishandled the Reiss affair (see *Writings of Leon Trotsky (1937–38)*, p. 340—"Again on the Reiss Case").

Dave Deutschmann and Keith Olerhead beaten at SLL meeting

AUSTRALIAN HEALYITES REVIVE STALINIST METHODS OF 1930S

By Dave Holmes

The following article appeared in the October 21 issue of *Direct Action*, a revolutionary-socialist weekly published in Sydney, Australia.

SYDNEY—In a year of escalating violence and disruption aimed by the Socialist Labour League against other organisations on the left, SLL thuggery reached new heights with a premeditated attack on members of the Socialist Workers party (SWP) and the Spartacist League (SL) on Sunday October 17.

There were two main incidents involved in the attack, which occurred outside the Sydney Trades Hall, where the SLL (which publishes the weekly paper *Workers News*) was holding a rally. Both incidents and other minor jostling which took place were entirely the result of open assaults on the part of the SLL, directed personally by its leading members including SLL National Secretary Jim Mulgrew.

During the afternoon, two people, Dave Deutschmann of the SWP and Keith Olerhead of the SL, were quite badly injured, both as a result of unprovoked assault by SLL members. Deutschmann needed hospital attention as a result of a vicious, intentional kick to the side of the head as he lay on the ground from a previous blow. Olerhead suffered a heavy blow to the stomach and a full-force elbow in the face. Another SWPer and an SL member received bloody noses from the assaults of the SLL thugs.

The central reason for this hooliganism was the Socialist Labour League's refusal to permit members of other political organisations to hand out and sell literature to SLL members, supporters, and independents entering the SLL's meeting. This is despite the fact that absolutely no obstruction was being caused to entry to the Trades Hall. The SLL leaders also objected to photographs being taken by SL and SWP members although SLLer Nick Beams insisted on taking a considerable number of photos throughout the episode.

Of course, the SLL insists on its right to distribute its literature and to take photographs outside meetings called by other organisations such as the SWP. Consistency is not their strong point.

The first major incident took place around 3:30 p.m., half an hour before the Healyite meeting was due to start. Dave Deutschmann, national organisation secretary of the Socialist Youth Alliance, which is the youth organisation in political solidarity with the SWP, was the first SWP supporter present at the hall. He gave the following account of the earlier incident.

Deutschmann stated that he went to the Trades Hall on October 17 in order

> to sell the Socialist Workers party newspaper *Direct Action* and to distribute replies to the slanderous accusations of the SLL that George Novack and Joseph Hansen of the SWP [Socialist Workers party] in the U. S. were accomplices of the GPU. This was my democratic right.
>
> The first incident arose when Jim Mulgrew of the SLL went across Dixon Street and approached a member of the Spartacist League who had a camera. He grabbed hold of the camera and proceeded to abuse the Spartacist League member. Mulgrew wouldn't let go of the camera and started jostling a bit. One or two members of the SL went over and I went over also and insisted that he let go of the camera, that he had no right to be holding on to it. Mulgrew went back over to the Trades

END VIOLENCE IN THE WORKERS MOVEMENT!

The following statement is being circulated by the Australian Socialist Workers party and Spartacist League as part of a public campaign to protest the attacks by the Socialist Labour League. We have taken the text from the October 21 issue of *Direct Action* (P. O. Box 151, Glebe 2037, New South Wales, Australia).

Reports have come to our attention that Socialist Labour League (SLL) members have used physical violence against members of the Socialist Workers party (SWP) and the Spartacist League (SL). It has been reported that several members of the SWP and the SL were set upon and severely beaten in a completely unprovoked attack outside the Sydney Trades Hall on October 17. Other reports of intimidation of sellers of *Tribune, Direct Action, Australasian Spartacist,* and the *Socialist* in the past months and the disruption of SWP public meetings have also disturbed us.

These incidents lead us to make this statement in favor of the free exchange of differing views within the labor movement without fear of physical reprisal from anyone. Taking such a stand certainly does not mean repudiating the right of self-defence against violent attacks. It means making clear that differences among those fighting for social justice cannot be resolved by fists or other weapons. Any attempt to do so simply provides openings for police and other enemies of the workers movement to tear us apart.

Further, it certainly does not help us oppose the Government's use of violence against us if some of us use it against people who may not agree with our points of view. These attacks must stop and we must respect each other's democratic rights if we are to have an environment where there can be progress in the struggles of the oppressed.

We call on all individuals and organisations of the labor and radical movements to support this stand and add their signatures to this statement.

Hall. He had already made it quite clear that he didn't want members of the SL on the footpath at all. Supposedly, they had been obstructing it, but that just wasn't the case. I don't know what happened as soon as he went back, but within a few seconds he was screaming out, "Get Logan, get Logan," and he repeated this several times. An SLL member—I think his name was Peter Soley (fairly short with long dark hair)—who was trying to provoke incidents most of the time, as well as another SLLer and Greg Adler commenced hitting people. Keith Olerhead of the SL was punched several times. Also Brett Stebbing of the SL finished up getting a bloody nose.

Deutschmann's account of this incident is verified in statements by other members of the SWP and of the SL.

Leading SWP member Gordon Adler commented on the situation at this time: "None of these people were obstructing the passage of people attending the meeting, nor was there any attempt by any of those gathered outside the entrance to interfere with the conduct of the meeting in any way." Adler also remarks on the incident of the Spartacist League member and the camera. "I heard Jim Mulgrew tell Greg Adler, 'If he takes any more pictures, smash his camera and then smash his face in.'"

The second major violent incident took place about half an hour after the first. In the meantime, SLLers continuously jostled, threatened, abused, and even spat at SL and SWP members. The second major assault occurred after SWPer Jon West was pushed by an SLL member against a parked car when West tried to hand out literature to people coming into the meeting. John Percy, *Direct Action* editor, took photos of the incident from Dixon Street.

A leading member of the Spartacist League, Bill Logan, related that Percy was then approached by several SLLers. He recounted that Jim Mulgrew, accompanied by several thugs, took the lead in trying to take the camera away from him. He explained that Mulgrew removed his glasses, discarded his cigarette and then hit Percy in the mouth.

From that point, things moved very fast. Logan said that he saw Dave Deutschmann lying on the ground groaning loudly and being kicked by SLLers, including Greg Adler. Logan said that shortly afterwards he himself was struck on the chin by one SLL thug.

> I tried to move towards John Percy [Dave Deutschmann recounted], and it was then that a tall blond SLLer moved in very quickly and looked as though he was going to get pretty vicious so I retreated to the other side of the road. He ran straight at me and hit me on the side of the head. There was someone behind him too, but I didn't see who it was. Before this character hit me I saw Greg Adler coming from the other direction screaming, "Get him!" After I was hit the first time, I went down to my knees and then Adler punched me on the other side of the head. This put me right down on the footpath and I tried to protect my chest and head. I know that at this stage I was kicked once in the head because that is the thing that I felt most, but I was also hit elsewhere. I also got kicked on the shoulder because there is a boot mark there. In short, I have bruises on the arms and thighs, so I must have been kicked and punched numerous times.

Jon West reported:

> I saw one SLLer approach Keith Olerhead and say something to the effect of "If you do it again I'll kill you." I clearly remember the words "I'll kill you." He turned, as if to go, and suddenly smashed his elbow into Olerhead's face. Olerhead fell to the ground.

This latest, and most serious, hooligan attack by the SLL against its political opponents peacefully exercising their democratic rights is part of a continuing pattern. They have regularly resorted to violence and disruption to settle political differences in the left and labor movement.

In this the Australian SLL are merely following the example of their parent organisation in Britain, the Workers Revolutionary party (formerly the Socialist Labour League) led by Gerry Healy.

On November 17, 1966, Ernest Tate was selling literature outside an SLL meeting in London's Caxton Hall. Six young SLL toughs under Healy's personal direction jumped Tate, smashing his glasses and bringing him to the pavement. They then repeatedly kicked him in the head, genitals, and kidneys. Tate had to be hospitalised. Healy later took legal action to intimidate several left papers which publicised an account of Tate's beating. This year, the SLL in Australia has further stepped up its acts of disruption and violence against left opponents.

Gerry Healy visited Australia in 1975 and spoke at a number of meetings organised by the SLL. At a meeting for Healy at the Sydney Trades Hall on June 16, members of the SWP (or Socialist Workers League as it then was) and the SL were distributing their literature outside the Goulburn Street entrance.

At one point Jim Mulgrew, the SLL's national secretary, was seen to point to the SL people standing on the steps. About six SLL thugs then tried

---

AGAINST HEALY'S FRAME-UP OF HANSEN AND NOVACK!

Following the publication of the statement denouncing the Healyite slander campaign against Joseph Hansen, George Novack, and the American Socialist Workers party (*Intercontinental Press*, September 6), additional signatures have been added to the document.

These include D. R. O'Connor Lysaght on behalf of the Movement for a Socialist Republic, Irish section of the Fourth International; and John Bryne, a veteran of the Irish Trotskyist movement of the 1940s.

Also, for the Revolutionary Communist party, Chinese section of the Fourth International: Lee See, Fong Shing, Lin Yuen, Kong Chi, and Yip Ning. The first four have been militants in the Chinese Trotskyist movement for more than thirty years.

In May sellers of the SLL paper *Workers News* harassed a woman Communist party member selling *Tribune* at Sydney's central station. SLLers later spat on other CPA members who were there to protect their sellers.

In July of this year the U. S. socialist Willie Mae Reid toured Australia for the Socialist Workers party. Her main Sydney meeting at the Teachers Federation on July 15 was subject to noisy disruption by thugs from the SLL and its youth group, the Young Socialists.

DIRECT ACTION

SYDNEY, July 15: Healyite thugs disrupt meeting for Willie Mae Reid.

to muscle the Spartacists off the steps and began punching them when they stood their ground. Bill Logan received a punch in the face. The SLL claimed that people were being "obstructed," but the way in to the Trades Hall was quite clear.

At assembly area for the Sydney May Day this year the SLL leaders attempted to prohibit other groups from distributing literature and selling papers to their contingent. Sellers of *Direct Action, Australasian Spartacist*, and the *Socialist* were all abused and threatened with physical violence if they attempted to sell to the SLL group.

There have been numerous incidents this year where SLL members have harassed and abused (usually in very sexist terms) sellers of other left papers. Sellers of *Direct Action* in the suburbs have been jostled by SLL members, had their toes trodden on, and papers knocked out of their hands.

During the question time the SLL-YS group of about 10 people yelled and screamed at the speaker and the chair. They stood up and chanted and waved their literature in the air. They were supported by nobody else in the audience and refused to obey the chairperson. Afterwards a broad cross-section of the audience signed a statement condemning this hooliganism.

Several other of Reid's meetings in Sydney and Canberra were also the subject of disruption by the SLL.

These examples show that the resort to physical violence by the Socialist Labour League is not simply a recent development. It has a lengthy history. In the October 17 assault on the SWP and the SL, two people were badly beaten. Next time the consequences could be truly tragic. Such violations of the norms of democracy in the left and labor movement must be condemned as widely as possible to ensure that there are no repetitions.

Text of official statement

VEREEKEN REGRETS HEALYITE TAINT IN ENGLISH EDITION OF HIS BOOK

The following statement appeared in the August issue of *le pouvoir aux travailleurs* (Power to the Workers), a copy of which was just received in New York. *Le pouvoir aux travailleurs* is the monthly mimeographed journal of the Belgian section of the Revolutionary Marxist Tendency (RMT). The statement bears the signature of that body and thus can be taken to represent the views of its leader, Georges Vereeken, whose book was subjected to gross misuse in its English translation.

Internationally, the leading figure of the RMT is Michel Pablo, who disagrees with the support offered by Vereeken to the slanderous campaign currently being waged by the Healyite "International Committee" against Trotsky's associates, Joseph Hansen and George Novack.

The translation from the French is by *Intercontinental Press*.

A year after it was originally published in France by Pensée Universelle (Paris), our comrade Vereeken's book has just appeared in an English translation put out by New Park Publications in London and illustrated with photocopies of a score of documents.

It goes without saying that the Belgian section of the Revolutionary Marxist Tendency is pleased that the way has thus been opened up for this book to reach the immense English-reading public.

We know that New Park Publications represents an English Trotskyist tendency, numerically the strongest one, we might add. It is known under the name of the "Healy tendency," and we have differences with it, as the publishers themselves say explicitly in the foreword to this English edition, signed "International Committee of the Fourth International." This is another aspect of the publication of this book that is pleasing to us. Differences have not prevented collaboration between heirs of the "Communist Left Opposition," the tendency that always opposed the Stalinist deviation from international communism, the tendency that was rather lightmindedly dubbed "Trotskyist," as if it itself were a deviation from communism. This fact is all the more pleasing to us since such collaboration points away from a long and pernicious tradition of splits, sterile factional struggles, and fragmentation.

Nonetheless, we still have to express two regrets about this edition in English. The first is that the preface to the original book, signed by J. Impens, was eliminated in the English edition. Why was this done? The second concerns the caption accompanying the picture of Joseph Hansen (of the Socialist Workers party of the United States), saying "indicted as an accomplice of the GPU."

We know that Hansen has in fact been so accused, but we do not think it was appropriate to mention this in the book, which does not deal at all with this militant. Like the International Committee, we are for forming a commission of inquiry, which should deliver a verdict on this

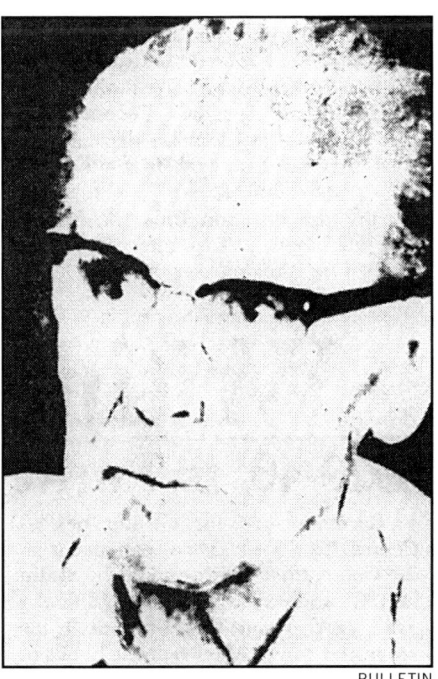
Vereeken

case. But, precisely for this reason, it seems out of place to already include Hansen's name, his picture, and this accusation in a book forever alongside the sinister Zborowsky, whose guilt is well and firmly established. It is true, on the other hand, that Hansen has unfortunately rejected even considering the idea of a commission of inquiry and that he has refused in advance to collaborate with such a commission, although it would give him a dream of an opportunity to clear himself. Nonetheless, we thought it necessary to call attention to this unfortunate fly in the ointment.

*The Belgian Section of the
Revolutionary Marxist Tendency*

The hard way

VEREEKEN BEGINS LEARNING ABOUT HEALYISM

By Joseph Hansen

Georges Vereeken, the author of *The GPU in the Trotskyist Movement*, has felt it necessary to indicate publicly his discomfort over two embellishments in the English edition of his book:

1. The insertion of a photograph of me, next to a photograph of GPU agent Zborowski, bearing a caption that reads in full as follows:

"Above: Joseph Hansen of the American Socialist Workers Party, indicted as an accomplice of the GPU

"Right: Marc Zborowski ('Etienne') after his arrest in the US"

2. The removal of a preface, signed by Jef Impens, that was included in the original French edition.

Vereeken's disavowal of responsibility for these alterations in the English edition of his book is less than forthright. He does not even speak as the injured author of a book that has been made subject to gross misinterpretation, but lets his complaint be voiced by "The Belgian Section of the Revolutionary Marxist Tendency."

Nonetheless, some meaningful conclusions can be drawn from the little that is said.

For instance, with regard to the elimination of the preface written by Jef Impens, the statement asks, "Why was this done?"

The implications are (a) that it was done without Vereeken's consent, (b) that Vereeken has been unable to ascertain through personal inquiry why it was done, (c) that he has no recourse but to make the matter public in hope that others, not involved in his transactions with the "Healy tendency," can cast light on the reason for this unilateral and arbitrary action.

Similar conclusions follow from the protest over the inclusion of my photograph and the lying caption accompanying it. As the statement declares, *Vereeken's book does not even mention the charges leveled by the Healyites against me.*

There is a third significant difference from the French original that is referred to only in passing. This is the inclusion of a foreword signed by the "International Committee of the Fourth International." How an introduction cooked up by this nameless and faceless body of frame-up artists came to be published in the English edition of Vereeken's book would seem to demand explanation.

Perhaps Vereeken can provide the necessary details. Did he agree with New Park Publications that a foreword of this kind was to be included? Who were the individuals he dealt with? Was he given an opportunity to read the text before it was published? Does he acknowledge responsibility for what the foreword says? Or was it included without his knowledge or consent? Why is Vereeken silent on this important point?

The significance of these questions can be judged in the light of the following sentences in the foreword written by the infamous Healyite committee:

> Sneevliet, murdered by the Nazis during the war, became the target of an especially vicious slander campaign after accusing Zborowski to his face to being a GPU agent.
>
> A sinister echo of these same slanders is renewed today by anti-Trotskyist elements gathered together under the Brussels-based umbrella organisation known as the "Unified Secretariat" of Ernest Mandel and the Socialist Workers Party (USA) of Joseph Hansen and George Novack.
>
> As soon as the International Committee of the Fourth International began to raise questions of elementary revolutionary security, it

was derided with the same insults and smears. The purpose is clear: to maintain the conspiracy of silence against the revelation of the full circumstances of Trotsky's murder and other GPU crimes. Vereeken records how at the Belgian revisionist conference in 1964 Ernest Mandel repeatedly tried to stop him reading out a document on the Zborowski affair.

Vereeken's book confirms the findings of *Security and the Fourth International* compiled by the International Committee of the Fourth International.

Security and the Fourth International is a poisonous brew that seeks to smear me, George Novack, and other leading figures in the Trotskyist movement as "accomplices of the GPU." The lies and falsifications worked up in the Healyite kitchen have been thoroughly exposed and refuted.* They are part of a frame-up put together in the tradition of the perpetrators of the infamous Moscow Trials.

The final sentence quoted above from the foreword to the English edition indicates the real interest of the Healyites in Vereeken's book. They concluded that the book could be converted, with a few deft touches, into "confirmation" of the frame-up charges directed against well-known leaders of the world Trotskyist movement. On that basis it is easy to understand why these specialists in the technique of the big lie fixed up Vereeken's book the way they did.

1. My photograph was placed in the book together with a caption composed in the manner of the late Senator McCarthy so as to make it appear that *Vereeken* "associated" me with GPU agent Zborowski.

2. A new foreword was written to make it appear that *Vereeken*, whose manuscript had been completed in 1972, had "confirmed" the newly hatched frame-up "findings" of the "International Committee." That the time sequence violated the most elementary rules of logic was of little concern to the Healyite forgers of "evidence." (Conceivably these forgers could "confirm" Vereeken's previous "findings" directed against Trotsky; but Vereeken's conclusions about Trotsky could not confirm their later "findings" directed against me, Novack, etc.)

3. The preface by Jef Impens was eliminated because it contained nothing whatsoever about me or George Novack, still less approval of the mud thrown at us by the "International Committee."

Instead, Impens described Vereeken's life from the viewpoint of an ardent admirer and stated the main purpose of his book, which was to try to demonstrate that Trotsky, unduly influenced by GPU agents in his staff, had made harsh—and incorrect—judgments of Vereeken's political positions on various points.

Here are two key paragraphs from the preface by Impens, indicating the theme of Vereeken's book:

> As a leader of the Revolutionary Socialist party, he was in touch with the International Secretariat led by the exiled Trotsky. Nonetheless, like his Dutch counterpart Sneevliet and many others (Nin, Landau . . .), he ended up quarreling with the "Old Man" over a certain number of points, in which—in all objectivity—history has shown him to have been right, if only by the fact that Trotsky himself later revised his own positions along similar lines, which came to light much later.
>
> A reconciliation never occurred, however, because another factor entered in: the infiltration of the secret Stalinist police in the so-called "Trotskyist" movement. Trotsky was not sufficiently distrustful on this point. The circumstances of his death prove it. This was decidedly one of his weakest sides. He had blind confidence in the imposters who

---

* See in particular: "On Healy's 'Investigation'—What the Facts Show" by Joseph Hansen; in the November 24, 1975, issue of *Intercontinental Press*, page 1636. "Healy's Frame-up Against Joseph Hansen" by George Novack; in the December 8, 1975, issue of *Intercontinental Press*, page 1710. "A Statement on Healy's Frame-up of Hansen and Novack" by Betty Hamilton and Pierre Lambert; in the March 15, 1976, issue of *Intercontinental Press*, page 397. "Healy's Smear Against Trotsky's Last Collaborators" by Sam Gordon; in the May 24, 1976, issue of *Intercontinental Press*, page 854. "Healy Caught in the Logic of the Big Lie" by Joseph Hansen; in the August 9, 1976, issue of *Intercontinental Press*, page 1188. "The Verdict: 'A Shameless Frame-up' (A Statement on the Slanders Circulated by the Healy Group Against Hansen, Novack, and the Socialist Workers Party)" in the September 6, 1976, issue of *Intercontinental Press*, page 1254.

had in mind only one aim—to break up the Left Communist Opposition completely by setting everyone against everyone else, using any means. Thus it was that they succeeded in making Trotsky believe that the Sneevliets, the Vereekens, and *tutti quanti* were nothing but sectarians, unstable types, etc.

These paragraphs, which are completely faithful to Vereeken's views, stood in the way of using the book to bolster the frame-up charges against me and Novack. That was why the Healyites decided to suppress them by eliminating the entire preface. In its place they inserted a new preface designed to shore up the frame-up.

Vereeken has joined the Healyites in calling for a commission of inquiry to investigate me, Novack, the Socialist Workers party, and various other victims of their frame-up. Let Vereeken begin his investigatory work at home.

Vereeken's first responsibility is to ascertain why the alterations he deplores in the English edition of his book were made, and who ordered them. His second responsibility is to investigate the way the Healyites have used his doctored-up book to advance a Stalinist-type frame-up.

I can assure Vereeken that whatever steps he takes in this direction will prove to be educational. It is to be hoped that he will keep the public informed of his progress.

'THESE ATTACKS MUST STOP'

The following statement condemning the use of violence in the labor movement is being circulated by the Australian Socialist Workers party and Spartacist League. Appended is the initial list of signers.

Reports have come to our attention that Socialist Labour League (SLL) members have used physical violence against members of the Socialist Workers Party (SWP) and the Spartacist League (SL). It has been reported that several members of the SWP and the SL were set upon and severely beaten in a completely unprovoked attack outside the Sydney Trades Hall on October 17. Other reports of intimidation of sellers of the Tribune, Direct Action, Australasian Spartacist and the Socialist in the past months and the disruption of the SWP public meetings have also disturbed us.

These incidents lead us to make this statement in favor of the free exchange of differing views within the labor movement without fear of physical reprisal from anyone. Taking such a stand certainly does not mean repudiating the right of self-defence against violent attacks. It means making clear that differences among those fighting for social justice cannot be resolved by fists or other weapons. Any attempt to do so simply provides openings for police and other enemies of the workers movement to tear us apart.

Further, it certainly does not help us oppose the Government's use of violence against us if some of us use it against people who may not agree with our points of view. These attacks must stop and we must respect each other's democratic rights if we are to have an environment where there can be progress in the struggles of the oppressed.

We call on all individuals and organisations of labor and radical movements to support this stand and add their signatures to this statement.

Brian Aarons (Sydney district organiser, Communist Party of Australia)
Eric Aarons (joint national secretary, CPA)
John Aarons (CPA)
Christine Allsopp (secretary, Sydney University Arts Society)
Jim Alexander
Mick Armstrong (South Coast organiser, International Socialists)
Phillip Bain (president, La Trobe University Students Representative Council)
Libby Barratt
Laurie Bebbington (women's officer, Australian Union of Students)
Gary Bennett (president, SU Labor Club)
Barbara Bound (Tasmanian State president, CPA)
Steve Bolt (Sydney University AUS secretary)
J.M. Brown (senior vice-president, South Coast Labor Council and organiser, Building Workers Industrial Union)
Dick Buchhorn
John Campbell (secretary, University of Queensland Union)
Peter Carruthers (Teachers Federation delegate to South Coast Trades and Labor Council)
Adrian Chan (lecturer in politics, University of NSW)
Ernie Chaples (lecturer in government, Sydney University)
Lloyd Churchward (reader in political science, Melbourne University)
Peter Cockcroft (South Coast organiser, CPA)
Mick Counihan (editorial collective, *Intervention*)
Peter Crawford (past president, NSW Young Labor Council)
Greg Cure (AUS chairperson, University of Tasmania)
Jenny Eastwood (women's officer, NSW Institute of Technology Students Association)
Grant Evans (editorial collective, *Intervention*)
Gwyn Farr (Communist League)
Terry Farr (Communist League)
Doug Fraser (AUS Queensland regional organiser)
Jim Frazer (Victorian State secretary, Australian Railways Union)
J. Goddard (Victorian State secretary, Liquor and Allied Trades Union)
Goh Siong Hoe (*Malaysian Socialist Review*)

Geoff Goullet (CPA)
Phil Griffiths (editor, *The Battler*)
Hugh Hamilton (Queensland State secretary, BWIU)
Joe Harris (Queensland BWIU organiser)
Trevor Hart (Brisbane organiser, CPA)
Kevin Healy (ALP councillor, Fitzroy)
Phil Herrington (organiser, CPA)
Andrew Hewett (co-ordinator, CICD)
Garry Hill (Adelaide Anarchists, ex-SLL member)
Ali Kazak
Dave Kerin (Libertarian Socialist Federation)
Peter King (member SU Trainee Teachers executive)
William Legge (La Trobe University SRC member)
Sian Lewis (secretary, Griffith University Union)
Steve Lewis (for SU Communist Group)
Bill Logan (for the Spartacist League)
John McCarthy (for the Communist League)
Anna McCormack (chairperson, University of Queensland women's rights committee)
Simon Marginson (co-editor, *Axis*)
Anthony Maron (secretary, Friends of Palestine)
Michael Matteson (Australasian Society of Engineers shop steward)
George Molnar (lecturer in department of general philosophy, Sydney University)
Fred Moore (central council, Miners Federation)
Michael Munday (president, University of Tasmania Union)
Judy Mundey (Sydney district organiser, CPA)
Judy Munro (co-editor, *Axis*)
Peter Murphy (co-ordinator, Alternative News Service)
Ted Murphy (secretary, Libertarian Socialist Federation)
George Murray (president, South Coast Trades and Labor Council)
Merv Nixon (secretary, South Coast Trades and Labor Council)
Tom O'Lincoln (national executive, International Socialists)
Dan O'Neill (lecturer, English department, University of Queensland)
Tasma Ockenden (president, Australian Union of Students
Joe Palmada (joint national secretary, CPA)
David Patch (president, Sydney University Students Representative Council)
Maxwell Pearce (executive member, NSW Young Labor Council).
Jim Percy (for the Socialist Workers Party)
Ron Poulsen (for the Communist League)
Barbara Ramjan (welfare officer, Sydney University Students Representative Council)
Abed Rizk (general secretary, United Arab Workers)
Mavis Robertson (joint national secretary, CPA)
Sarah Sheehan (NSW regional organiser, AUS)
Heinze Schutte (senior lecturer in sociology, La Trobe University)
Paul Slape (organiser, Municipal Officers Association)
Lesley Stern (lecturer, La Trobe University)
Peter Symon (general secretary, Socialist Party of Australia)
Bemie Taft (Victorian State secretary, CPA)
Anne Talve (AUS NSW regional women's organiser)
Sandy Thomas (co-editor, *Axis*)
Peter Tiernan
Frans Timmerman (executive member, Palestine-Australia Solidarity Committee)
Ted Tripp (secretary, Victoria Labor College)
Edith Turnewitsch
Peter Wertheim (lecturer in philosophy, University of Queensland)
Faye Westwood (editor, *Honi Soit*)
Harry Whitfield, (Seamen's Union delegate to South Coast Trades and Labor Council)
F. J. William (Victorian State secretary, Federated Engine Drivers and Firemen's Association)
Ivor Williams
Geoff Windon (secretary, Philip branch of the ALP)
S. Woodbury (president, Port Kemble Painters and Deckers Union)
A. N. Zeeno

BOOKS
VEREEKEN'S DIFFERENCES WITH TROTSKY
Reviewed by George Breitman

This is one of the most irresponsible books about the Trotskyist movement ever written by a former member. Its author, Georges Vereeken (he used to spell it Vereecken in the 1930s), is now eighty years old. Forty years ago he was a leader of the Belgian section of the movement that became the Fourth International. Politically, he is remembered as an inveterate sectarian and centrist. As a result he came into sharp conflict with the international leaders of the movement, both Leon Trotsky and the International Secretariat. On two occasions when his views did not prevail, he split away from the movement—the first time in 1935, when the Belgian section voted at a national conference to enter the Belgian Social Democracy; and again in 1938, two years after he had returned to the section,[1] when Trotsky and the IS made it plain that they wanted to found the Fourth International at an international conference being held that year.

These were not the only disputes Vereeken had with Trotsky in the thirties—just the ones over which he walked out. And they were not the only times he walked out: from his book we learn that the long-suffering Belgian section readmitted him two more times after World War II. His stay each time was brief, and today he is a member of the Revolutionary Marxist Tendency, led by M. Pablo.

Politically, Vereeken has not changed much. He is still incensed about his disputes with Trotsky and the IS in the thirties, and his book is an attempt to prove that he was right and they were wrong, dishonest and bureaucratic. It is filled therefore with long excerpts from what he and his adversaries said and wrote at meetings, in internal bulletins and newspaper articles, etc. Vereeken's style and his form of presentation can only confuse the uninitiated reader, but a useful book might have resulted from an objective discussion of the political and theoretical issues raised in the Vereeken-Trotsky disputes.

> *The GPU in the Trotskyist Movement*, by Georges Vereeken. London: New Park Publications, 1976, 390 pp., £3.00.

Unfortunately the number of people who would want to read so specialized a book is rather limited. Vereeken has met that problem by jazzing the thing up, as the title shows, through the addition of a theme that overshadows everything else. Briefly stated, it is that the leadership of the Fourth International and its predecessors in the thirties was infiltrated by a series of agents of Stalin's secret police in such numbers and so effectively that they were able, in addition to their other crimes, to dominate and disrupt the internal life of the organization, causing frequent splits and "factional struggles in which the GPU agents called the tune," and in other ways rendering it impotent as a political force. That, says Vereeken, is "how our movement was manipulated from Moscow." The corollary is that this explains why Trotsky, misinformed by these Stalinist provocateurs, disagreed so often with Vereeken (and with Landau, Rosmer, Nin, Sneevliet, and other people admired and defended by Vereeken, who all broke from the Fourth International).

It is well known, of course, that Stalin's agents sought to infiltrate Trotsky's secretariat and the

---

1. See the discussion about Vereeken between Trotsky and James P. Cannon in Mexico, March 1938, where Cannon complained about Vereeken being chosen political secretary of the Belgian section immediately after his return to the movement in 1936. *Writings of Leon Trotsky (1937–38)*, pp. 377–79.

Trotskyist movement from the time he was exiled to Turkey in 1929 until they succeeded in assassinating him in Mexico in 1940. The chief provocateur was the Ukrainian-Polish Marc Zborowski (Etienne), who joined the French Trotskyist movement in 1934, wormed his way into the confidence of Trotsky's son, Leon Sedov, and regularly supplied the GPU with information used to assassinate Sedov and several other leaders. His role as a GPU agent was not uncovered until 1955, when he was convicted of perjury in the U.S. Zborowski and other agents like him undoubtedly would have liked to play the major political role inside the Trotskyist movement that Vereeken attributes to them, but there is no evidence whatever to show they played more than secondary political roles.[2] Lacking such evidence does not stop Vereeken: he is good at spinning a fantasy. Since the number of known Stalinist agents is small, he expands the list to make a more substantial scenario. Let us now examine the five names he has added.

1. M. Mill (also known as J. Obin and Okun). A Ukrainian, he emigrated to Palestine and then France, where he joined the Communist party's Jewish Language Group in the 1920s. By 1929 he had joined the Oppositionist *Contre le Courant* group and after that the Oppositionist group around *La Verité*. He was a founding member of the French section and a member of its Jewish Group. Because he knew Russian, he was chosen to represent the Russian section on the IS in 1930 when Sedov was unable to leave Turkey for France. Dissatisfaction with his performance led to his removal from this post, whereupon he went over to the Stalinists in 1932.

2 and 3. The Sobolevicius brothers (Roman Well,

How Trotsky Viewed Vereeken's Approach

Vereekenism, a specific blend of sectarianism and centrism, was analyzed on several occasions by Leon Trotsky between 1933, when the call for a Fourth International was first advanced, and 1938, when the Fourth International was founded. These political articles and letters will be found in the Pathfinder series *Writings of Leon Trotsky* for the years 1934-35, 1935-36, and 1937-38. What follows are some excerpts from those articles about Vereeken's method that almost could have been written about Vereeken's 1975 book.

"Formalist minds [like Vereecken's] frequently seize upon altogether secondary questions to inflate them out of all proportion.
". . . his anti-Marxist journalist thought . . . flies from reality and concerns itself with phantoms.
". . . mountains of errors, distortions, unwarranted accusations and complete misconceptions on the part of Comrade Vereecken.
"[Vereecken should] strive to orient himself not in accord with his own texts but in accord with the reality of the struggle" (March 2, 1935).

"[Vereecken's negative qualities]: the absence of balance and a sense of proportion, the inclination to excessive exaggeration, indiscipline, and capriciousness—all these traits are characteristic of sectarianism" (November 17, 1935).

"[Vereecken combines] absolutely Menshevist ideas [on Spain with] leaps to the left, extravaganzas, and caprices" (December 24, 1937).

"The world appears to be upside down in Ver.'s head.
"[He engages in] factious distortion with regard to badly interpreted, isolated quotations" (January 2, 1938).

"It is necessary to . . . make him understand that one cannot practice politics with flights of fancy, improvisations, and petty personal combinations" (June 12, 1938).

"[Vereecken's] state of frenzy is not at all an individual quirk. Rather, it is characteristic of a particular political state of mind. This is what the draft Transitional Program says about it: 'Since sectarians, as in general every kind of blunderer and miracle-man, are toppled by reality at each step, they live in a state of perpetual exasperation, complaining about the "regime" and "the methods," and ceaselessly wallowing in small intrigues'" (June 22, 1938).

"The ancient Greeks used to parade drunken helots in order to turn their youth away from alcoholism. [Vereecken is among] the helots of sectarianism who fashion their grimaces and leaps as if with the special aim of repelling our youth from sterile and annoying sectarianism" (July 18, 1938).

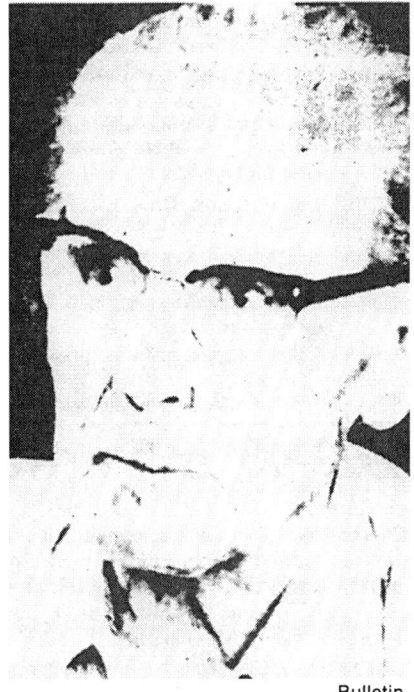
Bulletin

VEREEKEN

---

2. Vereeken unwittingly supports this estimate when he writes, "I know of no political document of theirs of any real value" (p. 27).

later called Robert Soblen, and Senin, later called Jack Soble). They were Latvians or Lithuanians. Senin reportedly joined the Left Opposition in the USSR in 1927. Later, in 1929, both were members of a Left Opposition group in Germany, and became leaders of the German section in 1931. In 1932 they began to criticize the Opposition's irreconcilable attitude to Stalinism and they split away, joining the German CP in January 1933 on the eve of Hitler's ascent to power. In 1957, Senin testified that he became a GPU agent in 1931.

Vereeken puts all three of these in the category of Stalinist infiltrator, part of the grand pattern of GPU subversion. But the facts point to something else.

There were more than a few politically unstable and irresponsible types who came around the Trotskyist movement in its early years. It took time and experience before their real quality became known—in fact, in some cases before they themselves realized they were in the wrong organization. Some dropped into inactivity and some became syndicalists or Social Democrats, while others became Stalinists, out of corrupt and careerist considerations or even out of political conviction. (This was during the Stalinist "third period," and similar defections were taking place at the same time among Oppositionists in the USSR, who were drawn to Stalinism by its ultraleftist line, and who were far more serious types than the Mills, Wells or Senins.) Mill became a Stalinist in 1932 because he was an opportunist, Well and Senin in 1933 perhaps for more ideological reasons, but that doesn't at all mean they *entered* the Trotskyist movement as GPU agents, which is Vereeken's contention.

Vereeken admits that neither Trotsky nor anyone else up to now believed Mill had been a Stalinist agent when he joined, but he says that Trotsky was "fooled" and the he, Vereeken, can prove this by "historical hindsight": Looking back, he sees that Mill always behaved the way Vereeken thinks a GPU agent would act—provoking splits, embittering personal relations, acting "more Trotskyist than Trotsky," etc. By such "logic," of course, Vereeken himself could fall under suspicion as a GPU agent—after all, he holds the all-time international record for the number of times he not only provoked but actually led splits from the movement.

As for Senin and Well, all that Vereeken knows about them he learned from Isaac Deutscher's The *Prophet Outcast* (1963). Deutscher reported that in 1957, when Senin was convicted in the United States as a Soviet spy, he testified that he had become a GPU agent in 1931. Deutscher was quite dubious about the accuracy of that date,[3] but in any case Vereeken has no other date than 1931 to go on. On what basis, then, does he set the time Senin became a GPU agent as 1927 or 1929? Never mind, Trotsky was wrong again and Vereeken *knows*. Along the way he forgets to ask himself, if Senin and Well were GPU agents in 1932 before they openly joined the CP, why (unlike Mill) was their course of action different from the one he thinks GPU agents follow? Why didn't they remain inside the Trotskyist movement, where they already had the authority of leadership in a national section, and, acting more Trotskyist than Trotsky, continue the disruptive work that they could not do on the outside? Why would they just walk out, or why would the GPU want them to just walk out, if they had joined in order to be able to destroy the movement from within?

4. Henri Lacroix (party name of Francisco García Lavid). In the twenties, a member of the Spanish Socialist party and then the Spanish CP. In exile in Belgium, he helped set up the first Spanish Left Opposition group, and then returned to Spain, where he became the section's general secretary until 1932, when he was replaced by Nin. He led a struggle against Nin, seeking Trotsky's support, until he was expelled in 1933. He then tried to get back into the CP and when that failed applied for readmission to the SP, which accepted him after he renounced his Trotskyist past. He was killed during the Spanish Civil War.[4]

To our knowledge, nobody, absolutely nobody

---

3. "Yet his [Senin-Sobolevicius's] whole correspondence with Trotsky and the circumstances of their break throw doubt on the veracity of this part of his confession. Sobolevicius himself broke with Trotsky after he had openly and repeatedly expressed important political disagreements, which was not the manner in which an *agent provocateur* would behave. Trotsky denounced him in the end as a Stalinist, but did not believe that he was an *agent provocateur*. Whatever the truth . . ." (*The Prophet Outcast*, p. 26).

4. According to a note by Pierre Broué, Lacroix was a commissar in the Republican Army, "reported to have been hanged a few meters from the French frontier by men of the Lister division." *La revolution espagnole* by Leon Trotsky, 1975, p. 761. The Lister division was dominated by the Stalinists.

has ever charged Lacroix with being a Stalinist or a GPU agent—except Vereeken. He has the right to dislike Lacroix and, as a partisan of Nin, to dislike him doubly, but what right has he to pin the "agent" label on him? Here is a sampling of his reasons: (1) When Mill was taken off the IS as the Russian section's representative, Lacroix wrote the IS saying the Spanish section wanted to put him back as its representative. Vereeken omits the well-documented fact that this was the position of the whole Spanish leadership, not just of Lacroix, preferring to speculate instead that Lacroix was "working in agreement with this agent" (Mill). (2) Lacroix wrote an internal article in 1933 arguing that the Spanish CP was stronger and had better prospects than some Oppositionists were willing to admit. Vereeken calls this "nothing but an apologia," although underestimating the Stalinists was one of the chronic and ultimately fatal weaknesses of the Spanish Oppositionists. (3) Lacroix's political position (faction not party) "was what suited the Stalinist bureaucracy best at this time." It was also the position at that time of the whole International Left Opposition, with few exceptions. And so on. Vereeken presents himself as a defender of democracy, fair play, honest discussion, and other excellent things, but I'd hate, on the basis of his hatchet job on Lacroix, to be on trial in a court where he was judge or jury.

5. Rudolf Klement. A young German, a secretary to Trotsky in Turkey and France, a member of the IS, he was the administrative secretary in charge of preparing the founding conference of the Fourth International when he was kidnapped and murdered by the GPU in 1938. As a member of the IS he was in several clashes with Vereeken over current political issues, including the Trotskyist movement's attitude to the centrist POUM (Workers Party of Marxist Unification) during the Spanish Civil War.

Vereeken disliked Klement intensely and entitles his chapter "Rudolf Klement: an agent? Certainly a coward." With a GPU revolver to his head, Klement may have signed his name to a GPU-type letter calling Trotsky an agent of Hitler after he was kidnapped (or his signature may have been forged). If that makes Klement a coward, what does saying such a thing make Vereeken? Is he utterly shameless? Not necessarily. Slandering a revolutionary victim of the GPU and being unable to distinguish between the victim and his murderers are little things, easily overlooked when you are obsessed with a fixed idea that supplies the key to all mysteries. ". . . the more I think over these extraordinary events," he confides, "the more I am convinced that he [Klement] was actually in the GPU, perhaps without even knowing that Zborowski and others were also in the game." There's no telling what else he will be convinced of if he continues to think more.

Anyhow, out of the five cases examined, two never had anything to do with the GPU, except that one was murdered by it, and the only evidence available about the other three is that they were not GPU infiltrators but capitulators to Stalinism who became agents of the GPU some time after they had joined or after they had quit. Saying that in no way extenuates the three or mitigates their crimes, but it does point up the total irresponsibility of Vereeken's deductions.

If Vereeken's book is worthless as interpretation, does it nevertheless have any of the "documentary" value that he claims for it? A little, but only a very little. Virtually all of the Trotsky citations he uses will be found in the *Writings of Leon Trotsky* series, usually better translated, complete and in their proper context. Vereeken's book has many factual errors. For example, Vereeken says—twice—that the Transitional Program (written by Trotsky in 1938) was adopted at an international conference in 1936. It also has many errors based on ignorance or distortion. For example, Vereeken says that in 1933 "not a voice was raised to demand that the lessons of the betrayal by the brothers Senin and Robert [sic] Well were learned. . . . [Two months after they left in January] they had still not been publicly denounced in the Trotskyist press." These were the months when Hitler came to power. But Trotsky's article, "Serious Lessons from an Inconsequential Thing," dated January 28, 1933, appeared in a February 1933 issue of *Die Permanente Revolution*, the German section's public paper.[5] Of course the lessons Trotsky drew are not the lessons Vereeken wants us to learn today, but that doesn't give him license to say that they were not drawn or that a public denunciation was not made. In general, his tendency is to deny something happened if he doesn't remember it or

---

5. See *Writings of Leon Trotsky (1932–33)* (Pathfinder, 1972), pp. 114–20 [2012 printing].

if it isn't mentioned in his documents.

Vereeken's method can be illustrated by a typical episode in the book. In 1935 his friends in the Spanish section, led by Nin, split from the Trotskyist movement and helped to found the POUM, affiliated to the centrist London-Amsterdam Bureau. In January 1936 the POUM signed a People's Front programmatic pact and Trotsky wrote an article, "The Treachery of the POUM," denouncing the signing of the pact as "a betrayal of the proletariat for the sake of an alliance with the bourgeoisie" and calling for a struggle to build a section of the Fourth International in Spain.[6] In August 1936, shortly after the Spanish Civil War had begun, the French Trotskyist paper published on its front page excerpts from a speech by Nin, describing him as a revolutionary, and on its second page Trotsky's January article denouncing the POUM. Vereeken's indignation knows no bounds. This for him is a clinching example of the GPU's sabotage inside the Trotskyist movement because, in his view, a rapprochement between the POUM and the Trotskyists was prevented by Trotsky's article, which, he says—twice—was "not intended for publication." He goes on at great length about the "fact" that since the French paper was published in Paris and Zborowski lived in Paris, "it can be deduced that it was Stalin's agent who translated this document and that he was also behind its publication. . . . Only Stalin's man, installed in a key position in our organisation, had any interest in seeing us isolated from the POUM," etc.

The whole construction rests on the absurd contention that Trotsky's article was not intended for publication; that he thought the POUM's capitulation to People's Frontism was a subject fit only for whispering into the ears of a few comrades. But the *fact* is that his article was published in English in the New Militant on February 15, 1936, in German in Unser Wort also in February 1936, and in French in the publicly sold Bulletin published by the IS in May 1936—all before the Civil War began. Only a crank could think that the POUM leaders were unaware of Trotsky's January article until it was printed in Paris in August 1936. Only a crank could think relations with the POUM depended in any serious way on the August publication.

In 1937 Trotsky wrote a letter about sectarians and ultraleftists on the fringes of the Fourth International that fits the Vereekens too, then and now.[7] They are political parasites, who help themselves to some idea from the Marxist movement (labor party, security or vigilance against infiltration by alien forces, or whatever), mangle the idea beyond recognition, twist it into a fetish to ward off all evils, and then counterpose this caricature to the Marxist movement and its program as a whole. Totally lacking in any sense of proportion, they can reduce the soundest concept to drivel.

It is fitting that the English translation of this 1975 French book has been published by the Healyite "International Committee of the Fourth International," because Trotsky's 1937 remarks apply with full force to this outfit too. There were a few embarrassing problems that arose. Technically, Vereeken is a Pabloite, and Pabloites are the most evil spirits in the Healyite demonology. In addition, some of Vereeken's charges are so patently groundless that even the Healyites want to avoid responsibility for them. Here, for example, is how Cliff Slaughter of the "International Committee" handles Vereeken's claim that Klement was in all probability a GPU agent who was liquidated after accomplishing his mission: "He arrives at this—still tentative—conclusion from various pieces of circumstantial evidence. . . . In our opinion, there is no basis for Vereeken's conclusion about Klement."[8] But if there is no basis for Vereeken's central "revelation" about

---

6. See *The Spanish Revolution (1931–39)* (Pathfinder, 1973), pp. 253–57 [2015 printing].

7. "Lenin called the ideas of these people 'infantile disorders.' A sick child arouses sympathy. But twenty years have passed since then. The children have become bearded and even bald. But they have not ceased their childish babblings. On the contrary, they have increased all their faults and all their foolishness tenfold and have added ignominies to them. They follow us step by step. They borrow some of the elements of our analysis. *They distort these elements without limit and counterpose them to the rest.* They correct us. When we draw a human figure, they add a deformity. When it is a woman, they decorate her with a heavy moustache. When we draw a rooster, they put an egg under it. And they call all this burlesque Marxism and Leninism" ("On the Sino-Japanese War," dated September 23, 1937, in *Leon Trotsky on China* [Pathfinder, 1976] pp. 721–22 [2015 printing], emphasis added).

8. See Slaughter's review of the Vereeken book, "Stalin's agents inside the Fourth International," in *The News Line*, August 21, 1976. But on exactly the same basis, or lack of it, Slaughter accepts and repeats Vereeken's slanders against Lacroix.

one of the martyrs of the Fourth International, what is the basis for translating, publishing, circulating, and touting the book that contains it?

Slaughter explains that too: "Clearing up these great historical questions [on the workings of the GPU in our movement] is the most important task of the preparation of the Trotskyist movement for the coming revolutionary struggles." If that is "the most important task," then of course everything else has to be subordinated to it, embarrassing or not. So the Healyites try to cover themselves in their introduction to the British edition by explaining that they have "no political agreement with Georges Vereeken."[9]

For them what counts is that Vereeken's book is "an invaluable contribution to the history of Trotskyism"—no, more than that, "an incomparable service to the Trotskyist movement and to the international working class." And even if that's a little hard to demonstrate, the book is still worth publishing because, they say, it "confirms" the slander campaign being conducted by the Healyites against Joseph Hansen and George Novack as "accomplices of the GPU." All we can say is that this campaign must be in really bad shape if they have to publish such wretched stuff to bolster it.

---

9. Depends on what is meant by "political." Vereeken says that the Trotskyist movement was "manipulated from Moscow" and the Healyites say, in the editorial introduction to Slaughter's article, that the GPU "actually gained control of the international [Trotskyist] organisation for a period." This certainly qualifies as "agreement," even though the Healyite statement in this case is the more extreme of the two. But is it possible to call such an agreement "non-political"? Can one make charges so monstrous, so fraught with the direst implications about a political organization created to fight Stalinism, and pretend that they are not political? I doubt it. In 1938, Vereeken quit rather than participate in the founding of the Fourth International, while Healy and the group he belonged to at that time also refused to attend the founding conference. They had differences at that time, but they were in political agreement against the Fourth International. Today Vereeken and Healy also have differences, but they are drawn into a bloc by their common animosity to the Fourth International and are in political agreement that, together or separately, they should throw whatever mud they can at the Fourth International and its history. We can only speculate as to which member of the Vereeken-Healy bloc will tell us in what specific "period" the GPU "actually gained control of the international organisation," and what effect this control had specifically on the politics of the "controlled" movement.

'Distortions, lies and concealment'

WSL CONDEMNS NEW BRAZEN MOVES IN HEALYITE FRAME-UP

The following article, under the title, "WRP Maintains Hansen Frame-up," appeared in the September 22 issue of the *Socialist Press*, the fortnightly paper of the Workers Socialist League, a British grouping that originated in a split from the Healyite Workers Revolutionary party.

As noted in the article itself, the Workers Socialist League had already condemned the frame-up. For the text of their original statement, see the January 19, 1976, issue of *Intercontinental Press*.

At the beginning of August Joseph Hansen, veteran member of the American Socialist Workers Party, published a lengthy reply to the slanders levelled against him in the publications of the Workers Revolutionary Party.

In his reply Hansen demolished the main pillars of the mountainous fabrication of "evidence" erected by the leading clique of Gerry Healy in the WRP who allege that he has been for almost 40 years an agent of the Stalinist GPU.

The reaction of the WRP leadership since Hansen's reply has confirmed to the hilt the assessment we made earlier of Healy's investigation—that it is a deliberate and cynical frame-up, which marshalls its "evidence" by distortions, lies and concealment, and which serves only to *divert* from the sharp political struggles which are necessary in the rebuilding of an international Trotskyist leadership of the working class. (See "WRP Frames Hansen" in *Socialist Press* of December 31st, 1975.)

Then as now, we spoke up in defence of Hansen against these slanders, despite the fundamental differences which divide us from the revisionist politics of the "United Secretariat of the Fourth International" (with which the Socialist Workers Party is in political sympathy, though prevented by reactionary legislation from affiliating).

We did so not only because we believe that slanders of such a vicious and serious character must be combatted on principle wherever they appear within the workers' movement, but because the political crisis of the world Trotskyist movement poses tasks of such urgency and importance for the international struggles of the working class that—more than at any other time in the post-war period—it is impermissible to allow methods such as those of Gerry Healy and Cliff Slaughter to foul and obstruct the political struggles that are on the agenda.

Nothing short of a book could examine in detail the whole of the WRP's accusations. But it will be highly illuminating of their methods to focus on the key items. Examining in detail the *reactions* of the WRP leadership to Hansen's reply will make clear the character of the frame-up.

Among all the volume of "evidence" unearthed by Healy's "investigators" only *one* single item is related to Hansen individually. This was a report prepared by an official of the US Consulate in Mexico City of his conversation with Hansen on Saturday August 31st, 1940.

This was eleven days after Trotsky was murdered at his house in Mexico City by Stalin's agent, Mercader.

The report was forwarded to the State Department in Washington the day after it was written and was recently unearthed in the State Department archives by the WRP's "investigating" team (who give no precise location for the document).

In his report, the consular official, Robert G. McGregor, wrote that Hansen had suggested various lines of enquiry in the United States which might uncover the responsibility of the GPU apparatus for Trotsky's murder.

Hansen reportedly told McGregor that he himself had been in contact with a GPU agent in the US for several months. The passage reads:

> For, while Hansen is convinced that the murder is a GPU job, that very fact makes it hard to unravel. Hansen stated that when in New York in 1938 he was himself approached by an agent of the GPU and asked to desert the Fourth International and join the Third.
>
> He referred the matter to Trotsky who asked him to go as far with the matter as possible. For three months Hansen had relations with a man who merely identified himself as "John," and did not otherwise reveal his real identity.

(Quoted in *How the GPU Murdered Trotsky*, Chapter 17, no page number.)

McGregor's memorandum immediately became the star exhibit in Healy's "case." It had the advantage for them that—unlike virtually all the rest of the material—it related to Hansen as a named individual, rather that just the SWP or its leadership as a whole and it showed a conscious contact with the GPU.

The WRP used it to try to establish *two* distinct, and in fact mutually exclusive, charges against Hansen. (Perhaps there were at one stage too many cooks stirring the broth.)

Firstly: that Hansen had some kind of illegitimate relationship with the US authorities and/or the FBI, concealed from the Trotskyist movement, and (they insinuated) that he might even be an FBI agent.

The "evidence" for this was the fact that Hansen met McGregor on a Saturday (i.e. outside normal office hours) and appeared to have "a familiar relationship" with him.

But this allegation simply collapsed under the fact that (as is clear even from the WRP's own material) Hansen was only one of several members of the Fourth International (including Trotsky himself) who had had quite open conversations with McGregor.

The document was thus used as the number one prop in the allegation that Hansen was and is an "accomplice of the GPU."

> Is it seriously suggested [the WRP asked] that Trotsky, the leader of the Red Army, would ask a relatively inexperienced newcomer from Salt Lake City [i.e. Hansen] to infiltrate the most skilled terror machine of the GPU? What could have been the purpose of this infiltration? There are no published records to show that Trotsky evinced an interest in infiltrating the GPU.

(*How the GPU Murdered Trotsky*, Chapter 17.)

The WRP's rhetorical questions are answered in what is perhaps the most important item in Hansen's reply.

Trotsky *did* (Hansen relates) attempt to use him to infiltrate the GPU apparatus in the US and thereby to gain vital knowledge of the Stalinists' plots against the movement and Trotsky himself.

This took place in 1939—McGregor is mistaken in placing it in 1938. Secret communications between Hansen in New York and Trotsky in Mexico went through one V. T. O'Brien, an American guard of Trotsky, who is still alive and has testified in writing to his role in the operation.

And moreover, on Trotsky's advice, the SWP leadership in New York drew up a confidential record of the matter, which was signed by James Cannon, Max Shachtman and Hansen himself (though Hansen was not then a member of the leadership).

Hansen has now published this report (*Intercontinental Press*, 9th August, 1976, p. 1210).

It is worth reprinting, both for the light it sheds on the serious manner in which Trotsky and the American Trotskyist leadership approached the overwhelming task of protecting the movement against Stalin's murder-squads, and in order to appreciate the utter cynicism of the WRP's reaction to it.

April 7, 1939

> To the Political Committee
> of the Socialist Workers Party.
> Comrades:
>
> Upon his return to the United States from Mexico, Comrade Joe Hansen chanced to meet an agent of the G.P.U. This agent introduced Hansen to a superior in the G.P.U., a man apparently the head or one of the heads of the American division of the G.P.U. This man whose real name Hansen does not know but

who may be called "Y" sounded out the possibilities of converting Hansen into an agent of the G.P.U. Hansen immediately informed Comrades Trotsky, Cannon, and Shachtman. Under their direction and with their full approval he conducted for purposes of reconnaisance in the American G.P.U. organization a series of conversations with "Y" upon the Stalin book which Comrade Trotsky is now writing, the internal status of the S.W.P. and the internal conditions at Mexico, in all cases giving equivocal, misleading answers to "Y's" questions or telling him things that are semi-public knowledge, reporting in detail after each meeting to Comrades Trotsky, Cannon, and Shachtman. Through these conversations valuable information has been gained for the Fourth International. Hansen is disinclined—for fear that the story might leak out and because the reconnaisance is not yet completed—that the entire P. C. should be made aware of this affair at present without full guarantees that his personal safety and the further political gains which might accrue be safe-guarded by complete silence on the part of P. C. members with their friends, political associates, and correspondents regarding this affair. Even the most guarded allusions or hints might cause the failure of further work in this respect.

J.P. Cannon
Max Shachtman
Joe Hansen

How have the WRP responded to this document? *At no point* have they challenged its authenticity. On the contrary they have—in an astonishing logical somersault—taken it as *additional* evidence for their "indictment"!

A hurriedly-prepared leaflet issued to the WRP's London meeting on August 15th—ostensibly organised to "commemorate" Trotsky, in reality to "indict" Hansen and pollute Trotsky's memory—carried the astonishing headline "Hansen Admits the Charges!"

This leaflet—like the other statements on the matter produced by the WRP since then—manages to avoid *any* explicit mention of the very existence of the document quoted above, although the leaflet is quite obviously an attempt to obfuscate the fact that it destroys the only item in the WRP's "case" that had any direct bearing on Hansen's individual role.

Healy

As Cliff Slaughter, Secretary of Healy's "International Committee" (and now coming forward as one of the main architects in the attempt to shore up the fabrications) has rightly commented it is "circumstantial evidence" that "abounds in situations of this sort." (*News Line*, August 21st.)

Evidently, a report dealing in detail with the matter, clearing Hansen and signed by James Cannon, is so "circumstantial" that its very existence must not be mentioned by Healy's allegedly "meticulous" investigators!

The *political* direction of the WRP's "investigation" emerged with dazzling clarity over the weekend of Sunday, August 15th.

Far from pausing for even the briefest re-evaluation of their case, the WRP leadership turned immediately to the capitalist press (as they have accurately described them, "the sewers of Fleet Street").

Healy's apprentices in the matter of frame-ups turned without hesitation to experienced practitioners.

The *Sunday Times* of August 15th carried an article by Anthony Holden summarising uncritically the WRP's case, and including a plug for their meeting that day.

It is impossible to avoid the supposition that Mr. Holden—at best—naively swallowed "information" offered by courtesy of his former colleague as a

Sunday Times journalist Alex Mitchell, now editor of the *News Line*.

Next day the campaign hotted up. Revealing the leverage they seem to have over the "jackals" who inhabit "the sewers of Fleet Street" (*their* epithets, though we agree with the spirit!) the WRP called a "press conference" to which the capitalist press *and only the capitalist press* were invited!

Pieces duly appeared in the *Guardian* and *The Times* the next day. They did not, of course, mention Hansen's reply nor has any of the capitalist press yet done so.

And to top it off, an interview was conveniently arranged on the BBC's Radio 4 "PM" programme on Monday evening for Harold Robins, a former SWP member and one of Trotsky's guards in Mexico, who has lent his name to the WRP's campaign.

In it, Robins—though not completely coherent—attempted to revive the theory that Hansen was (and is?) an agent *both* of the GPU and the FBI:

> The Socialist Workers Party ... was successfully penetrated by GPU agents, and they weren't just GPU agents, I'm convinced that some of them were double agents, agents for the American Government who wanted to kill Trotsky precisely because they didn't want to have what they had after World War 1 ("PM", August 16th).

From their proposals for a "parity commission" of the Trotskyist movement to investigate their spurious allegations, the WRP leadership overnight switched horses, apparently without batting an eyelid, to attempt to get a witch-hunt rolling through the capitalist press and media.

There could be no clearer indictment of the factional, slanderous and *anti-political character of their campaign*.

Any honest assessment of the evidence highlights, in fact, the serious and revolutionary manner in which Trotsky and the small cadres of the Fourth International in the 1930s faced up to the task of defence against the avalanche of slander and violence launched by Stalin.

And, if the SWP report which Hansen publishes is authentic (which the WRP have at no point challenged) it shows that his own role, though secondary, was a courageous one.

Not only was he in the firing line as one of Trotsky's guards in Mexico, but he exposed himself to the serious risk of "liquidation" at the hands of the GPU if they discovered he was hoodwinking them: a GPU machine which had already taken the lives of thousands of Stalin's political opponents.

It is necessary to comment also on the way in which the slander campaign against Hansen highlights the enormous acceleration in the political degeneration of the WRP and its leadership, a degeneration in the fight against which the founding members of the Workers Socialist League were illegally and bureaucratically expelled by Healy at the end of 1974.

Cutting themselves off from their base in the organised workers' movement, turning their backs on the day-to-day struggle for leadership in the unions, mouthing a few sectarian slogans to cover over their opportunist adaptation *in practice* to the labour bureaucrats (including entry into scab "participation" committees)—all these tendencies show Healy's "Trotskyism" being driven swiftly under pressure of the class struggle, into its opposite: phrase-mongering and intrigue.

Healy and his associates move increasingly in a narrow circle of petit-bourgeois dilettantes, actresses and bourgeois journalists.

In such circles the fraudulent and frenzied search for "conspiracies" to explain the problems of the organisation easily push out any *serious* attention to questions of security against agents provocateurs and spies.

Similarly, light-minded speculation and metaphysics take the place of the political, scientific study of real developments in the workers' movement.

In this atmosphere the most ethereal "explanations" can flourish. It has been suggested (though this is not a version the WRP leadership has yet put into print) that there *is* a version of Hansen's "complicity" with the GPU which could survive the evidence he presents in his defence.

It is this—that Hansen was a trained agent of the GPU, in place in the SWP since well before the events of 1938–40. As a skilled operator in intrigue he (or his masters) conceived a plan which would allow him to meet more openly with his GPU controllers in New York, and at the same time protect himself against accusations from the Trotskyist ranks that he should *pretend* to infiltrate the GPU on behalf of the SWP, meanwhile pretending to the SWP leadership that he was pretending to do the opposite on behalf of the GPU, and getting a report signed by Cannon on file to cover himself.

He thus became an agent (or "accomplice") of the GPU within the SWP, cunningly disguising himself as an agent of the SWP inside the GPU ostensibly *pretending* to be an agent of the GPU in the SWP—or so on ad nauseam!

No doubt, if the WRP leadership chooses to come forward with this version, they will find excellent "philosophical" and "dialectical" reasons to buttress it with.

And these are the best reasons they can find, since in the nature of the case, the "facts" of the matter as they have emerged so far can—"logically"—neither prove nor disprove it.

It is, like all the WRP's recent "philosophy," inherently metaphysical.

It is the sort of "theory" which would allow the WRP's "investigators" to leave aside all the "circumstantial evidence"—including the detailed history of Joseph Hansen's more than forty years in the Trotskyist movement—except where it was convenient for them to select from it.

It allows Healy's International Committee to represent all the important post-war splits of the Trotskyist movement not as real political battles but as crises fomented and manipulated by Stalinist agents.

And, like their campaign against Hansen to date, it represents not an attempt to protect and strengthen the Trotskyist movement, but a slanderous and incompetent invention.

Greek Trotskyist group give their verdict

HEALY'S 'POLITICAL BANKRUPTCY' SHOWN IN FRAME-UP OF HANSEN AND NOVACK

A group of former members of the "International Committee" (IC) in Greece have examined the charges made by Gerry Healy and associates that the editor of *Intercontinental Press* and other veteran Trotskyists are "accomplices" of the GPU. The group published the results of their study in the October issue of their magazine, *Nea Poreia*, the organ of the Kommounistike Diethnistike Enosi (KDE—Internationalist Communist Union).

The KDE was formed this year by activists expelled from the Workers Internationalist League (WIL), the Greek organization affiliated to the "IC."

Following the fall of the dictatorship in 1974, the WIL was one of the larger groups in Greece claiming adherence to Trotskyism. It was one of the few groups of any significance belonging to the "International Committee." The IC now is little more than the rubric used for international operations by the English Workers Revolutionary party (WRP) of Gerry Healy.

At the beginning of 1976, however, the WIL suffered a shattering split. In its May 4 issue, *Newsline*, the organ of the WRP, said that one of the main leaders of the WIL, L. Sklavos, had been expelled for "engineering a provocation." What that meant, *Newsline* did not indicate. It ran this leader's picture under the caption, "The Renegade Sklavos." The differences that led to the rupture were outlined as follows:

> When LS [L. Sklavos] developed his philosophical differences, denying the conflict of opposites as the source of development, he took a course which was calculated to destroy all that had been built in Greece....
>
> In essentials, he wanted a theoretical rationalisation for opportunist adaptation to the national political milieu, dominated as always by "democratic" opportunism. For this it was necessary, just as it was for Wohlforth and Hansen in the United States and Thornett in England, to build up a smokescreen of lies and slanders about the "intervention" and "bureaucratic" dictatorship of the IC and WRP leadership. LS's resignation and disruption was designed to do exactly this. His conduct was a continuation of his previous opposition to publishing in Greece the material of the IC on Wohlforth.
>
> All sections of the IC, already forewarned by the work on Security and the Fourth International, which followed the struggle against Wohlforth, are warned to be vigilant and completely firm against all such disruptions.
>
> They are not accidental, on the contrary, are characteristic of the period in which we now fight. Trotskyism has been successfully wrested from the hands of agents and those who capitulated to agents through theoretical neglect, political adaptation, and organisational softness. The middle class propagandists who want Trotskyism tied to the coattails of the reformists and Stalinists grow more hysterical and resort to sheer provocations, because they hate being politically defeated; they are caught like rats in a trap.

Clearly the group expelled from the WIL went through an intense experience with Healy's methods of dealing with political opposition. As a precedent for their campaign against this group, the Healyites cited their previous "exposures" of Tim Wohlforth, former leader of the American affiliate of the IC, the Workers League, and Joseph Hansen.

When Healy decided to remove Wohlforth from

Gerry Healy

the Workers League leadership, he claimed that his experts on "security" had discovered that Wohlforth's companion was a CIA agent.

In escalating their attacks on Hansen in 1975, the Healyites claimed to have discovered that he had been an "accomplice" of the GPU, and possibly the FBI as well, for at least the last thirty-six years. As Trotsky's secretary and participant in his defense, Hansen was smeared as an accomplice in the murder of the revolutionary leader.

When George Novack denounced the Healyites' charges, he also was accused of being an "accomplice." Novack, like Hansen, has been a leading member of the Trotskyist movement for almost forty years. He was the organizer of the Dewey Commission, which found Trotsky not guilty of the charges levelled by Stalin in the Moscow Trials.

As victims of the same frame-up technique, the leaders and members of the Greek KDE were in a good position to understand the meaning of Healy's charges against Hansen and Novack. In the article on this case in the October *Nea Poreia*, the authors, D. Veros and S. Dharakis, made it clear that they continue to defend the general political outlook they learned in the "International Committee." "The KDE opposes Hansen and Novack, their method, and the program of the SWP [Socialist Workers party] in general."

However, whatever their differences with the SWP and its leaders, the KDE writers said,

> This is no reason to accept slander and character assassination as a method of combating political opponents. To the contrary, a genuinely revolutionary movement is obliged to keep the air clear, to remove obstacles from the way of a struggle on the basis of principled differences, differences that must be clearly defined and not obscured by personal attacks and foul slanders.
>
> Healy's method is the same as Stalin's—worthy of a bureaucracy that falsifies. Left without political weapons, he has no choice but to transfer the fight to a "different level." Trotskyism developed in the fight against bureaucracy, and the introduction of the method of this bureaucracy by people who call themselves supporters of the Fourth International is not only an attack on certain persons, organizations, or political currents, but an attack on the very principles of Trotskyism and on the Trotskyist movement itself.
>
> It is no accident that the bourgeois press (the *Washington Post, Ta Nea*) as well as the Stalinist bureaucrats have taken the opportunity presented by Healy's slander campaign to obscure the circumstances of Trotsky's murder and to present him not as a victim of Stalin but of his own collaborators.

Veros and Dharakis state that Healy's use of such methods led him deeper and deeper into a campaign against the entire historic Trotskyist movement:

> The only way Hansen can defend himself against such charges is to turn to the old practice of revolutionary parties and cite the testimony of Trotsky's closest collaborators, such as James Cannon. The logic of the lie leads Healy into attacks not only against Trotsky's unworthy epigones, but against the Fourth International in Trotsky's day and those closest to its founder. It is revealing how Healy is now moving closer and closer, in this campaign, to the Belgian Vereeken and other such types who broke with Trotsky and polemicized and fought against the building of the Fourth International. It is the duty of every Trotskyist to refute and reject the method of Healy. This is not a matter of defending Hansen, Novack, and the opportunist line of the SWP and

the United Secretariat, but of defending the Trotskyist movement itself!

Vereeken disagreed with Trotsky's criticisms of the POUM in Spain, among other things, and left the Trotskyist movement in the 1930s. He has developed the theory that the differences between him and Trotsky arose because Trotsky was fooled by GPU agents planted in the Fourth International movement. Vereeken wrote a book to support this claim, which the Healyites translated and published under the title, *The GPU in the Trotskyist Movement.*

The Healyites apparently found Vereeken so useful that they were willing to overlook some articles of faith of the "IC," to say nothing of the logic of their arguments about "agents," in order to avail themselves of his services as a "historian" of Trotskyism. Veros and Dharakis note this:

> Vereeken was an official speaker at the WRP rally on the thirty-sixth anniversary of Trotsky's murder. He said quite a lot about the GPU in the Fourth International. What he neglected to inform the audience about . . . was that he is a follower of Michel Pablo—the Pablo that Healy has also accused of being a possible GPU agent in the Fourth International, the Pablo that the International Committee was built to fight.

As for the "evidence" presented by the Healyites to support their charges, Veros and Dharakis write:

> After constant and diligent research, it says, in the U.S. official archives, Healy's "Committee" recently published a series of articles against Hansen and Novack. With half-truths, insinuations, and slanders, they claimed to support their charges. Healy's concept of "impartiality" can be seen from the following unbelievable phrase in the statement of his "Committee," which has been published in the Healyite press: "Until they answer before an international commission of inquiry, our charges are proved and they are guilty as charged." This is the concept of justice maintained in reactionary bourgeois courts. . . .

> This is the kind of justice that was practiced under fascism as well as Stalinism at the time of the worst persecution of the opposition and of the frame-up trials.

Veros and Dharakis deal with Healy's call for a "commission of inquiry." They note that the Healyite press claimed that Hansen's answer[*] to the IC's charges amounted to a "confession." They comment:

> If Hansen "accepted" the charges, what is the need for a commission of inquiry? If Hansen did not accept the charges, then by saying he did, Healy lied to the activists who work for his press. If he is not lying to them, and Hansen did "accept" the charges, then the proposal for a commission of inquiry is a maneuver, or a deception of his own activists.

> Healy is falling into contradictions and exposing himself. In making this claim about Hansen's "confession," he lied again. In fact in his article in *Intercontinental Press*, Hansen incontrovertibly refuted these charges and did an excellent job of making their author a laughing stock.

In their eleven-page-long article Veros and Dharakis examine Healy's charges in detail and show them to be without foundation.

These former members of the "IC" argue that Healy resorted to this campaign because he could not respond to the crisis that opened in England in 1971. In a situation that demanded that he get out of the rut of routine propaganda activity and apply his proclaimed revolutionary principles in practice, they write, Healy lost his bearings. He had to invent conspiracies to explain his failures. The expulsion of Wohlforth in the U.S. was also an example of this. Healy invented a conspiracy to explain the losses the Workers League suffered because it tried to follow a sectarian line set from London.

> This is not a simple slander campaign and still less is it a campaign for "security" in

---

[*] See the article published in the August 9, 1976, *Intercontinental Press*, p. 1188, entitled "Healy Caught in the Logic of the Big Lie: More Facts on a Stalinist-Type Frame-up."

the Fourth International against infiltration by agents. It is the expression of political bankruptcy. . . . Healy and his followers are turning away from dialectical materialism to an un-Marxist method that resembles the method of the worst reactionary bourgeois journalism. It is a method that does not focus on the class struggle but explains history by the conspiratorial activity of obscure forces.

The reason for the campaign against Hansen and Novack is that "only by such methods can sectarian leaders deal with their own internal problems and strangle all criticism within their own ranks."

The KDE has had a vivid experience of such methods.

It is to be hoped that they will disclose the details to the Trotskyist movement along with the conclusions they draw from it.

Prominent figures in labor movement agree to serve on panel

LET COMMISSION INVESTIGATE CHARGES OF HEALYITE VIOLENCE!

By Dave Holmes

JOHN PERCY/DIRECT ACTION

Healyite leader Greg Adler scatters SWP literature following assault.

The following article appeared in the November 25 issue of *Direct Action*, a revolutionary-socialist newsweekly published in Sydney, Australia.

For some weeks now *Direct Action* has extensively covered the defence campaign of the Socialist Workers Party and the Spartacist League against the physical violence of the Socialist Labour League (publishers of *Workers News*).[1] On October 17 SWP and SL members were assaulted by SLL toughs outside Sydney Trades Hall. Participating in and directing the assault were top leaders of the SLL.

This attack was completely unprovoked. The SWP and SL were peacefully and nonobstructively selling their papers and distributing literature outside an SLL-sponsored meeting.

In the attack Dave Deutschmann, a member of the SWP and the editor of the Socialist Youth Alliance newspaper *Young Socialist*, was punched to the ground. While he was lying on the ground trying to protect himself he was kicked in the head and body by an SLL leader and another SLL member. Deutschmann had to be taken to hospital for treatment. Keith Olerhead of the SL was also viciously beaten during the attack. He was punched and elbowed violently in the face. Full details of the attack are contained in a pamphlet being circulated nationally by the SWP and the SL.

This wanton attack by the SLL has met with a strong response from activists in the labor and radical movement. A large and very representative number of people have endorsed a statement expressing concern at the SLL's violations of the norms of workers democracy.[2]

In articles in *Workers News* the SLL has attempted

---

1. See "Australian Healyites Revive Stalinist Methods" (*Intercontinental Press*, November 8, p. 1588) and "Healyites Continue to Claim Right to Beat Up Working-Class Opponents" (*Intercontinental Press*, November 22, p. 1656).

2. See statement and partial listing of endorsers in, *Intercontinental Press*, November 22, p. 1657.

to dismiss these very serious charges. They claim that only minor "scuffles" took place. They allege that the SWP and SL were provocative in having cameras outside the Trades Hall. These claims have been exposed as lies in previous articles in *Direct Action*.

The Socialist Workers Party and the Spartacist League have proposed the establishment of an impartial commission of inquiry to determine the truth of the October 17 incident before the whole Radical and labor movement. Such a commission would be made up of respected and authoritative figures from the left and working-class movement belonging neither to the SWP, the SL or the SLL.

The SWP has already stated that it will publicise the findings of such a commission whatever its verdict.

The SWP and the SL propose a commission made up of, or at least including, the following labor movement figures. They have all agreed to serve on a commission of inquiry:

George Petersen, Labor member for Illawarra of the NSW Legislative Assembly and a well-known figure on the left for many years;

Ted Wheelwright, associate professor of economics at Sydney University and author of several books on political economy and a leading proponent of the campus movement for political economy;

Lester Bostock, administrator of the Black Theater in Sydney and a long-time activist in the Black movement and the Labor Party.

The SWP and SL would like to know the views of the SLL on the idea of a commission of inquiry, the above specific proposals for commissioners, and the details of its operation.

If the Socialist Labour League has any confidence that it can substantiate its account of the October 17 incident and back up its motivations, then let it do so before such an independent labor tribunal.

Such a commission of inquiry would do far more than establish the truth of the Trades Hall incident. It would demonstrate the seriousness with which the labor movement views democracy in its internal life and its determination to stamp out all tendencies to substitute hooliganism and gangsterism for the free debate of political differences.

WORKING-CLASS LEADERSHIP AND THE SOCIALIST REVOLUTION

The Case of Leon Trotsky
Testimony Before 1937 Commission Investigating Charges Made against Him in Moscow Trials
LEON TROTSKY

Was the regime of Joseph Stalin and his heirs a continuation of the Bolshevik-led workers and peasants government established by the October 1917 Revolution? No! says Bolshevik leader Leon Trotsky in testimony before a 1937 international commission of inquiry into Stalin's Moscow frame-up trials. Reviewing forty years of working-class struggle in which Trotsky was a participant and leader, he discusses the fight to restore V.I. Lenin's revolutionary internationalist course and why the Stalin regime organized the Moscow Trials. $28

To Speak the Truth
Why Washington's 'Cold War' against Cuba Doesn't End
FIDEL CASTRO, CHE GUEVARA

In historic speeches before the United Nations and UN bodies, Guevara and Castro address the peoples of the world, explaining why the US government so fears the example set by the socialist revolution in Cuba and why Washington's efforts to destroy it will fail. $15

The Communist Manifesto
KARL MARX AND FREDERICK ENGELS

Communism, say the founding leaders of the revolutionary workers movement, is not a set of ideas or preconceived "principles" but workers' line of march to power, springing from a "movement going on under our very eyes." $5. Also in Spanish, French, Farsi, Arabic.

Our History Is Still Being Written
The Story of Three Chinese Cuban Generals in the Cuban Revolution
ARMANDO CHOY, GUSTAVO CHUI, MOISÉS SÍO WONG, MARY-ALICE WATERS

"What was the key measure to uproot discrimination against Chinese and blacks in Cuba? It was the socialist revolution itself." New edition sheds light on Chinese Cubans' involvement in Cuba's internationalist course, including in Africa and Latin America. $15. Also in Spanish, French, Farsi, Greek, Chinese.

Thomas Sankara Speaks
The Burkina Faso Revolution, 1983–87

Under Sankara's guidance, Burkina Faso's revolutionary government led peasants, workers, women, and youth to expand literacy; to sink wells, plant trees, erect housing; to combat women's oppression; to carry out land reform; to join others worldwide to free themselves from the imperialist yoke. $15. Also in French.

The Teamster Series
FARRELL DOBBS

Four books on the strikes, organizing drives, and political campaigns that transformed the Teamsters across the Midwest in the 1930s into a militant industrial union movement. Written by Farrell Dobbs, the general organizer of these Teamster battles and leader of the Socialist Workers Party.

$16 each, series $50. Also in Spanish. *Teamster Rebellion* is also available in French, Farsi, Greek.

PATHFINDERPRESS.COM

THE WORKING CLASS AND THE FIGHT AGAINST JEW-HATRED

New!
The Fight against Jew-Hatred and Pogroms in the Imperialist Epoch
Stakes for the International Working Class
V.I. LENIN, LEON TROTSKY
FARRELL DOBBS
JAMES P. CANNON
JACK BARNES
DAVE PRINCE

Jew-hatred and pogroms—like Hamas carried out on October 7, 2023—are now part of the permanent social convulsions and wars of the imperialist epoch. That's why fighting Jew-hatred is of decisive importance to the working class and oppressed nations of the entire world. The authors answer the all-important question: *What is to be done to end it*—for all time. $10. Also in Spanish and French.

Fascism: What It Is and How to Fight It
LEON TROTSKY

Writing in the heat of struggle against the rising fascist movement in Europe in the 1930s, Russian communist leader Leon Trotsky examines the origins and nature of fascism and advances, for the first time, a working-class strategy to combat and defeat it. $5. Also in Farsi.

The Socialist Workers Party in World War II, 1940–43
JAMES P. CANNON

Preparing the communist workers movement in the United States to campaign against wartime censorship, repression, and anti-union assaults. $23

The Jewish Question
A Marxist Interpretation
ABRAM LEON

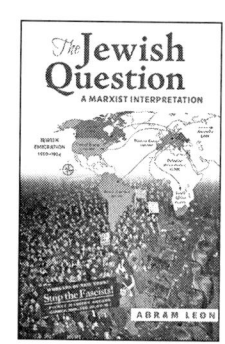

The battle against reactionary forces aiming to exterminate the Jews remains central to world politics, as shown by the genocidal October 2023 pogrom in Israel. Why is Jew-hatred still raising its ugly head? What are its class roots? Why, as Abram Leon explains, is there no solution "independent of the world proletarian revolution"? Revised translation, new introduction, 40 pages of illustrations and maps. $17. Also in Spanish and French.

The Low Point of Labor Resistance Is Behind Us
The Socialist Workers Party Looks Forward
JACK BARNES, MARY-ALICE WATERS
STEVE CLARK

The global order imposed by Washington after its victory in World War II is shattering. A long retreat by the working class and unions has come to an end. The bosses and their government are stepping up attacks on our wages, conditions, and constitutional rights. This book highlights opportunities for building a mass proletarian party able to lead the struggle to end capitalist rule, opening a socialist future for humanity. $10. Also in Spanish, French, Greek.

Imperialism's March toward Fascism and War
JACK BARNES

"There will be new Hitlers, new Mussolinis. That is inevitable. What is not inevitable is that they will triumph. The working-class vanguard will organize our class to fight back against the devastating toll we are made to pay for the capitalist crisis. The future of humanity will be decided in the contest between these contending class forces." In *New International* no. 10. $14. Also in Spanish, French, Farsi, Greek.

EXPAND YOUR REVOLUTIONARY LIBRARY

Are They Rich Because They're Smart?
Class, Privilege, and Learning under Capitalism
JACK BARNES

Exposes growing class inequalities in the US and the self-serving rationalizations of well-paid professionals who think their "brilliance" equips them to "regulate" working people, who don't know what's in our own best interest. $10. Also in Spanish, French, Farsi, Arabic, Greek.

Writings of Leon Trotsky
Fourteen volumes covering the period of Trotsky's exile from the Soviet Union in 1929 until his assassination at Stalin's orders in 1940. $270 set

The Origin of the Family, Private Property, and the State
FREDERICK ENGELS

The emergence of class-divided society gave rise to repressive state bodies and the oppression of women to enable the ruling classes to pass along wealth and privilege. Engels discusses the consequences for working people of these class institutions—from their ancient forms to their modern versions. $15. Also in Spanish and Farsi.

Cosmetics, Fashions, and the Exploitation of Women
JOSEPH HANSEN, EVELYN REED, MARY-ALICE WATERS

How big business reinforces women's second-class status and uses it to rake in profits. Where does women's oppression come from? How has the entry of millions of women into the workforce strengthened the battle for emancipation, still to be won? $12. Also in Spanish, Farsi, Greek.

Women in Cuba: The Making of a Revolution within the Revolution
VILMA ESPÍN, ASELA DE LOS SANTOS, YOLANDA FERRER

The integration of women in the ranks and leadership of the Cuban Revolution was intertwined with the proletarian course of the leadership of the revolution from the start. This is the story of that revolution and how it transformed the women and men who made it. $17. Also in Spanish, Farsi, Greek.

50 Years of Covert Operations in the US
Washington's Political Police and the American Working Class
LARRY SEIGLE, FARRELL DOBBS, STEVE CLARK

How class-conscious workers have defended constitutional freedoms and fought the capitalists' drive to build the "national security" state essential to maintaining their rule. $10. Also in Spanish and Farsi.

Pathfinder Press accessible e-books for the blind, those with low vision, or other challenges reading print books

For a list of current accessible titles, go to: pathfinderpress.com/collections/books-for-the-blind.

Visit bookshare.org for information on how to sign up.

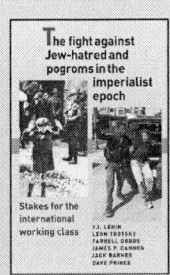 

PATHFINDERPRESS.COM

BUILDING A PROLETARIAN PARTY

New Edition!
Che Guevara on Economics and Politics in the Transition to Socialism
CARLOS TABLADA

It's essential for working people to win state power, said Ernesto Che Guevara. "Then there's the second stage, maybe more difficult than the first"—the transition from dog-eat-dog capitalism to socialism. That includes moving from work as a condition for survival, to voluntary social labor through which we express our common humanity. Includes Fidel Castro's 1987 speech "Che's Ideas are Absolutely Relevant Today." New edition with substantially expanded selections from Guevara's writings. $17. Also in Spanish, coming in French.

Revolutionary Continuity
Marxist Leadership in the U.S.
The Early Years, 1848–1917
Birth of the Communist Movement, 1918–1922
FARRELL DOBBS

"Successive generations of proletarian revolutionists have participated in the movements of the working class and its allies. . . . Marxists today owe them not only homage for their deeds. We also have a duty to learn what they did wrong as well as right so their errors are not repeated." —*Farrell Dobbs*
Two volumes, $17 each.

The Clintons' Anti-Working-Class Record
Why Washington Fears Working People
JACK BARNES

What working people need to know about the profit-driven course of Democrats and Republicans alike over the last three decades. And the political awakening of workers seeking to understand and resist the capitalist rulers' assaults. $10. Also in Spanish, French, Farsi, Greek.

The Working Class and the Transformation of Learning
The Fraud of Education Reform under Capitalism
JACK BARNES

"Until society is reorganized so that education is a human activity from the time we are very young until the time we die, there will be no education worthy of working, creating humanity." $3. Also in Spanish, French, Farsi, Greek.

The Struggle for a Proletarian Party
JAMES P. CANNON

"The workers of America have power enough to topple the structure of capitalism at home and to lift the whole world with them when they rise," Cannon asserts. On the eve of World War II, a founder of the communist movement in the US and leader of the Communist International in Lenin's time defends the program and party-building norms of Bolshevism. $20. Also in Spanish and Farsi.

Labor, Nature, and the Evolution of Humanity
The Long View of History
FREDERICK ENGELS, KARL MARX
GEORGE NOVACK
MARY-ALICE WATERS

Without understanding that social labor, transforming nature, has driven humanity's evolution for millions of years, working people are unable to see beyond the capitalist epoch of class exploitation that warps all human relations, ideas, and values. Only the revolutionary conquest of state power by the working class can open the door to a world free of capitalist exploitation, degradation of nature, subjugation of women, racism, and war. A world built on human solidarity. A socialist world. $12. Also in Spanish and French.

Lenin's Final Fight
Speeches and Writings, 1922–23
V.I. LENIN

In 1922 and 1923, V.I. Lenin, central leader of the world's first socialist revolution, waged what was to be his last political battle—one that was lost following his death. At stake was whether that revolution, and the international communist movement it led, would remain on the revolutionary proletarian course that brought workers and peasants to power in October 1917. $17. Also in Spanish, Farsi, Greek.

The Organizational Character of the Socialist Workers Party
1965 Resolution of the SWP
The Structure and Organizational Principles of the Party
FARRELL DOBBS

Deepening capitalist crisis and sharpening class conflict demand a revolutionary solution. Active preparation for such struggles determines the kind of organization the Socialist Workers Party has set out to build from its birth. $5 each.
The Organizational Character of the Socialist Workers Party also available in Spanish.

The Transitional Program for Socialist Revolution
LEON TROTSKY

The Socialist Workers Party program, drafted by Trotsky in 1938, still guides the SWP and communists the world over. The party "uncompromisingly gives battle to all political groupings tied to the apron strings of the bourgeoisie. Its task—the abolition of capitalism's domination. Its aim—socialism. Its method—the proletarian revolution." $17. Also in Farsi.

Malcolm X Talks to Young People

"The young generation of whites, Blacks, browns, whatever else—you're living at a time of revolution," said Malcolm in 1964. "And I for one will join with anyone, I don't care what color you are, as long as you want to change this miserable condition that exists on this earth." Four talks and an interview in the last months of Malcolm's life. $12. Also in Spanish, French, Farsi, Greek.

The History of American Trotskyism, 1928–38
Report of a Participant
JAMES P. CANNON

"Trotskyism is not a new movement, a new doctrine," Cannon says, "but the restoration, the revival of genuine Marxism as it was expounded and practiced in the Russian Revolution and in the early days of the Communist International." Talks by a founding leader of American communism on building a proletarian party in the United States. $17. Also in Spanish and French.

Cuba and the Coming American Revolution
JACK BARNES

This is a book about the example set by the Cuban people that socialist revolution is not only necessary—it can be made. A book about the struggles of workers and other exploited producers in the imperialist heartland, and the youth attracted to them. About the class struggle in the US, where the revolutionary capacities of working people are as utterly discounted by the ruling powers as were those of the Cuban toilers. And just as wrongly. $10. Also in Spanish, French, Farsi.

PATHFINDERPRESS.COM

COMMUNIST CONTINUITY AND PROGRAM

The First and Second Declarations of Havana

Nowhere are the questions of revolutionary strategy that today confront men and women on the front lines of struggles in the Americas addressed with greater truthfulness and clarity than in these uncompromising indictments of imperialist plunder and "the exploitation of man by man." Adopted by million-strong assemblies of the Cuban people in 1960 and 1962. $10. Also in Spanish, French, Farsi, Arabic, Greek.

Dynamics of the Cuban Revolution
A Marxist Appreciation
JOSEPH HANSEN

How did the Cuban Revolution unfold? Why is it an "unbearable challenge" to US imperialism? Why are its lessons important to working people everywhere?

In "Cuba—The acid test: A reply to ultraleft sectarians," one of more than 20 articles here, Hansen starts with facts—not doctrine pretending to be theory—to examine the class struggle unfolding in Cuba in the 1960s. He refutes the political blindness of leftists who denied the dialectical richness of the socialist revolution and communist leadership developing before their eyes. $23

The First Ten Years of American Communism
Report of a Participant
JAMES P. CANNON

A founding leader of the communist movement in the US tells the story of the early years of the effort to build a proletarian party emulating the Bolshevik leadership of the October 1917 revolution in Russia. Among other things, Cannon writes, "Everything new and progressive on the Negro question came from Moscow, after the Bolshevik revolution and as a result of it." $17

The First Five Years of the Communist International
LEON TROTSKY

During its first five years, the Communist International, guided by V.I. Lenin, Leon Trotsky, and other central Bolshevik leaders, sought to build a world movement of Communist Parties capable of leading the toilers to overthrow capitalist exploitation and colonial oppression. This two-volume collection contains Trotsky's speeches and writings from the first four Comintern congresses. Volume 1, $22; volume 2, $22.

Socialism on Trial
Testimony at Minneapolis Sedition Trial
JAMES P. CANNON

The revolutionary program of the working class, presented in response to frame-up charges of "seditious conspiracy" in 1941, on the eve of US entry into World War II. The defendants were leaders of the Minneapolis labor movement and the Socialist Workers Party. $15. Also in Spanish, French, Farsi.

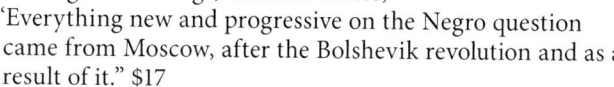

My Life
An Attempt at an Autobiography
LEON TROTSKY

A leader of the Russian Revolution, Red Army, and the fight to maintain Lenin's continuity recounts lessons from battles he took part in from the early 1900s to his forced exile in 1929 from the Soviet Union by Stalin's counterrevolutionary regime. $27

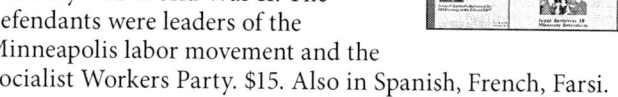